GUIDEBOOK

For **Publishing**

Philosophy

1997 edition

Edited

By Eric Hoffman

Published
*By the Philosophy Documentation Center
in cooperation with
the American Philosophical Association*

Published by Philosophy Documentation Center
Bowling Green State University
Bowling Green, Ohio, 43403

ph: 1-800-444-2419 (US and Canada)
fax: (419) 372-6987
e-mail: phildoc@opie.bgsu.edu
http://www.bgsu.edu/pdc/

in cooperation with the

American Philosophical Association
University of Delaware
Newark, DE 19716

ph: (302) 831-1112
fax: (302) 831-8690
http://www.udel.edu/apa

Cover and book design by Todd Childers, Todd Childers Graphic Design

ISBN: 0-912632-62-3

Table of Contents

Preface

by Eric Hoffman

The present *Guidebook for Publishing Philosophy* owes its inspiration, if not its form, to the work of Janice Moulton and Marcia Yudkin. The history of the project was set forth in the last edition of the *Guidebook*, which was published in 1986. The history begins with a symposium entitled "Alternatives to Perishing" at a 1973 conference of the Society for Women in Philosophy. Several editions followed, and the last edition rested on questionnaires circulated to publishers and journal editors, on the participation of an editorial board with over 30 active participants, and on the overall coordination of Moulton and Yudkin.

The purpose of the present edition, as articulated in the previous edition, remains the same: "to provide, in a single source, helpful information for those who want to make public their work in philosophy." The present edition, however, represents a cooperative venture between the American Philosophical Association and the Philosophy Documentation Center. The venture draws on the strengths of both organizations to provide members of the profession with the most helpful information possible. The APA is grateful to be working with George Leaman and Lori Fells of the PDC on this important project.

Unlike previous editions, the present edition is set up in a manner that will permit it to be more easily updated. Short pieces prepared by experienced members of the profession are supplemented by information about journals and publishers collected by the Philosophy Documentation Center. Republication of this information in a more accessible and affordable form will certainly support those who are looking for advice and information about how to make their work public.

In addition to Janice Moulton and Marcia Yudkin, whose inspiration continues to move the present edition and whose words continue to offer wisdom to philosophical writers, I want to thank the other authors of pieces published here: Samuel Gorovitz, Nancy Simco, Thomas Magnell, and Francis Crawley. Also, I want to thank Sanford Thatcher, Ernest Sosa, John Lawrence, Jacques Catudal, and Terry Bynum, all of whom reviewed and commented upon parts of the current manuscript.

While we are pleased to present this new edition, we are aware that experience with our new format for a new audience in a new environment will enable us to make improvements we have not yet considered. In this spirit I ask that suggestions for improvements in future editions be forwarded to me at the APA National Office.

Eric Hoffman, Executive Director
American Philosophical Association

The Perils of Publishing

by Samuel Gorovitz

We don't warn our young associates, struggling toward tenure, that publishing can feel very much like perishing. We ought to ready them for the battles ahead. It's not that publishers are personally perverse. I've liked most of those I've dealt with; I've learned from and enjoyed working with them-up to a point. But their business has perverse dimensions–from small university presses to big commercial houses–and we don't prepare young colleagues well for that.

Few professors who have written books are without horror stories. The rest of us are another matter. Someone should gather our laments; as *Cautionary Tales for the Aspiring Professor*, they'd arm young authors to deal with publishers more effectively.

That collection first occurred to me following a visit in 1982 by a sales representative from Macmillan. An earnest young woman, she was promoting texts for logic and introductory philosophy. But the next course I would teach was on ethics in medicine. Her reaction got my attention: "That's a great area; I wish we had something to offer. But we haven't gotten into it yet. I hope we will soon."

I expressed surprise at her response, since I was sure Macmillan did have something in the field, but she stood firm. So I handed her a copy of *Doctors' Dilemmas: Moral Conflict and Medical Care*, and said, "Well, this is in the area, and it says Macmillan on it." In retrospect, I could have been kinder, but I'd already had enough of Macmillan.

She looked at the book and at me with bewilderment and distress, and then, with an audible gasp, noticed that I was its author. Later, after the tears, she surmised that it had been published on a trade list, and its existence had simply not been revealed to the text side of the house. Some marketing!

I might have been more tolerant but for a Los Angeles talk show from which I was still smarting. There, as the make-up guy was finishing, a producer swooshed in and said "I don't know if we can use you. No books." Macmillan, despite arranging that TV appearance, hadn't sent books to stores in LA. "They don't like us to plug a book that's not in the stores," the producer explained. "We get complaints. Viewers and stores. So we check. The stores don't have your book."

"When am I on?" I asked.

"Right after the peanut butter fudge lady. Ten minutes. You get seven minutes, then Hodding Carter."

"Nothing I can do now. Let's do the segment; then, I promise, I'll call New York and try to get fast action."

So I had my seven minutes while a slick-looking guy read questions he seemed not to understand from a card he had been given, then I sizzled the phone lines to New York, and tried to leave.

"How do I get a taxi?"

"Why do you want one?"

"To go back to my hotel. I'm finished here."

"Didn't you come in a limo?"

"No, in a taxi."

"Why?"

"It was just a short ride. It seemed crazy to ask for a limo just for a few miles. It was totally unnecessary."

"Hey, Tom, this guy wants a taxi. He didn't ask for a limo! Any idea how we do that?"

"Dunno. Try the newsroom. They might know." So I got a taxi. Some glamour! Some fun!

What tore it for me with Macmillan, however, was when they later said they'd decided against a paperback, because the hardback hadn't sold enough. Much correspondence ensued, including a request that they return the rights to me, but to no avail. Then I wrote, in part:

> The United States Court of Appeals for the Second Circuit held that the contract between publisher and author establishes a relationship that "implies an obligation on the former" to make "a good faith effort to promote the book . . . to give the book a reasonable chance of achieving market success in light of the subject matter and likely audience." Publisher's Weekly observed that, "For the first time, the scope of a publisher's duty to advertise and promote the books it publishes had been defined." . . . I can demonstrate beyond any reasonable doubt that Macmillan's handling of my book failed–by a wide margin–to meet the standard implied by the Court's opinion.

Back came the rights; I was free to find a paperback publisher. I nearly had a deal with a fine university press, whose director said, "We're all set; it's just a formality now of presenting our recommendations to the board." But nothing is all set until something binding is in hand. That director, professing the most profound embarrassment, then reported that the board dissented– "highly unusual," and all that.

No matter—a brief delay, and then the good people at Oxford University Press did the paperback. They did it well, and sold it well. So I turned to them with another book, and was delighted with their handling of it—until *they* abruptly and inexplicably decided not to issue a paperback! Once burned, however, means more savvy. I invoked a clause I had added to the original contract: if they did not do a paperback by a date certain, the rights automatically returned to me. A lovely new paperback was then published by Temple University Press (and the wizards at Oxford then reprinted the hardback).

This loony behavior is nothing new. In 1975 I called Random House, my first publisher, to offer a co-edited anthology in medical ethics—because we had enjoyed such a good prior relationship. Don't even send it, they replied, explaining that they would not consider the book because there was no such field. Many other publishers were comparably dismissive, but I was buoyed by recalling a conversation I'd had with Paul Goodman a decade earlier. *Growing up Absurd*, then selling thousands of copies a week, had been rejected by more than 20 publishers before Random House (of all places) took it. "How did you muster the tenacity to keep at it?" I asked. "What sustained you through all those rejections?"

"Easy," he answered. "They were wrong, and I knew it. It was just a question of how long before someone figured it out."

I, too, kept on. One day a visiting Prentice Hall representative asked what I was working on. My reply was essentially, "What's the difference? You folks are all too dumb to know what's worth considering anyway." But he wasn't dumb.

"Have you had some kind of bad experience?" he inquired. "If so, I'd like to hear about it." So I told him that PH was among the many who had rejected the anthology, and that this was further evidence of the hidebound, short-sighted, unimaginative, hyper-conservative, moss-backed, narrow-minded, reactionary mentality of his whole tedious industry—explaining in detail why I thought so. A few weeks later he returned with his chief editor.

"Tell him what you told me," he said. "The whole thing." So I did, for over an hour. (I'd progressed from advanced dudgeon to full diatribe.) In three weeks we had a contract with Prentice Hall; in two years the anthology had adoptions on more than 100 campuses. Is this, at least, a purely happy story?

One day the mail brought an advance copy of a promotional flyer extolling the wonders of the book and describing me as a physician. The medical world is skeptical enough about outsiders probing their affairs, and they have little use for philosophers who masquerade as physicians. As soon as I got down from the ceiling, I phoned the editor, who intercepted 6000 outgoing copies of the erroneous flyer in the mailroom. Now I check absolutely everything a publisher will allow me to see.

It hasn't been all bad, of course. I've had good interviews as well as bad, and the publishers cited here for intermittent buffoonery are basically good ones. I don't counsel against working with them; I counsel only caution and competence.

Some of the interactions with publishers even provided treasured memories. The manuscript for *Doctors' Dilemmas* had the working title *Doctors of Virtue.* How clever, I'd thought—we want physicians to be virtuous as well as competent, moral philosophers study virtue, and this book is about the relationship between them, hence, ambiguously, *Doctors of Virtue.* "The subtitle's okay, but you'll have to change the title," my editor said, explaining that "we can't sell a book with 'virtue' in the title." (This was just before Alasdair MacIntyre's masterful *After Virtue* was published to national acclaim.)

"Okay, what should I call it?"

"We can't tell you. It's your book. Something punchy."

"Punchy? What's that, a technical term in publishing? Give me an example."
"Well, we sold six million copies of *Jonathan Livingston Seagull.*"

"Fine. So call it *Samuel Gorovitz Penguin.*"

"You're not taking the problem seriously."

"Everyone I've asked likes the title I had."

"They're irrelevant. Titles aren't for people you interact with. They're for browsers. The judgment of the people in your circle doesn't matter."

"But I'm in that circle, so how can I pick the title?"

"Something really catchy, but with some relation to the content."

"Okay, how about *The Hourly Orgasm Weight Loss Plan*"

"You're still not taking the problem seriously."

Indeed. A certain propensity for mirth is essential in these matters. Yet it remains important to be cautious, because the perils are real. The contract offered by a publisher—written by their lawyers to protect their interests—is typically poor as first presented. It can almost always be improved through cordial negotiation. No young academic should assess that first contract without the help of a battle-scarred warhorse, and it is wise to insist on various extra protections. Your editor—that nurturing and enthusiastic advocate, champion, and protector of your book, may be gone just after it appears (this has happened to me several times), leaving the book "orphaned." Large publishers, especially, despite the literary character of their product and the image they may have as marketing powerhouses, have the same vulnerabilities and foibles as any other large bureaucracy.

THE PERILS OF PUBLISHING

The immobilizing fear of rejection that keeps young faculty from dealing competently with publishers is the unfortunate result of a naivete we do too little to dispel. This has heightened significance when publishers themselves are marketed properties. Random House is now McGraw Hill; Prentice Hall is now Simon and Schuster, which is part of Paramount. Who will own what tomorrow can't be guessed, but can have powerful impact. A manuscript submitted to a publisher may be shunted aside in a transition of ownership or management, whether it is under consideration, already accepted, or in production. Without contractual protection, the author may be unable to retrieve it. (Even publication is no guarantee of availability; one colleague tried to obtain his own book only to be thwarted for a time when the warehouse at Pergamon was sealed in the aftermath of Robert Maxwell's death.)

Our inadequate mentoring of young faculty about these matters is, of course, only one facet of a broader problem–the general laxity of academe about the professionalization of its entrants. Many large law firms have sophisticated programs specifically designed to introduce lawyers into the ways of the profession, and physicians at least have residency requirements containing some formal structure. But we tend to leave new professors largely to their own devices with respect to many aspects of professional life, including dealing with publishers. We should at least let them in on the nasty secrets it took us so much time and pain to learn.

On Avoiding Rejection by Journals

by Nancy D. Simco

There may be people who enjoy reading rejection letters from journal editors, but most of us would rather avoid that. What follows is advice on how to avoid that. It does not contain new insights into the "art" of being published. There probably are no new insights on this subject, but it always seems useful to review the old insights.

Before Submission

Journal editors are often asked, "*What is the most common reason for rejecting papers?*" Many journal editors will agree that *the answer is that the authors of those papers have failed to convince the reviewers that they have anything to say.* With continual pressure to publish in order to obtain tenure, promotions, and salary increases, or even to remain in the profession, it is not surprising that some papers which have nothing to say are submitted to journals. However, a large number of papers which initially appear to fall into this category actually do not. The problem is an old one. Journalists are admonished not to "bury the lead." Journal referees, and grant proposal reviewers, are generally very busy people who do not see it as their jobs to sift through pages of prose to find out what the author's project is. A related adage is that papers in professional journals should not be candidates for mystery magazines. So, if there is a *first* rule regarding getting papers into print, it is to announce the point of the paper at the very beginning, and then to let the reader know how that point will be developed. It is not just reviewers one is apt to lose by burying the lead; since journal *readers* are deluged with material, they want to know right away whether *this* is a paper they want to read. If the central point of the paper has a reader's attention, the next step is to help the reader along throughout its development. The author can do this best by trying to see the paper as the reader sees it. Be conscious of what the reader has been told—and not been told—at each step in the process.

Further, there should not be too many steps in the process. Papers which are the average length of most current journal articles usually cannot adequately address a very complex point, even if the author is quite skillful. If your idea for a paper cannot be stated in a short paragraph of no more than three to four sentences (many reviewers would say one or two sentences!), it probably should be developed in a more extended format than a journal article.

But what if your problem is that you *do not* have a journal-article-sized idea? The best sources of such ideas are philosophical discussions with your colleagues and reading journals. Both are useful in focusing attention on a manageable sized issue. When you talk about and read philosophy the point you wish to interject in the on-going philosophical conversation, and where it fits in that conversation, is likely to emerge quite naturally.

While you are reading journals you will also be learning about the characteristics of particular journals. These characteristics need to be recalled when you are ready to submit your work. A useful practice is to keep your own notes, or log, on what you learn about each journal. The ultimate question your notes should be able to answer is, "Is there any reason to believe this journal will publish my paper on X?"

The answer to this question is the result of the answers to a number of prior questions. Has this journal published other papers on X? Are the papers in this journal written in a particular philosophical style? What is the normal length of papers in this journal? Does this journal publish comments? Discussion notes? Reviews? Let us look at these questions in a bit more detail.

First, let us consider **topics**. The clear case in which authors can be sure that their paper's topic will be appropriate is when an invitation to submit papers for a special issue on that topic has been announced. There is at least one journal which publishes only special topics issues, and the topics are announced well in advance. Of course, most of the papers one writes will not have such an obvious target.

There are topical trends within our discipline, just as there are in other disciplines, and those trends affect what is published. (Being able to see these trends develop and run their course prior to appearance in print is one of the reasons over-worked academics are willing to serve as journal referees.) It is difficult, perhaps impossible, to tell how long a trend will last, or where a particular journal is in relation to a trend, because authors do not have access to the papers accepted for publication that are "forthcoming." Nevertheless, your perusal of journals will tell you quite a lot. If several papers have appeared on a particular topic, they will almost always be clustered in a few of the journals. There will be journals which have published no papers on the subject and that should usually be taken as an indication that those journals are interested in something else.

When a trend is at its peak, papers in the thematic region become more difficult to get accepted. The greater the number of papers in an area, the harder it is to find something which has not already been said. Sometimes editors find themselves in the position of receiving a high-quality paper which makes the same point as a lower-quality paper they have already accepted. In this situation both the editor and the author of the higher-quality paper are disappointed, but timing in this sense is under the control of neither. The point here is that the disappointed author had in fact done the work needed to choose an appropriate journal. That this work did not result in an acceptance was more a matter of luck than ability. In publishing journal articles, at least, *ability and persistence will eventually overcome bad luck.* We will return to this important point later, but for now, let us note that it is usually the case that the work, which led one to submit the paper to the journal that turned it down under these circumstances, will also have produced a set of alternative journals. It is a good idea to get the paper right back into the mail and on its way to one of the alternatives.

Philosophical style also follows trends, and inexperienced authors should beware of getting too caught up in them. Attempting to write like someone else tends to trivialize your work. Remember that you are not Wittgenstein, Derrida, or your major professor. The best way for most of us to get into print is to say what we have to say as clearly as we can.

Clarity also involves not sending unintended messages to readers by the insensitive use of language. The American Philosophical Association publishes and distributes *Guidelines for Non-Sexist Use of Language.* Although this publication is directed toward making our use of language neutral with respect to gender, a number of people in the profession have reported that drawing attention to this issue has made them much more sensitive to other value-laden expressions which can interfere with communication.

There are other more specific senses of style with respect to which journals vary in what they accept. But, if you have been *reading* journals, there should be little confusion about most of these differences. For example, a piece of historical scholarship differs from a short discussion of a technical point in analytic philosophy in almost every detail. Papers on the same topic are written differently for subdisciplinary specialty journals than they are for general journals. The readership of a specialty journal can be expected to have a greater command of detail with the material. In general, readers of different journals have different expectations regarding the amount of tight argument or analysis, exposition, interpretation, background information, number of footnotes, content of footnotes, bibliographies, and length.

Journal editors scratch their heads when they are sent book-length manuscripts, or one-page political or religious harangues. But between these extremes paper length does raise some tricky questions. Some journals have explicit length specifications, for example, the "normal word limit is from 3,000 to 5,000 words." But even when editorial instructions are so precise, one often finds that a high percentage of the work which actually appears in the journal is approximately the same length, say, for example, close to one end or the other of the range. The most reliable guide to the length acceptable to particular journals is their *most recent* issues. I stress "most recent" because healthy journals are not static. The people making the decisions change, the reviewers change, the topics of interest change (and different topics may require development at different lengths), and financial situations change (perhaps resulting in increases or decreases in the number of printed pages). Such changes may result in only minor variations, but they can also produce abrupt shifts. Being aware of the major shifts can obviously save authors from submissions which are no longer appropriate for a given journal. And, if one can pick up on the minor variations, one has undoubtedly already achieved "pro" status.

Length is not even a constant with respect to discussion notes and book reviews. We tend to think of both of these forms as significantly shorter than articles, but a survey of journals produces quite a large number of counter-examples. Again, the most reliable guide will be a few of the journal's most recent issues. Canvassing journals also indicates whether they publish **discussion notes or book reviews**. Beginning authors are frequently advised to start their publishing careers by producing work in one, or both, of these forms. Many authors have found this to be very good advice, but one still has to get the work to the "right" journal. Discussion notes should enter some on-going *discussion*. The "best bet" for acceptance should be the journal which is home to the particular point at which your work enters the philosophical conversation. Be aware that journals rarely (almost never) publish discussion notes which continue the discussion from a *different* journal. Particular journals cater to their own readers, and do not expect them to "jump" to another journal for a part of an on-going conversation.

There are wide variations in book review practices. Journals which never publish book reviews, or which publish reviews written only by their own staff, will not welcome unsolicited work of this form. However, some journals list book titles with an invitation to volunteer to review them. Journals which issue such invitations tend to be in subdisciplinary areas. That this is the case is an advantage for a beginning scholar in a particular subdisciplinary area. Since the number of people in our profession is relatively small, and the number is even smaller in any subdisciplinary areas, and most of the people in a given area will read reviews of the books in that area, one can become known to the people with whom one hopes to "do philosophy" by producing work in this form.

Although volunteering for a specialized journal may offer the highest success rate, other types of journals do publish unsolicited reviews. However, before you spend your time in this manner, it is worth asking if an unsolicited review will be considered. A letter of inquiry, phone call, or e-mail message to the editor will help you judge whether to spend time on a particular review or move on to another project.

Regardless of which form your work takes, one of the primary characteristics sought by its reviewers is **originality**. If the first commandment of publishing in journals is "Don't bury the lead," the second may well be "Don't reinvent the wheel!" Here again, the best guide will be a thorough knowledge of the literature and journals in the area in which you are writing. The ultimate transgression of this commandment occurs when a reviewer comes upon a wheel of his or her own invention!

A related point is that it is always a good idea to let reviewers know that you are aware of work which is close to your own. For most journals, the accepted means of doing this is a brief footnote. This is part of **situating** your work within the literature. Both reviewers and readers want to know where your work is located in the on-going philosophical conversation. In some instances situating your work may require only a sentence (e.g., in a brief discussion piece), and in some instances it may require the bulk of the paper (e.g., in a piece attempting to persuade the reader of a point of interpretation regarding an historical figure). In any case, authors improve their chances of acceptance by locating their work.

And, what is sometimes more important, they improve their chances of getting an evaluation that is useful for helping the author improve the work. Reviewers often express location failure by saying that the author has failed to **motivate** the work.

'Motivation' has several connotations in this context. Does the paper indicate right away why its topic is important? Why the reader should be interested? Why this topic at this time? Against which background? All of these questions should be answered directly, or the reader should find them obviously answerable from what is said directly. The answers locate your work. And, if a reviewer says things which indicate that you have a location failure, that is *almost* good news. Making sure that your paper answers the above questions is something you can readily determine and repair. This minor repair may be all that is needed for acceptance.

Submitting your Paper

When you have settled on the journal to which you will submit your work, you can help your case by giving a little thought to what it would be like to be on the receiving end of your paper, plus a large number of other papers. A simple approach is best. The traditional "plain brown wrapper" is sturdy enough to protect a manuscript. Binding the envelope with yards of strapping tape is not necessary. And, special mail services are usually an unnecessary expense for the author and sometimes an inconvenience for the editor or journal staff. Anyone who handles a lot of mail can tell you that regular first class mail rarely fails. However, beware of anything which calls special attention to your package, especially if you are trying to save time! Special handling often adds unnecessary steps to the process. For example, a specially handled item may have to wait until an individual is available to deliver it, or a campus post office may send the journal office a notice by regular mail that there is a package to be picked up! An editor of a well-known journal told me that he has to drive to an off-campus post office to pick up certified mail.

Cover letters which describe the paper, or why the paper was written, are also unnecessary. Unless there is some particular reason the editor should be interested in the life history of a paper, all that is needed in the cover letter is the author's name, address, and the paper title.

Advocating such a sparse approach to cover letters might lead one to think that they should be dispensed with all together. But this is not the case. Because of their editorial experience, editors are very often in the position of receiving papers which are not submissions for their journals. For example, they may chair program committees, review for other journals, or collect papers for an anthology. So, it is useful to include a cover letter which indicates why the paper is being sent.

Reviewers need to know even less about the paper's circumstances than does the editor. There is no reason they should know the author's name. Blind refereeing is a common practice in philosophy, but if it is to be effective the author has to make it possible. Publishing philosophy journals is hardly a big business, so journals do not have sufficient staff members to remove the authors' identity from papers. The easiest means, for both authors and editors, of preparing papers for blind refereeing is to put any information which identifies the author on a removable cover sheet, or simply in the cover letter.

If one really wants refereeing to be blind, then care must be taken not to reveal the author's identity in either the text or the footnotes. There are some obvious instances in which footnotes are actually designed to "let" the referee "figure out" the author's identity. Some referees find this practice to be pretentious and annoying. In this case authors would better serve their interests by making no effort to conceal their identities.

So, is blind refereeing worth the extra effort? It has been argued that blind refereeing results in more papers by women, minorities, and unknown philosophers being published. Critics of blind refereeing have argued that it results in fewer publications by under represented groups. The Association of Philosophy Journal Editors (APJE) in cooperation with the APA Committee on the Status of Women and the APA Committee on Blacks in Philosophy tried to obtain information relevant to answering this question. In 1993 the APJE sent questionnaires to journals asking for information about the representation of women, minorities, and unaffiliated philosophers among the journal's submissions and acceptances, and the journal's policies on blind refereeing. No one expected conclusive results from the survey, but the data collected was not very useful in determining the correlation between blind refereeing policies and the issue of representation because there are too many cases in which the relevant factors are unknown. For example, what can one report about "E. P. Johnson" who uses a home address in a large metropolitan area? The data showed a higher average acceptance rate for women authors (31.99% for 22.26% of total submissions) than men authors (20.27% for 77.41% of total submissions), but fewer than a third of the journals made an attempt to separate acceptances by gender. (Acceptance rates of 31.99% and 20.27% are much higher, at least double, the mean acceptance rates in philosophy journals.) So, the jury is still out on the value of blind refereeing. In the absence of concrete evidence, authors can only follow the established practice of journals (and program committees) which have definite policies, and make their own decisions when submitting to others. One of the virtues of word processing equipment is that it is fairly easy to keep more than one version of a paper. So, if you are undecided about the blind-refereeing issue, it is feasible to have two versions until some factor tips the scale toward one of the alternatives.

The greatest virtue of word processing capabilities is the ease with which we can make changes. However, this also raises the expectation that authors will take advantage of this virtue and present clean, accurate text. Poor proof-reading, or no proof-reading, prior to submission is not viewed charitably by reviewers. And don't pass up the spellcheck option. One reviewer expressed this quite succinctly: "Why should I spend my time on something the author cared about so little?"

Part of the proof-reading routine should be to format your work so that it meets any special directions for manuscript preparation announced by the journal to which it is being submitted. Almost all philosophy journals ask for double-spaced text, footnotes at the end of the text, and adherence to some commonly used style specifications. Reviewers are so accustomed to work meeting these basic requirements that they often find it distracting when they are not met. Some journals will return papers unread if these requirements are not met.

Having said all this about what authors can do to enhance the probability of acceptance of their work, it is important to be explicit about what authors should be able to expect from journals. In 1974, in an effort to help both authors and editorial personnel, the Association of Philosophy Journal Editors adopted a set of guidelines for the handling of manuscripts. The Guidelines were also endorsed by the American Philosophical Association. However, since neither of these bodies have legislative authority over journals, they serve as recommendations rather than mandatory policy. Journals do operate at least in the spirit of these guidelines, but only minor revisions have been made in them over the past twenty years and some particular points need to be up-dated given changes in the mechanics of journal publishing.

Suggested Guidelines for the Handling of Manuscripts
by the Editors of Philosophy Journals

The following guidelines are given with the recognition that the Association cannot, and has no wish to, legislate for its members. They are designed merely to facilitate and clarify the processing of manuscripts and to communicate general policy. It is understood that variations from these guidelines may be necessitated by a variety of editorial conditions. When so necessitated, differing editorial practices are within the spirit of the guidelines, though editors are urged to announce or communicate their special policies.

Philosophy journals exist to serve the community of philosophers and to promote and further philosophical inquiry. The following professional guidelines regarding the processing of manuscripts are designed to facilitate these goals.

---

1. Special directions for the preparation of manuscripts shall be publicly announced by journals which have them.

2. Journals shall notify authors by return mail of the receipt of manuscripts and where possible indicate the approximate time needed for evaluation procedures.

3. Unless authors are notified to the contrary, such evaluation procedures will normally not extend beyond four months from the date of receipt. After this period of time authors are encouraged to inquire concerning the status of their manuscripts.

4. Authors of accepted manuscripts shall be notified in the letter of acceptance of the approximate date of the publication of their manuscript.

5. If articles are held for two months or more, letters of rejection shall normally include one of the following: a) the comments of the referees, b) a brief summary of the referee's comments, or c) the editor's reasons for rejecting the paper. The signed comments of a referee may be forwarded to the author only with the referee's explicit permission. Editors shall not be expected to reply to further inquiries about their evaluations.

6. Editors shall not suggest other specific journals to authors.

7. Authors have full responsibility for the proper preparation of manuscripts. When the manuscript is not properly prepared, services performed for them by editorial offices, as well as author changes in proof, are properly chargeable to them.

8. Changes in manuscripts by an editor other than those necessary for the style of the journal (footnotes, spelling, layout, etc.) shall be made only with the approval of the author.

9. Authors shall normally review their articles in proof before printing.

10. Authors shall submit the same manuscript to only one journal at a time.

11. Authors have responsibility for arranging (through envelopes, return postage, etc.) for return of their manuscripts.

12. A letter of acceptance from an editor is normally an agreement to publish the article in the journal.

The items in the Guidelines were intended to be straightforward, but some of them deserve comment.

Number 3 encourages authors to inquire about the status of manuscripts after four months. Many authors are convinced that such inquiries will prejudice editors against their work. Editors say emphatically that it does not. What produces this apparent discrepancy? One can only guess, but busy editors' *abrupt* demeanor in response to telephone inquiries has frequently been cited! I believe that editors do genuinely encourage inquiries, *after a reasonable amount of time.* Weekly calls from an anxious author may not really prejudice the decision, but the editor is not likely to be pleased to see more submissions from this author.

E-mail is quickly becoming the choice medium for inquiries. For both authors and editors, e-mail accomplishes the purpose without being as time consuming as letters back and forth by regular or "snail" mail, or as a game of "telephone tag."

There are some pitfalls in Guideline 5. The widest procedural variation among journals probably occurs with respect to how they handle referee's comments. Similar to several items mentioned earlier, the most reliable guide on what to expect is the author's most recent experience with that journal (as well as the recent experience of one's professors and colleagues). Some journals never try to explain why papers are rejected while some try to give a thorough explanation on every occasion. The reason there is so much variation is that providing authors with *good* explanations, which are accurate, fair, and not misleading, is by far the most time consuming task editors face. Some would rather offer no explanation at all than one which will be useless or harmful.

There is significant disagreement among editors regarding whether it is ever appropriate to reveal a referee's identity. The reasons for not revealing the identity of the reviewer when the report is negative seem obvious, but problems also arise when the report is positive. The most extreme case may have occurred when the author of a rejected paper tried to get the favorable referee to join in a lawsuit against the editor! A more common problem is authors contacting favorable referees to read more of their work or help them find publishers. Even if the referee is disposed toward offering this kind of help, it can easily create unfair demands on the referee's time.

There is also disagreement about whether editors should "be expected to reply to further inquiries about their evaluations." Many editors want to know when authors believe something has gone wrong with the evaluation of their work. A large part of the editor's job is to make the review process as fair, intelligent, and humane as possible. But if the editor does not know the process is failing, it won't be fixed. Editors need to continually and open-mindedly scrutinize their own review processes, but this does not mean they should see them as having failed each time they are questioned. Editors will sometimes re-enter a paper whose author has questioned the process, or its results, so it is reasonable to ask for this treatment. At the same time, it should be recognized that given the large number of submissions to most journals, editors may be forced to avoid engaging in this practice.

Guideline 6 has raised a considerable amount of curiosity. The reason the APJE adopted it was that some authors mistakenly took the advice of the editor of journal X to send a paper to journal Y as a commitment on the part of the editor of journal Y. There is also a danger of an author taking a suggestion that a paper be sent to a specific journal as amounting to a recommendation to that journal to publish the paper. These kinds of situations have caused friction between authors and editors and between editors and editors.

The unique submission policy, Guideline 10, is common practice in philosophy, but not in other disciplines. This policy is designed to avoid the abuse of journal personnel, especially reviewers. Disciplines which allow multiple, simultaneous submissions are generally those in which reviewers are paid for their time. Since reviewers' time is professional *service* in our discipline, it is a very precious commodity. Without people willing to donate this service there would be no journals–or, at least, very few. If two or three referees have given careful consideration to a paper, and the editor then receives a letter saying that the paper is being published by another journal, its author should probably not send any more papers to that editor.

Guideline 11 is clearly a case in which this document is out of date. Journals no longer return manuscripts because word processing and photocopying facilities have made this practice unnecessary.

Submitting Your Paper Again

Even if you have great ideas and take all of the advice available, the probability that you will never receive a rejection letter is quite low. Acceptance rates in philosophy journals are among the lowest in academia. However, there are several variations on the rejection theme and on most of them, you should submit your paper again.

On some occasions your paper will be returned with referee's comments which suggest improvements, and an invitation to resubmit to that journal. Because editors have so many papers from which to choose, an invitation to resubmit is a clear indication that your paper is a strong candidate for publication in that journal. If you revise your paper as suggested and resubmit it to the same journal, that does not guarantee that the journal will publish it, but it does enormously increase the odds in its favor. Journal practices vary regarding whether revised, resubmitted papers are reviewed by the referee whose comments on the earlier version were sent to the author, or to new referees, or to both. But, regardless of the practice, an invited resubmission already has the editor's attention and interest. In most cases editors only invite resubmission of papers which can be revised in light of the referee's comments with a modest amount of work. Papers seen as requiring substantial revision are also seen as too great a risk to encourage their return.

Not all referee's comments will be as useful as those accompanied by an invitation to resubmit, but they should always be considered as a potentially valuable resource. The most common complaint about referees from authors is that their work has been misunderstood. When this happens one should remember that referees generally read a large number of papers and know what to look for in them, so if they have misunderstood, the average journal reader is likely to have a much harder time. Study the comments to see if you can determine what misled the referee. It is not always easy to adopt a reader's point of view with respect to your own work, but it may be the most useful skill you can acquire. Referee's reports, as well as your colleagues' comments and your commenting on your colleagues' work, are important resources for developing this skill. After you have done what is needed to get the reader on track, mail the paper to another of the journals you believe might be interested in it. Guiding the reader through the paper usually does not require extensive revision. It will almost certainly require less time than writing another paper.

Occasionally you may find that a referee's comments just "miss the mark." After you have ruled out the sort of misunderstanding discussed above, you may still believe that your work received an inappropriate evaluation. You have to be the judge of which revisions and how much revision is needed on the basis of any report. Sending the paper to another journal without revision is sometimes the best course of action. It is also a professional courtesy to let the editor know that you found the evaluation inappropriate. As indicated in discussing the Guidelines, this information helps the editor continually improve the review process, which contributes to upgrading publishing in the profession as a whole.

You may want to send an unrevised paper out again even if the referee's comments do not fall in the "off the mark" category. Not every set of referees will see the merits of a particular paper in the same way. For one thing, different sets of referees read different sets of competing papers. A particular paper can obviously be judged as the best of the lot with respect to one set of papers, but have a much lower ranking in another set.

If the referee's comments are useful, and you decide to make the suggested revisions, you then have the option of sending the paper back to the same journal. However, if you do send it back to the same journal, the cover letter should indicate that the paper is a revised version of a paper reviewed by the journal. Authors frequently include a copy of the referee's report with the resubmission. This information is useful to the editor in selecting which referees will be most helpful for both the author and editor. If you send the revised piece to another journal, you need not indicate that it is a revision. It has a clean slate with the new journal. Some people recommend sending unsolicited revisions to a different journal in every case because of the clean slate feature. This may be good advice when decisions at the first journal are made by one, or a small number, of people. But, for most journals which use a large number of reviewers, unsolicited revisions are not disadvantaged.

There is really only one crucial point to be made with respect to papers which have not been accepted: Submit the paper again! Earlier we saw that a paper may not be accepted because of bad luck in timing. There are also other reasons for rejections which are not based on the quality of work. In discussing trends within the discipline, we noted that there can just be too many papers at one time on a particular theme. An editor may believe that the journal has published so many papers on a topic that the readership has tired of them. There are also questions of balance. Whatever the journal's established readership, the editor will want to print papers which appeal to as many interest groups within the readership as is feasible.

After your Paper Has Been Accepted

The letter of acceptance will tell you what happens next. Sometimes you will be asked to do minor revisions. If the acceptance letter gives you a publication date, you should do the revisions as quickly as possible. Otherwise, your paper might have to be rescheduled. Some journals do not schedule papers for publication until they have the final copy. In this case, the speed at which the author makes revisions determines how soon the paper will appear in print.

Most journals now ask for disk copies of accepted papers. This saves production costs and staff hours for journals, and significantly increases accuracy. In spite of beginning with electronic copy, most journals still send page proofs to authors. This is another occasion on which you should respond promptly. Journals with tight publication schedules may have to delay publication of a paper if the page proofs arrive late, or they may publish the paper as is.

If a journal asks for disk copy and you cannot provide it, just explain this to the editor. This should not result in the journal's inability to print your paper. It has been projected that in a few years journals will be forced to charge authors for producing electronic copy of their texts, but there is no indication that this is necessary at this time.

24

However, as indicated above in the APJE Guidelines, it is sometimes necessary to charge for author-errors corrected at the page proof stage. Corrections at page proof can be minimized if you do a good job of proofing before submission. The old advice about proof reading is still best: read with a helper if possible, with one of you reading the copy aloud and spelling any unusual words; or if you proof alone, follow along one line at a time with a straight edge underneath the line, and avoid reading for content.

If the journal which accepts your paper has a copy editor, when you receive page proofs you may find that your text has been altered to conform to the journal's style. If changes made by a copy editor change the meaning, or even the tone, of your work, you should mark the proof to indicate that you want to retain the original copy and include a brief explanation.

Presenting Work and Delivering Papers

by Thomas Magnell

Most philosophers have delivered papers or otherwise presented work before colleagues and the educated public as a means of furthering their own intellectual development. Plato and Aristotle went so far as to create colleagues for the purpose. Medieval scholastics became itinerant speakers, in part to fill the void of monkish seclusion. Worldly philosophers such as Russell have sought all manner of occasions to speak their minds, as well as to write their thoughts. There is much to be said for this.

More or less formal venues for presenting work give you the opportunity to engage others in discussions of your developing thought. Through their questions and comments, you can learn what needs to be said more clearly; which arguments need to be tightened up; and which points might even need further thought. Criticism is usually friendly. Intemperate speechifying by others is not likely to be well received. Killer questions are always possible, though rare. In any event, difficult questions can spur you on to further reflection after the fact. All of this is difficult to obtain through the printed word. Moreover, occasions for speaking allow you to present work in various stages of completion, from early thoughts, to work in progress, to work ready for publication. Delivering papers is no substitute for publishing papers, but it is one way to go about publishing better papers.

Meetings of the American Philosophical Association

The meetings of the American Philosophical Association (APA) are obvious occasions for presenting work. They are the largest annual gatherings of philosophers in the United States. There are three sets of meetings: Eastern Division Meetings, held in the last week of December; Pacific Division Meetings, held at the end of March or the beginning of April; and Central Division Meetings, held at the end of April or the beginning of May. The Eastern Division Meetings are attended by the largest number of people, but the Pacific and Central Division Meetings are otherwise comparable. The programs at the meetings of each division are separated into sessions sponsored by the division and sessions sponsored by smaller philosophical societies that focus on a particular area of philosophy, a philosophical movement, or a prominent philosophical figure. In recent years, the portion of the program sponsored by the smaller philosophical societies has grown to be as large as the APA portion of the program.

Each division of the APA has its own program committee, which makes decisions about invited papers, commentators, and chairs of sessions for the APA portion of a divisional meeting. The divisional program committee will consider requests for chairing or commenting on sessions. The program committee is also the body that makes the decisions on which submitted papers will be accepted for the APA portion of a divisional meeting. Guidelines for submissions are set forth below on pages 29-31.

There is no single rule for submitting papers to the smaller societies. Each society is autonomous and has its own guidelines. Some societies will only accept submissions from members. Others do not impose conditions of membership. Some societies meet regularly with all three divisions. Societies that have sessions at only one of the divisional meetings are likely to have them at the Eastern Division Meetings.

When submitting a paper to a society, it is usually a good idea to follow the general guidelines for APA submissions. Deadlines may be a little more flexible, as may the lengths of papers. It is prudent, however, to check this out ahead of time. Some societies review submissions by committee. The president of a society can be expected to forward submissions to the appropriate individuals. Requests for chairing a session or commenting on a paper can also be made to the president.

Most philosophical societies belong to the Conference of Philosophical Societies, an umbrella organization of which even the APA is a member. A list of member philosophical societies and information on the societies may be requested from the National Office of the American Philosophical Association. Information on philosophical societies is also published in *The Directory of American Philosophers*, published by the Philosophy Documentation Center.

International Conferences

The largest international gatherings of philosophers are the World Congresses of Philosophy. They are sponsored by the *Fédération Internationale des Sociétés de Philosophie* and held once every five years. In addition to the invited papers, the program committee for a World Congress of Philosophy reviews submissions for sessions in sections on specified topics announced in a circular that is made available ahead of time. International societies and some of the societies that meet regularly with the APA also hold sessions in conjunction with World Congresses of Philosophy. Inquiries, requests for guidelines, and submissions may be directed to the president of a participating society. The XXth World Congress of Philosophy will be held in Boston in the summer of 1998. This will be only the second time in over seventy years that a World Congress of Philosophy will have been held in the United States.

Occasionally, the *Fédération Internationale des Sociétés de Philosophie* sponsors smaller interim conferences in the off years between World Congresses of Philosophy. International societies also meet on their own, sometimes in exotic locales. Nationwide and regional philosophical groups outside the United States, such as the Canadian Philosophical Association, the Australasian Association of Philosophy, and the Aristotelian Society and Mind Association hold annual meetings. Many local conferences are also held throughout the world. Presenting work in another country among scholars who may have sometimes remarkably different philosophical backgrounds and perspectives can be highly stimulating.

PRESENTING WORK AND DELIVERING PAPERS

Conferences in the United States

Some philosophical societies, such as the American Society for Aesthetics, and the Metaphysical Society of America choose to hold large annual meetings apart from the divisional meetings of the APA. Other groups, such as the Conference on Value Inquiry, and the Association for Practical and Professional Ethics hold independent, annual conferences. Geographically based associations, such as the Creighton Club, the New Jersey Regional Philosophical Association, the Northern New England Philosophical Association, the Ohio Philosophical Association, and the Washington Philosophy Club hold regular meetings, some of them more than once a year. Graduate students are often made particularly welcome. The review process for submissions varies from group to group, and sometimes meeting to meeting. The geographically based meetings offer excellent opportunities to try out new arguments, to garner critical comments on works in progress, and to meet nearby philosophers.

The dates and locations of conferences can be found in the Philosophical Calendar. Some international conferences, as well as annual conferences and special conferences on particular topics are listed. The Philosophical Calendar also contains information on persons to contact and deadlines for submissions. It is published by the Conference of Philosophical Societies, and is available by mail through subscriptions. Some issues appear in the *Proceedings and Addresses of the American Philosophical Association* and can be viewed through the home page of the APA on the world wide web. All the issues are mailed to subscribers and to all member societies.

Departmental Colloquia and Other Engagements

Departmental colloquia and lectures, and undergraduate and graduate student philosophy clubs provide still more opportunities for presenting work. The selection of speakers is almost always by invitation. The engagements range from small, informal gatherings, to large, formal lectures. It is wise to determine the nature of the engagement at the time of the invitation. A paper focusing on scholarly minutiae that only a specialist could love would be as out of place at an undergraduate philosophy club as a laid back, directed discussion would be at a formal lecture. Whatever the venue, presenting work before others can promote lively, edifying discourse.

APA Paper Submission Guidelines

The following guidelines are those in effect for 1997-98. Please check current issues of the Proceedings and Addresses of the American Philosophical Association *or the APA website for current guidelines.*

Information For All Three Divisions

• Author must be a member in good standing of the APA.

• Papers in any area are welcome.

• All paper submissions are blind reviewed. Therefore, the name, institution, and references pertaining to the identity of the author are to be omitted from the actual manuscript, notes and bibliography.

• Submitted papers are not returned to the author.

• Paper deadlines falling on a weekend or holiday will be extended to the next business day.

• Any submitted paper which is under consideration for publication elsewhere will be considered, provided it will not appear in print until after the Division meeting is held. If this is the case, indicate when and where the paper is expected to be published.

• The envelope containing a paper submission should be clearly marked on the lower left side with the name of the appropriate Divisional Meeting.

• The receipt of a paper submission will be acknowledged if a self-addressed, stamped envelope or postcard is included.

• Papers not accepted by one Division may be resubmitted for consideration by another Division; however, the author will be required to send a new set of submission materials.

• Papers and abstracts must be typed, double-spaced, prepared with no less than one-inch margins on all sides, typed on one side of the page with all pages numbered, prepared in standard 10 or 12 point font.

• Three copies of the paper and three copies of an abstract are required; abstract is limited to 150 words.

• Author's name, institution, address, and telephone number should appear on a separate cover page, *and should not appear elsewhere in the manuscript.* Author should also indicate on the cover page which Division should receive the manuscript.

- Paper submissions for all Divisions should be sent to:
  Linda Smallbrook, Meeting Coordinator
  The American Philosophical Association
  University of Delaware
  Newark, Delaware 19716

Central Division Paper Submission Information

- Postmarked deadline for submission of papers is September 1 (prior to meeting).

- Meeting is usually held the end of April.

- Selections are announced in January, or before, when possible.

- Papers under consideration by the Pacific Division will not be reviewed by the Central Division Program Committee.

- No more than two submissions by the same author will be considered by the Program Committee.

- Papers must observe a limit of 3,000 actual words, and must include a word count on the title page. Papers exceeding specified length will not be considered by the Program Committee.

Eastern Division Paper Submission Information

- Postmarked deadline for submission of papers is March 1 (prior to meeting).

- Meeting is held December 27-30.

- Selections are announced in May, or early June.

- No more than one submission by the same author will be considered by the Program Committee.

- Submissions for consideration as colloquium papers must not exceed a length of 3,000 words. Authors must include a word count on the title page. Papers exceeding 3,000 words will not be considered as colloquium papers.

- Submissions for consideration as symposium papers must not exceed a length of 5,000 words. Abstracts for symposium papers must not exceed a length of 300 words. Authors must include a word count of the paper's text and the abstract on the title page. Authors should be aware that only a few papers are selected for presentation as symposium papers. If authors wish to have a shortened version of their paper considered as a colloquium paper, they should submit the appropriately shortened version, along with a shortened abstract, simultaneously with the submission of the symposium paper.

- Any paper submitted without an abstract will not be considered. Any paper whose abstract is deemed unacceptable by the Program Committee will not be accepted. No revised abstract submitted after the paper's acceptance will be published in the *Proceedings and Addresses of the American Philosophical Association* without the approval of the Program Committee.

Pacific Division Paper Submission Information

- Postmarked deadline for submission of papers is September 1 (prior to meeting).

- Meeting is usually held the end of March.

- Selections are announced in December.

- Papers under consideration by the Central Division will not be reviewed by the Pacific Division Program Committee.

- No more than one submission by the same author will be considered by the Program Committee.

- Submissions for consideration as colloquium papers must not exceed the length of 3,000 words. Authors must include a word count on the title page.

- Submissions for consideration as symposium papers must not exceed the length of 5,000 words. Abstracts for symposium papers must not exceed a length of 150 words. Authors must include a word count of the paper's text and of the abstract on the title page. Authors should be aware that only a few papers are selected for presentation as symposium papers. If authors wish to have a shortened version of their paper considered as a colloquium paper, they should submit the appropriately shortened version, along with a shortened abstract, simultaneously with the submission of the symposium paper. (This will be considered a single submission.)

General Advice About Book Publishing

by Marcia Yudkin and Janice Moulton

One acquisitions editor at a university press wrote us, "There are no unsung Miltons lurking in the halls of academy. Maybe Vico was ignored for 200 years, but it's most unlikely that a first-rate book will go unpublished, and it will be published well." We think this is somewhat too optimistic; much evidence points to quite a contrary moral. First of all, in the twentieth century publishing is a business. Even at nonprofit university presses, a variety of criteria besides the quality of a manuscript influences the decision of whether or not to publish it. With a little imagination, anyone can dream up an unprofitable project that would not fit the specialization of any existing press. Secondly, compared with journal publishing, book publishing is haphazard and undemocratic. With blind review, a bright but completely unknown author from an obscure college has a fair chance of a journal accepting her article; but that same author, submitting an uninvited book proposal or manuscript of similar quality, has the odds stacked much higher against her. Without understanding the realities of publishing, she might try 20 wrong publishers, or 20 suitable publishers with the wrong approach, fail, and then give up. On the other hand, she can greatly improve her odds of getting published by using a knowledge of how publishing works to her advantage.

We recommend that anyone writing or considering writing a book read *Books: The Culture and Commerce of Publishing*, by sociologists Lewis A. Coser, Charles Kadushin and Walter W. Powell (see "Resources"), particularly chapters 5 and 9. Based on formal and informal interviews with more than 100 editors in different sectors of publishing and more than 200 authors, they explain how various pressures on editors lead them to acquire manuscripts in a manner that slights poorly connected, unsavvy hopefuls. They also document the unbalanced power relation between authors and publishers and its consequences. Anyone who doubts that their conclusions apply to the presses that publish philosophers should also read *Getting into Print: The Decision-Making Process in Scholarly Publishing*, Walter W. Powell's case study of two scholarly publishing houses (see "Resources").

What are you writing?

We don't mean to scare anyone into a cynical, sale-oriented approach to writing a book. We assume that you want to write a book because you believe you have something worthwhile to say and would like to communicate it in print. Our advice consists mainly of adding several steps to those you would probably take anyway and omitting others that editors and other experts on publishing consider unlikely to lead to publication. Rather early in the planning stage of your book project, for example, you should decide what *kind* of book you want to make it. There are three main types: scholarly books, trade books, and textbooks.

Scholarly books, both monographs and anthologies, are aimed at libraries and specialists in a certain field and distributed through mail order, some specialized bookstores, and at professional conventions. Trade books, aimed at general (including highly educated) audiences, are distributed primarily through bookstores. They tend to go out of print much sooner than scholarly books, and there are relatively few by philosophers. Textbooks, of course, whether unitary ones or anthologies, sell almost exclusively to college students through college bookstores. In addition to different audiences and distribution systems, each of these kinds of books represents a different set of constraints and opportunities. While royalty rates and contracts for each differ also, the main reason this classification system matters for authors is its relevance for choosing an appropriate publishing house for your book and then contacting it and following through effectively.

Finding out about publishers

Once you have an idea of your topic and target audience, you should start collecting information about potential publishers. While this *Guidebook* includes listings for a number of publishers, this far from exhausts the publishing houses that put out philosophy books. If you become interested in a publisher, you can call or write to request their philosophy catalog and examine it closely, looking to see who they publish, what kinds of books, in what subject areas and at what levels. Notice whether or not there are any philosophy series, and if so, who the series editor is. If you can attend an APA meeting, go and take notes on various publishers' offerings and talk to the representatives there, some of whom may be even be the acquisitions editors. At the exhibits or in your library, look over samples of different publishers' books to see how well executed they are. You may also want to contact some philosophers who have published books with the publishers you are investigating to ask them how satisfied they feel with the process and the result.

One strange fact is that many publishers seem reluctant to specify their preferences even when the preferences are very well established. One acquisitions editor has defended his inability to explain what he called "editorial judgment" thusly: "It's a bit like asking a centipede how he or she can coordinate all those legs. Thinking about it too closely means you can't do it." Surely, formulating and publicizing the preferences that guide a company's choices should pull in more appropriate submissions and discourage inappropriate ones, but until publishers believe that, careful review of their offerings will be critical.

When it comes to matters like how long it takes for a final manuscript to make it into print, or whether or not they will consider Festschriften, editors are a good deal more cooperative. If you have these sorts of questions about publishers, call and ask.

Choosing a publisher

We think that you will be more satisfied when your book is published if, from the start, you formulate your goal as not merely getting your book published, but getting it published well. If yours is a scholarly book, you will want it to accurately reflect the final manuscript you turn in, to be reviewed, to sell to libraries, and to stay in print at least long enough for it to reach its audience. Since relatively few academic authors find themselves with offers from more than one publisher, you should carefully choose a target publisher, or list several in order of priority, before you submit. As Coser, Kadushin and Powell document, once the book is accepted and you have signed a contract, you are in a poor position to protest poor-quality editing, poor-quality bindings, printing or paper, a tasteless cover or a plan to omit an index. The best way to assure that yours will be a quality product is to choose a publisher that does your sort of book well consistently.

You may decide to shoot for the prestige publishers first, or you may decide on another strategy. Suppose, for example, that your book is a new translation of a classic, or on a relatively specialized subject or rather technical; you might be better off aiming at a publisher that has carved out that particular market niche. Not only might the latter be more receptive to your submission, as publishers generally prefer to keep accepting manuscripts in the specialties they have established; the more specialized publisher might also be able to reach the potential audience for your book more effectively.

Price is another factor to consider in drawing up your list of potential publishers. If your book is designed for students, it shouldn't be priced out of their reach. If your book is aimed at your professional peers, you wouldn't want it to threaten the budget of an assistant professor. One author wrote to Janice Moulton for the last edition of the *Guidebook* about the author's book, which was supposed to be available for courses and yet cost $40 for under 350 pages. The author lamented, "It cannot be required for courses and is virtually unsaleable except to a few affluent libraries....I cannot now utilize portions of the book in Xerox form for my students without violation of the explicit copyright warning." When we asked publishers to report the range of book prices to help make comparisons several editors indicated that they had no idea how much the books their company published cost.

Contacting the publisher

Here is where the research of Coser, Kadushin and Powell is most helpful. They divided the various sources of the manuscripts that editors ended up purchasing into three main categories: (1) those that resulted from the editor's active searching; (2) those that were personally recommended by someone the editor could trust; and (3) "over-the-transom" submissions, those simply mailed in without any prior contact between the author and editor. They found that most editors coped with limited time for a great number of submissions by setting up a priority system, in which they turned first to the category of submissions they could least afford to ignore and gave the other categories whatever time they had left. At all publishing houses, categories (1) and (2) received by far the most attention. Powell, who observed two scholarly publishers for an extended time at close range, found that at "Apple Press," manuscripts in category (1) had a roughly one in three chance of being published, those in category (2) slightly less than one in ten and those in category (3) considerably less than one in a hundred. "The message to authors should be clear," concluded Coser, Kadushin and Powell (p. 132). "Use whatever contacts you have. Given the large number of projects that cross an editor's desk, any type of serious, personal recommendation that will attract someone's attention can only help."

For academic authors, the recommender who pulled a submission out of the lowest-priority category was either a more well-known mentor, friend or colleague of the author, anyone else the editor happened to know and trust, or a series editor. (Russell, you may recall, intervened and secured the publication of Wittgenstein's *Tractatus Logico-Philosophicus* for his friend and former student.) Powell emphasized that academic authors have a better chance than non-academic authors when submitting a manuscript without any intermediary or prior contact, but his statistics reinforce the recommendation of the earlier book that you should submit "over the transom" only as a last resort.

If you can't think of or can't (or don't want to) persuade a suitable intermediary to help you get the editor's attention, then it's especially crucial that you prepare your book submission with care. The following suggestions also apply if you've used an intermediary, for even a recommendation by the most eminent philosopher will rarely override a bad proposal or manuscript.

First, find out how much material you need to submit. There are three main kinds of preferences. Some textbook and scholarly publishers request only a proposal and detailed outline or table of contents. Others request in addition several sample chapters, which should be the strongest or most characteristic ones, not necessarily the first ones. Textbook publishers will almost never want more than that, because they like to be able to influence the form and content of the book. But many scholarly publishers, particularly some university presses, cannot reply without having had the complete manuscript to read and referee. Submitting less than what a publisher wants will either yield a refusal or a noncommittal request for more material. Submitting more than what a publisher wants, on the other hand may result in a considerable delay when it lands in the editor's "when-I-have-time" pile.

Second, prepare the submission. Most of the procedural recommendations in the section on journal publishing apply here as well. There is one big difference between journal and book submissions, though; along with making your writing lucid and your typing or printout neat, in the latter case you must also, however genteelly, try to sell the publisher your book. Either in a proposal, or, if you prefer, in a long cover letter that performs the function of a proposal, you must explain what is distinctive about your book, who the potential audience would be and why buyers will prefer your book over other similar ones in its general subject area. For a book you think would be adopted for courses, be specific about courses that it would suit, even estimating the number of those courses and their enrollments if you can. For a monograph that is not designed for courses, you should still give every kind of evidence you can think of (the number of people working in that subfield, the groundswell of interest and controversy about journal articles that your book is based on) of who is likely to buy your book and why. Do not assume that publishers know as much as you about current trends in philosophy; their information and impressions may be out of date.

Make sure that your proposal can be understood by an intelligent non-philosopher. Although the editor you are contacting may know quite a lot about philosophy, he or she will probably circulate the proposal to other editors or editorial board members who will also need to be convinced that your book is marketable and important. Your outline or table of contents should be informative enough to show that you have already thought through the book in detail and that your material will be well chosen, complete and logically organized. Ten or even 20 pages for the plan of a book when you are not submitting the whole manuscript is not too much. If you are not submitting the whole manuscript, mention how long you expect it to be and when you expect to complete it. Most publishers want you to enclose your vita as well, and you may also suggest getting together to discuss your project in person, at an APA meeting, for example, or at the office of the publisher. For incomplete projects, editors often like personal contact with authors in order to gauge their ability to complete what they have proposed.

37

Unlike journals, only a few book publishers strenuously object to simultaneous submissions. Some university presses require in cases of multiple submissions that you promise not to commit yourself to another publisher before their review process is complete. You may want to put those publishers that demand exclusive submissions at the top of your priority list if they say they are quick and at the bottom of your list if they are slow. One reason response times of different houses vary is that some send proposals out to specialists in the project's field, while others reserve that method of review for the final manuscript.

Last, address both the package and your cover letter to an editor by name. Otherwise, especially at a larger house, your submission may be shunted around among different departments or lost. Most publishers will be glad to tell you the name of the editor who handles philosophy submissions if you call them.

Negotiating with the publisher

Many publishers use a two-stage review process: initial screening of the proposal or the proposal and sample chapters, and later formal review, including outside referees' reports, of the complete manuscript. Some of these publishers can offer what is called an "advance contract," basically a promise to publish the book should the final manuscript be acceptable, on the basis of their initial screening. Others encourage certain authors to submit a complete manuscript, but without promising to publish it; they can offer a contract only on the basis of a complete manuscript. Since a publisher may request quite extensive changes in a complete manuscript, the latter is not equivalent to a final manuscript. And every publishing contract contains an escape clause that allows the publisher to back out of the agreement if the final manuscript is not satisfactory. Although this escape clause is rarely invoked in academic publishing, you should be aware of its existence.

Virtually every other clause in a contract is negotiable to some extent. Do not assume, if you are presented with a preprinted contract form with your name, book title and other particulars typed in, that you must accept the standard printed terms. Any number, phrase or paragraph can be x'd out and another number, phrase or paragraph substituted. Several books listed under "Resources" explain various terms and clauses of publishing contracts in detail. Since agents work on commission, it's probably not convenient to use an agent to help you negotiate your contract. But you may want to ask a lawyer to explain the legal terms in the contract to you, particularly if it's your first contract.

Before you sign the contract is the time to discuss when the book will appear, how the book will be advertised, whether or not you will have the right to approve the cover and text design and whatever other similar factors matter to you. If you agree on something that your editor says is not appropriate to insert in the contract, try to get it down in writing with the editor's signature. This is important not because editors are unreliable and tend to go back on their word, but as a way to prevent misunderstanding. Also, throughout publishing editors change jobs frequently; if your editor leaves the house you contracted with before your book finishes the publication cycle, his or her successor may be reluctant to proceed as you verbally agreed. Anything in writing has more moral weight than a verbal agreement with someone who no longer works there.

After acceptance

After you sign the contract, you will probably receive a production timetable and detailed instructions for preparing the final manuscript. You will have to send off not only what you might think of as the book itself, but also the "front matter"— title page, table of contents, preface and acknowledgments—and permissions to reprint copyrighted material. Not long afterwards, just when you are enjoying being rid of your project, the copy-edited manuscript will arrive in the mail. These days, many publishers use freelance copy editors, and the extent to which they wreak refinement or havoc on your writing varies. In *One Book/Five Ways* (see "Resources") you can see what five different copy editors did to the same two chapters of a manuscript. Their changes range from minor polishing to restyling of almost every sentence. One copy editor deleted material that she considered redundant but that the other four left in; she also explained to the author the reasons for many of her changes, while the other four did not. It's best to keep an open mind about whether or not your prose can bear improvement and to remain calm when you see the extent of the markings on your manuscript. If you find changes that are positively wrong, awkward or misleading, explain why you find them so in a letter to your contact with the publishing house.

Your subsequent responsibilities will include proofreading and, usually, preparing an index. Both of these tasks will have to be completed within a very short time, about two weeks, so make sure you have an idea when the proofs will be arriving. Set aside enough time to do a thorough job or make arrangements beforehand for someone to help you out. Your publisher will probably give you detailed instructions on how to perform these tasks; you may also find the *Chicago Manual of Style* or other style manuals helpful (see "Resources"). Around this time, the marketing department will send you an author's questionnaire to fill out. Think through your answers to the questions about journals and magazines for advertising, specific professional groups for mailings, courses for which your book is appropriate and so on, as the marketing department will probably rely on your suggestions in its sales strategy for the book.

Special situations

Dissertations. Contacting a press about publishing your Ph.D. thesis won't provoke a frenzy of enthusiasm, not even if you are the hottest protégé to come along since Plato, and your mentor has written that ahead to the publisher. You'll get a better response if you play down the fact that it's your thesis and make it clear in your proposal and sample material that this is an original, well-written and significant work of philosophy that has already been through several stages of revision. Dissertations that make it into print have usually had boring, pedantic chapters cut and other material added; do the surgery and reconstruction before you submit.

39

Anthologies. What could be more of a scam than making money and tenure by editing an anthology? If you have the idea that an anthology editor just thinks up a concept while the authors and the publisher do all the work, then you'd better talk to someone who has coordinated contributions from ten or more authors about the tribulations and ordeal that may be involved. For a collection that includes new work, you will be responsible for soliciting articles and ensuring that they are completed on time, of sufficient quality and within the budgeted length. This may require considerable tact and organizational skills. Using already published selections, on the other hand, will involve a lot of correspondence and follow-up; an anthology cannot go into production until you furnish the publisher with all the appropriate copyright permissions.

If you decide you're up to the task, your proposal should be clear about whether the selections will be new or originally published, whether the appeal will be primarily the authors' ideas or well-known names or both and how tightly the articles will be connected, as well as the level or background the articles will assume. Estimate the total length of the volume, the average length of selections, and the length of the interpretive introduction you will undoubtedly want to include.

Textbooks. The most market-oriented of the various types of books you might write, textbooks involve some peculiar dangers and requirements. Because sizable profits are at stake, textbook publishers compete fiercely with one another. Beginning in the 1970s, several larger publishers, including McGraw-Hill, Harper and Row, and Little-Brown, tried to improve on the slow, uncertain process of hiring an academic to produce a textbook. A more controlled process evolved of concocting a marketable educational formula, hiring non-academics to do the writing and finding an academic, preferably well known, willing to receive credit as the author. Chapter 10 of *Books* describes and condemns these essentially ghost-written "managed texts" and warns professors not to be deluded into cooperating with them. If a textbook sales representative or editor approaches you about writing a textbook, you owe it to yourself to read this chapter and discuss its points with them before you commit yourself.

Although editors at textbook houses tend to be more aggressive in soliciting authors than editors at scholarly or university presses, they are also receptive to good proposals. Some houses have a bias in favor of authors who teach at large, not necessarily prestigious universities, because such schools often account for most of the textbook orders. If you teach a large course that your proposed book would suit, be sure to mention it. In any case, your research and knowledge of the college market must be evident in both the proposal and the eventual contents once you have won a contract. Remember that professors, not students, decide which books will be ordered for which courses.

Even if you write an entire textbook yourself, in the traditional fashion, many publishers will intervene or at least advise with respect to certain aspects of the content. You will probably have to avoid sexist language (see "Resources") and remove any inadvertent sexual, racial, ethnic, religious, age, or other stereotypes. For an introductory text, you may also be edited down to a particular reading level. None of these demands are likely to be as silly as the strictures of some elementary-school publishers against the mere mention of any kind of "junk food" (even ice cream!), but still, some people will find them irritating. If you undertake to write a textbook, you should be prepared to tolerate this kind of guidance.

Electronic Publishing and Philosophy

by Francis P. Crawley

Philosophers today know what they need to do in order to secure a position and move toward advancement in their profession. No one continues to assume that good teaching and active departmental work alone will provide job security or the possibility for promotion. Perhaps more than ever, today's philosopher must continually produce high-quality scholarly writings, if not original contributions to the field, which are open to peer scrutiny, evaluation, and rebuttal. The pressure to produce publishable material begins in graduate school and continues beyond one's first appointment, into the years of tenure, even at times into retirement (when there is finally time). The growing number of conferences and publications in philosophy attests to the insistent demand that philosophers publicly take well defined positions, ones based on research and ones they are ready to defend.

Only ten years ago, when the second edition of this *Guidebook* was in preparation, the choice among media for publication was obvious: the philosopher needed to decide whether her ideas and the supporting research would be best presented in the concise form of a scholarly article in a journal or the more extended form of a monograph. Of course, there was always room for variations on a theme; however, the final product sought lay in the structuring of research and ideas in such a way that they received the kind of permanence we had been taught to expect of worthwhile achievements in philosophy: the printed word on paper. CD-ROM, the Internet, and electronic journals were still very much in their infancy, only playing a marginal role in academic publishing.

The last edition of this *Guidebook* did contain, for the first time, "A Note on Word Processing," which celebrated the advantages of using word processing programs for preparing texts and encouraged professional philosophers to explore the possibilities. However, times are rapidly changing. Among my freshmen today, although there are some struggles during the first weeks of the academic year regarding my insistence that all papers must be typed, ninety percent of the papers I receive are produced with the assistance of a word processing program; the remaining ten percent are typed on the more traditional typewriter. I do not know a single masters or PhD student today preparing a thesis or dissertation without the assistance of word processing. "Ten years ago" in the history of philosophy may not be much more than the wink of an eye; in the history of electronic technology "ten years ago" is an enormous geological time span.

Today, the choice of media for publishing in philosophy is many and varied, and expanding rapidly. If the changes in publishing were simply quantitative, opening up more places to publish and creating a rapid increase in the volume of philosophy literature annually available, then—while there would remain cause for investigation and analysis—this *Guidebook* would itself need do little more than list the changes. However, the use of electronic, especially digital, media has an increasing qualitative (as well as quantitative) effect on publishing in philosophy. Since published works largely define philosophy as a discipline, the current changes in publishing are inevitably having their effects on how we practice philosophy. Philosophers today are becoming increasingly aware of the uses new media open up for expressing ideas within the arena of philosophical debate. More importantly, that arena itself is taking on new dimensions.

Words and Places

Two fundamental factors play a central role in philosophical writing: one is the message or idea we want to convey; the other is the audience to whom we address ourselves. We are usually quite conscious of the first, the thesis, struggling to make our points clear, avoiding ambiguity, arguing sensibly, and simply getting matters right. At the same time, although we are usually more or less aware of whom we are addressing, the audience often plays a more distant role in the development of our ideas. While such things as tone, references, and length are readily adapted to the situation in which we are either presenting or publishing a paper, the central idea and the structure of the argument need hardly change. Making allowance for a few minor adaptations, the "same" paper can be presented at a local inter-departmental meeting where we know all of the participants well, presented again at an international conference where most of the participants are new faces for us, and then published in a journal that enjoys either limited or wide circulation.

As more and more academics, scientists, and philosophers take to alternative media for developing and communicating their ideas, the questions "What is my thesis?" and "Who is my audience?" begin to play a more prominent role in deciding where to publish. The more traditional media of books and journals still hold center stage when it comes to establishing oneself within the profession. However, while books and journals provide the most secure channels for attaining professional recognition, they are increasingly viewed as limited by scientists and scholars alike. The Internet is moving in as the preferred vehicle for exchanging ideas and information. A key factor here is time. The manuscript for a journal article or book may take up to a year or more to get through the editor and reviewers before appearing in print. This means that often the focus of a scientist or academic has shifted by the time her research appears in print and receives comment from the audience she is addressing.

Computers and computer networks today come ever closer to conveying ideas and arguments at the speed of thought. Though philosophy has always been a reflective activity, philosophers today are discovering a new and stimulating field for developing their ideas. The ability to publish in real time and the availability of more immediate responses are structural changes in the profession that are rapidly influencing the practice of philosophy. Philosophy is becoming less an account of debates between established texts and leading commentaries, and much more a lived discourse on problems and issues in contemporary society. Cyperspace has made it possible for philosophy to return to the much more public space of the agora, where daily conversation among philosophers and sophists is not subject to the bureaucracy of publishing houses and a litany of reviewers.

In the agora of cyberspace the philosopher also finds an audience (or audiences) of a greater variety from the ones she had grown accustomed to with the printed word. The first reference to the identity of a correspondent is usually an address— not a name or a face, not a man or a woman, not even professor or student. The discussants on the Internet begin to know one another in the unprejudiced and egalitarian atmosphere of conversation structured entirely by its participants. It is essentially an interactive community where participants are, not simply the passive recipients of ideas or information, but active contributors to the development and dissemination of the ideas and information they receive. The pursuit of knowledge, as well as the sharing of acquired knowledge, becomes increasingly a community activity.

Within this community, knowledge itself takes on a much more public face. The traditional distinctions between the categories of author, publisher, reviewer, commentator, reader, and archivist begin to fade as the texts or conversations themselves gain their authority from their use. The stronger and more attractive works in cyberspace tend to be the ones to which many hands (minds) have contributed, ones where it is increasingly difficult to identify either authorship or date of origin. These works tend to adapt the shape of an active, living conversation. Critique and rebuttal take on new forms, as do exegesis and interpretation, when philosophers encounter words and arguments in the dynamic medium of electronic interchange as opposed to the more embedded medium of the printed word.

The discussion groups are the bedrock of the Internet. These discussion groups allow philosophers a daily forum for engaging specific topics in their area of specialization or in related areas. The discussion groups are generally headed by a manager, who is responsible for maintaining the list of subscribers and seeing to it that ideas and information circulate smoothly. Managers are not authors and they are not publishers; neither are they final authorities. They devote their time and energy (and often quite a bit of extra-curricular time and energy) to ensuring the smooth flow of discourse. The subscribers post ideas they have on the topic of the discussion group and they respond to messages posted by other members of the group. Thus, the ideas develop and build through a natural process of discussion, argumentation, dispute, and rhetoric.

The discussion groups have become places for presenting scientific findings and engaging pressing concerns in society, as well as a medium for quibble and gossip. Today, in many areas of academics and even philosophy, these discussion groups are setting the research agenda and acting as the first line for sifting through the chaff. If you have an idea concerning philosopher 'x' or theory 'y', and you are considering developing it into a publishable article, you might do well to read through the postings on or related to your topic and then e-mail one or two subscribers who appear particularly knowledgeable. In the short run, it is likely to save you valuable time in research and also provide you with several different approaches to consider in developing your idea. In the long run, it may very well save your article from either outright rejection by a journal editor or a thorough rewrite.

Finally, although a contribution to a discussion group does not warrant an entry under Publications on your vita, colleges and universities are beginning to understand the added value active participation brings to the intellectual life of an academic. Within a discussion group one acts (or interacts) in a more or less public domain without a need to claim uniqueness in authorship or point of view. The Internet opens up the opportunity for philosophers to act both publicly and privately in a community that is fundamentally democratic, international, and multicultural. Even the philosopher who stubbornly refuses to yield to the arguments of others has a role to play in a community whose first interest is the conversation that increases our knowledge.

Perish the Word

In the last ten years there has been an enormous growth in the number of journals in philosophy and related fields. Much of this has to do with increased specialization in the discipline as well as the growth and splintering of science itself into further subdivisions. In the same period subscription prices for academic journals have more than doubled. The budgets of university libraries simply have not been able to keep pace, and there is a growing tendency of deacquisition among libraries as they struggle between the demands of professors and students and the soaring prices of journals and books. At the same time, academics, scientists, and publishers have been exploring alternative media in order to reduce costs and establish more efficient means for accessing and storing publications. One important innovation here has been the use of CD-ROMs as a medium for recording and distributing journals and books. Anyone who has used, for example, *The Philosopher's Index* on CD-ROM for more than half an hour would consider it enormous punishment to have to return to the library stacks the next time she wanted to find the latest publication by her favorite philosopher.

Perhaps the most remarkable innovation here has been the enormous growth in electronic journals and newsletters. Although few E-journals have gained the professional prestige of the more established printed journal, this is by far the fastest growing area in publishing today. One of the most attractive aspects of the Internet for scholars is its unfettered and egalitarian atmosphere; but this is also seen by many as one of the biggest threats to serious academic and scientific work. In this environment of "anything goes," where there can be few established rules for order or authority, science (and with it philosophy) risk spinning off into an unwieldy hegemony of babble. While the Internet enlarges the freedom of speech and the freedom of access to information, it also endangers the traditional standards that have guided scientific investigation and discourse. This situation is further complicated by the fact that there is, as of yet, no broadly reliable system in place to ensure that the costs of producing E-journals will be recovered. Up until now most online journals and newsletters have been the result of volunteer efforts by scientists and academics eager to decrease the time needed to broadcast new ideas.

However, recent developments in producing high-quality scholarly journals in a purely electronic format have shown that these problems can be overcome. Scholars no longer need to push aside fundamental standards in favor of expediency. Indeed, many E-journals now publish according to strict requirements of peer review. There is even good reason to believe that the peer-review process can be improved through the use of the Internet. Following in the footsteps of scientists and academics, some of the larger publishers of journals are beginning to put their journals online while still running a profitable business. Indeed, if the trend continues, many publishers of academic journals will find it necessary to place their publications online if they want to stay in business.

The printed word in philosophy has, since even before the time of the Greeks, enjoyed an enormous degree of constancy and duration. The author of a work, once penned and published, had secured a place in the great tradition—even if that place was lost and needed to be recovered by someone at a later date.

We are still far from either printing or entering the final word on publishing philosophy. In many ways, we are fortunate to have the advantage of a crossroads, with the choices and possibilities that it both holds open and opens up. Clearly, the future for the media of publishing philosophy has little to do with the plans or decisions any group or institution would want to enforce. How we publish philosophy in the future will depend on the practices we individually and collectively adopt today in the face of the technological developments in the communications media. Indeed, one is tempted to say that the very nature of philosophy itself will, in the future, depend on these practices.

Beyond the Ivory Tower: Publishing in Newspapers and Magazines

by Marcia Yudkin

Once you have had the thrill of seeing your name and your words in print, you may fantasize about your byline over articles in larger-circulation publications. Or you may read some slick, sloppily argued commentary and think, "I can do better." Or perhaps you just have some ideas that you want to communicate to the broadly educated public. Whatever the source of your urge to publish in non-professional outlets, we want to encourage you. The world at large can certainly use more of the clear, logical thinking many philosophers specialize in. Procedures, customs, and preferences in the world of general-audience publications differ somewhat from those discussed elsewhere in this *Guidebook*, but with the following orientation, you should have a fighting chance of making the transition.

Virtually all freelance contributions to newspapers and magazines originate in one of three methods of contact with an editor: an in-person or telephone conversation about a writer's proposed idea or ideas; a query letter in which the writer outlines a proposed article and explains why he or she is the person to write it; or a completed manuscript that the writer submits with a cover letter. Unless you already know an editor personally or the editor is likely to recognize your name, you shouldn't try to get an assignment by calling the editor or dropping into the publication's office. Most editors do not appreciate casual interruptions of their already fragmented time. More importantly, an editor cannot judge by talking to you whether or not you can write a suitable article for that publication; the conversation is likely to be inconclusive. But except for short (under 1,200 words) opinion pieces or personal-experience articles, neither should you go ahead and write the whole manuscript first and send it in. For all other submissions, newspaper and magazine editors prefer query letters.

What should a query letter be like? First, it should be short, no more than one or two single-spaced pages. Second, it should be addressed to a specific editor at your target publication; you can find out the name of the appropriate editor from this year's edition of *Writer's Market*, from the masthead of the publication (if no title jumps out at you as appropriate, try the managing editor or the associate editor) or by calling the publication to ask who handles freelance articles on your subject. Third, it must be polished, lively, and specific. The editor will be looking for evidence that you can write an interesting, readable article that will engage that publication's readers. One formula is to open the letter with a vignette or anecdote that encapsulates the importance or appeal of your topic, use the second paragraph to explain the scope of your article and sources of information, tell who you are and why you're qualified to write this article in the third paragraph and close with something like "I look forward to hearing from you soon." Finally, you must enclose a self-addressed stamped envelope for the editor's reply.

A query letter is like a try-out for a job, the job of writing a certain article for a certain publication. Besides checking and rewriting your letter if necessary, you can maximize your chances of being taken seriously by keeping in mind the different purposes of scholarly and non-scholarly publications. Most journals set up a gauntlet of referees in order to try to strike down earlier rather than later those papers that will not survive an onslaught of critical attention. Consequently, academic style is usually defensive. For professional journals, it is reasonable to hedge each sentence with qualifiers, announce, make, and then repeat one's point and expunge any signs of personality. But for general audiences, that kind of writing is deadly. In a query letter you have to plunge right in without any throat-clearing, rely on one vivid example or anecdote and one fact to imply an argument and use concrete nouns and active verbs to form fresh, lucid sentences. If this advice rankles your sense of propriety, you are probably better off sticking to academic publications.

Because of the differences between academic and non-academic writing, you should probably not enclose a copy of your discussion note in *Mind* or book review in *Philosophy and Public Affairs* with your query letter as a sample of your writing. Mention previous publications if you like, but unless you have samples that would be appropriate for your target publication, let the query letter itself be your showcase. If, in addition to your scholarly credentials, you demonstrate that you can write crisply and concretely, the editor will most likely be extremely impressed.

After sending off a query letter, it may take as short a time as a week for your self-addressed stamped envelope to reappear in your mailbox. If more than two months elapse without a reply, feel free to write a polite inquiry about the status of your query. When you do receive a reply, it will take one of several forms. Best of all is an assignment to prepare the article you suggested, along with instructions about length and date of delivery for the article and perhaps a specified payment for a satisfactory result. You may even receive a written contract and the promise of a "kill fee"—that is, a fee (usually 10 to 33 percent of what a magazine would pay for the article if published) for an article that fulfills the magazine's specifications but nevertheless won't be published. Second best is an invitation to submit the article "on speculation" or "on spec." This means that the editor is interested in what you proposed but doesn't want to make any promises. Although you must bear all the risk of preparing the article, it still represents a good opportunity, and you should go ahead and do your best. Next best is any kind of personal rejection from the editor, even a handwritten "Sorry" at the bottom of a printed rejection slip, which in that world counts as encouragement. But even a completely impersonal, unspecific rejection need not be a sign that you ought to give up; the magazine may just have accepted an article on your topic or had its freelance budget reduced, or your idea may appear inappropriate to that magazine but exactly right to its competitor.

Much of what I have said about query letters applies also to short opinion and personal-experience pieces, which you should submit as completed articles.

Always send the article, a self-addressed stamped envelope, and a cover letter explaining who you are and why you have some authority on your topic to a specific editor by name. Neatness, spelling, grammar, tone, detail, and style count here as well. It also helps to check your target publication to make sure that they do publish pieces like the one you would like to submit and of roughly that length. Editors appreciate a word count either on the manuscript or in your cover letter. The first paragraph of your article ("the lead") should be an example, anecdote, quote, or controversial suggestion that that will hook the reader; then make sure that you don't let the reader down. Use more concrete examples and specific details than you would for a scholarly article.

If your article is accepted, you may be asked what rights you wish to sell or be told that the publication is buying "first North American rights" or "all rights." Try not to sell or transfer "all rights"; that means that the publication may republish or resell your work, to a syndicate, to another publication, in an anthology or even to the movies without consulting you and without paying you any additional money. If a newspaper or magazine acquires "first rights," you must make sure the article appears there first, but afterwards it belongs to you again. "First North American Rights" means the right to first publication in North America; "first serial rights" means the right to first publication in a newspaper or magazine; and "one-time rights" means the right to publish an article one time only, without regard for priority.

49

A lot of neophyte writers wonder about agents. Would it help to sell something to the Op-Ed page of *The New York Times* if you had an agent? It might, but unless you are writing a non-fiction book with commercial potential or a novel, no agent would want you as a client. Reputable agents work solely on commission (generally 15 percent) and the amount you would make for such an article is simply too small to be worth the trouble to sell it for you.

A worry peculiar to academics who are interested in publishing for general audiences is whether or not non-professional publications can backfire on their career. That depends on what you write about and your ratio of scholarly to non-scholarly publications. If you want to write about your recent divorce, your secret drug habit or your disillusionment or scorn for your profession, you should consider adopting a pseudonym. Your correspondence with editors should still be under your own name, but if you explain why you prefer to publish under a pseudonym, most editors will understand and cooperate. If you want to win tenure and promotion, you should beware of a publication record that is heavier in non-scholarly than scholarly credits. But if it's a matter of a first or occasional opinion piece or article on Tahiti, where you spend summer vacations, you needn't worry. Your colleagues will probably react with mild, harmless envy and everyone else with congratulations and praise.

Resources for Writing
and Publishing Philosophy

by Francis P. Crawley

Provided here is a selective bibliography whose primary purpose is to assist philosophers in the preparation of manuscripts for publication.

Style Manuals

Nearly all journal and book publishers in philosophy require their authors to follow established styles for such scholarly devices as notes and bibliography. Listed below are the style manuals most often designated. In each of these manuals you will find useful information on the writing process as well as on grammatical considerations such as spelling and punctuation.

The Chicago Manual of Style. 14th ed. Chicago: University of Chicago Press, 1993. ix & 921 pages. ISBN 0-226-10389-7. One of the most complete style manuals, including sections on bookmaking and printing. The 14th edition has been revised and updated to include a comprehensive coverage of electronic writing and documentation. Chapter 4 presents an excellent discussion of the respective responsibilities of author and editor, as well as a discussion on copyright law. Chapter 16 presents a comprehensive discussion of documentation, strongly recommending the author-date system. This is often a required style by publishers in philosophy.

A Manual for Writers of Term Papers, Theses, and Dissertations. 6th ed. Kate L. Turabian. Revised by John Grossman and Alice Bennett. Chicago: The University of Chicago Press, 1996. ix & 308 pages. ISBN 0-226-81626-5. Based on the 14th edition of *The Chicago Manual of Style.* This is considerably easier to use and contains the most important information on research mechanics found in the parent publication. This new edition provides up-to-date advice on preparing manuscripts with the assistance of electronic word processing.

A Manual of Style. U.S. Government Printing Office. Gramercy Publishing Company, 1986. xi & 479 pages. ISBN 0-517-60526-0. Used by the US government for its own publications. Although never required by publishers in academia, this style manual provides detailed guidance on technical issues not covered with as much depth in other style manuals (e.g., capitalization, compound words, abbreviations). It is also essential for philosophers concerned with policy issues and working with US government publications.

MLA Handbook for Writers of Research Papers. 4th ed. Joseph Gibaldi. The Modern Language Association of America, 1995. 293 pages. ISBN 0-87352-565-5. Similar to *The MLA Style Manual.* Although intended for undergraduates, this is more up-to-date than its sister publication and, thus, recommended more highly. The 4th edition incorporates considerable expansion into researching and documenting electronic information sources and publications.

The MLA Style Manual. Walter S. Achtert and Joseph Gibaldi. The Modern Language Association of America, 1995. 293 pages. ISBN 0-87352-565-5. Similar to The MLA Style Manual. Although intended for undergraduates, this is more up-to-date than its sister publication and, thus, recommended more highly. The 4th edition incorporates considerable expansion into researching and documenting electronic information sources and publications.

Publication Manual of the American Psychological Association. 4th ed. Washington, DC: American Psychological Association, 1994. 368 pages. ISBN 1-55798-243-0. The standard style manual for publishing in psychology and the social sciences. One of the earliest champions of the author-date system, this style is also required by many publishers in philosophy.

Usage

The works listed here give practical advice for the clear and effective use of words and phrases in writing.

The Complete Plain Words. Sir Ernest Gowers. Revised by Sidney Greenbaum and Janet Whitcut. Joseph Epstein, intro. Boston: David R. Godine, 1986. xxvii & 288 pages. ISBN 0-87923-733-3. A lively and sensible presentation on how to write clearly and avoid trouble spots in the language. Although not written for philosophers, this is a book you will want to pass on to colleagues.

A Dictionary of Modern English Usage. 2nd ed. H. W. Fowler, revised by Sir Ernest Gowers. Oxford: Clarendon Press, 1968. xxii & 725 pages. The classic guide to English usage and for many years the standard. Although now somewhat dated in both its method and conclusions, it remains a valuable reference for accepted usage.

Line by Line: How to Improve Your Own Writing. Claire Kehrwald Cook. Boston: Houghton Mifflin Co., 1985. xx & 219 pages. ISBN 0-395-39391-4. A book written specifically for scholars who publish. This is a direct and engaging step-by-step guide for improving one's own writing.

The New York Public Library Writer's Guide to Style and Usage. New York: HarperCollins, 1994. xiii & 838 pages. ISBN 0-06-270064. One of the best thought out, most judicious, and complete presentations of usage, grammar, style, editing, and text production. It presents succinct opinions based on a thorough review of the current literature.

Webster's Dictionary of English Usage. Springfield, MA: Merriam-Webster, 1989. xii & 978 pages. ISBN 0-87779-032-9. By far the finest reference available on English usage. The articles demonstrate the scientific use of historical principles in analysis, combined with judiciousness and sobriety in reaching conclusions.

Style and Publishing Guides

These works assist the writer in the revision of prose for clarity of expression. Several of the books also discuss editorial considerations when preparing manuscripts for publication.

Author and Editor at Work: Making a Better Book. Elsie M. Stainton. Toronto: University of Toronto Press, 1981. 96 pages. ISBN 0-8020-6449-3. A concise guide to the relationship between author and editor. This book also includes an extensive discussion on difference between dictionaries and an annotated bibliography of style manuals.

Books: The Culture and the Commerce of Publishing. Lewis A. Coser, Charles Kadushin, and Walter W. Powell. NY: Basic Books, 1982. xiii & 411 pages. ISBN 0465007457. Describes the historical, social, cultural, and commercial context and structure of book publishing. Practical advice is woven into a social science approach. A strong index is appended.

The Elements of Style. 3rd ed. William Strunk, Jr. With revisions, an Introduction, and a Chapter on Writing by E. B. White. Macmillan, 1979. ix & 92 pages. ISBN 0-02-41890-0. A sound, sensible, and simple set of guidelines for improving your writing style. This small book begins with a discussion of usage and moves through composition and form to style itself.

Freelance Writing for Magazines & Newspapers: Breaking in Without Selling Out. Marcia Yudkin. NY: HarperCollins Publishers, 1993. ISBN 0-06-273278-1. A solid hands-on approach to publishing in the popular press from someone with extensive experience.

Getting Published: The Acquisition Process of University Presses. Paul Persons. Knoxville: University of Tenessee Press, 1989. Product of four years of research by a professor of journalism and mass communications.

Getting into Print: The Decision-Making Process in Scholarly Publishing. Walter W. Powell. Chicago: University of Chicago Press, 1985. xxxi & 260 pages. ISBN 0-226-67704-4. Presents a detailed study on the process involved in selecting and editing manuscripts for book publication. Provides and extensive list of references and an index.

Handbook for Academic Authors. Beth Luey. Cambridge: Cambridge University Press, 1987, revised edition 1990. Guide to academic publishing, including both journals and books, by the longtime director of the Scholarly Publishing Program at Arizona State University. Includes advice on negotiating contracts, handling permissions, and other practical matters. Excellent bibliography.

One Book, Five Ways: The Publishing Procedures of Five University Presses. 2nd ed. Association of American University Presses Staff, ed. Joyce Kachergis, intro. Chicago: University of Chicago Press, 1994. xiv & 330 pages. ISBN 0-226-03024-5. Tracks the publication process for a manuscript through five university presses. A useful way of finding out what to expect when publishing a book-length manuscript.

"Listbuilding at University Presses." Sanford G. Thatcher in *Editors as Gatekeepers: Getting Published in the Social Sciences*, ed. Rita J. Simm and James J. Fyfe. Lanham, MD: Rowman & Littlefield, 1994. Situates decisions of acquiring editors in context of higher education and publishing industry based on 25 years experience as acquisitions editor at university presses.

Revising Prose. 3rd ed. Richard A. Lanham. New York: Macmillan, 1994. 144 pages. ISBN 0-02-367445-8. Provides solid advice and concrete examples on revising for clearer and more concise prose.

Writing Philosophy: A Guide to Professional Writing and Publishing. Richard A. Watson. Carbondale, IL: Southern Illinois University Press, 1992. xiv & 97 pages. ISBN 0-8093-1810-5. Approaches philosophy as a kind of technical writing. There is a chapter on the philosophy paper, one on the dissertation, and two on critiquing. In the middle are some abrupt notes on style. The book is completed with a slim bibliography.

Guides to Avoiding Sexism in Language

The following publications provide sound advice for avoiding bias in expressions and constructions.

Guidelines for Bias-Free Writing. Marilyn Schwartz and the Task Force of the Association of American University Presses. Bloomington, IN: Indiana University Press, 1995. xii & 100 pages. ISBN 0-253-35102-2. A practical and well-designed handbook for bias-free writing. This guide makes use of a number of other guidelines in providing clear and well-illustrated suggestions for eliminating prejudices from language. There is a well selected bibliography and an extensive bibliography.

"Guidelines for Non-Sexist Use of Language." Virginia L. Warren and the APA Committee on the Status of Women in the Profession. *Proceedings and Addresses of the American Philosophical Association,* 59 (1986): 471-482. An essential guideline for avoiding sexism in the use of language by philosophers. An updated version is now available as a separate publication from the APA National Office and on the APA web site.

The Handbook of Nonsexist Writing: For Writers, Editors and Speakers. 2nd ed. Casey Miller and Kate Swift. HarperCollins, 1988. 160 pages. Balanced advice for avoiding sexism in language. This is a classic handbook on the subject. It is well researched, providing strong historical background.

Writing and Research Guides

The books listed here provide general considerations for writing academic papers. They also provide valuable assistance for pursuing a research strategy and locating resources.

Library Research Guide to Philosophy. Charles J. List and Stephen H. Plum. Ann Arbor, MI: Pierian Press, 1990. ix & 102 pages. ISBN 0-87650-264-8. Provides an excellent introduction to library research in philosophy. Primarily geared toward undergraduates, the book concludes with a well selected and partially annotated list of reference sources in philosophy.

The Modern Researcher. 5th ed. Jacques Barzun and Henry F. Graff. New York: Harcourt, Brace and World, Inc., 1992. 416 pages. ISBN 0-395-64494-1. A standard research guide for work in the humanities. This handbook is particularly helpful for historical research.

Philosophical Writing: An Introduction. A. P. Martinich. Englewood Cliffs, NJ: Prentice Hall, 1989. xvii & 125 pages. ISBN 0-13-664103-2. Discusses composition in philosophy primarily from the point of view of the logical structure of argumentation. Little attention is paid to research and style. No bibliography.

Research Guide to Philosophy. Terence N. Tice and Thomas P. Slavens. Sources of Information in the Humanities, no. 3. Chicago: American Library Association, 1983. xii & 608 pages. ISBN 0-8389-0333-9. Provides an introductory overview of the different periods and areas in philosophy. Each section contains a short description of a period, figure, or division in philosophy followed by basic bibliographic sources. The book is completed with an annotated bibliography, an author-title index, and a subject index.

Philosophy Indexes

Listed here are the two most important philosophy indexes, used for locating recent and past publications in the field.

International Philosophical Bibliography/Répertoire bibliographique de la philosophie/Bibliografisch Repertorium van de Wijsbegeerte. Louvain-la-Neuve: Éditions de l'Institut Supérieur de Philosophie/Leuven: Hoger Instituut voor Wijsbegeerte, 1939-. ISBN 0034-4567. A successor to the *Répetoire Bibliographique.* Without abstracts, but more complete than The *Philosopher's Index* for non-English publications. The November issue contains book reviews and an index of names.

The Philosopher's Index: An International Index to Philosophical Periodicals and Books. Bowling Green, OH: Philosophy Documentation Center. 1967-. [From 1996 published by The Philosopher's Information Center (Bowling Green, OH).] Contains a subject index, an author index, and a book review index. The author's index is with abstracts. This index is now available online (DIA-LOG) and on CD-ROM.

General Indexes

These indexes include publications outside the field of philosophy.

Arts and Humanities Citation Index. Philadelphia: Institute for Scientific Information, 1976-. ISBN 0162-8445. Provides detailed indexing and searching possibilities for over 2000 titles from more than 40 countries. The index is divided into 4 parts: the citation index, the source index, the corporate index, and the permuterm index. Available online.

British Humanities Index. London: Library Association Publishing, 1962-. ISSN 0007-0815. Indexes approximately 350 titles, mostly British.

Hispanic American Periodical Index. Los Angeles: UCLA Latin American Center Publications, 1974-. ISSN 0270-8558. Indexes more than 250 titles focused on Hispanic America and Hispanic groups in the US. It has separate author and subject indexes.

Humanities Index. New York: H. W. Wilson, 1974-. ISSN 0095-5981. Indexes approximately 350 titles in the humanities. Available online and on CD-ROM.

The Index and Abstract Directory: An International Guide to Services and Serials Coverage. Birmingham, AL: EBSCO Publishing, 1989. 2177 pages. ISBN 0-913956-42-2. The most complete guide to indexing and abstracting services. Section 1 lists, by subject, approximately 30,000 titles providing histories of title, frequency, editors, addresses, prices, and indexing and abstracting services covering that title. Section 2 lists approximately 700 indexing and abstracting services.

Social Sciences Citation Index. Philadelphia: Institute for Scientific Information, 1972-. ISSN 0091-3707. Indexes just under 6000 periodicals. Divided into four parts: the citation index, the source index, the corporate index, and the permuterm index. Available online and on CD-ROM.

Social Sciences Index. New York: H. W. Wilson, 1974-. ISSN 0094-4920. Provides broad coverage the social sciences, indexing approximately 350 titles. Available online and on CD-ROM.

RESOURCES FOR WRITING AND PUBLISHING

Directories

The two directories listed here provide not only information on individual philosophers and their institutions, but also on publishers in philosophy. The listings contained in this *Guidebook* come from the editions of the *Directories* listed below.

Directory of American Philosophers: 1996-1997. Archie J. Bahm, ed. 18th ed. Bowling Green, OH: Philosophy Documentation Center, 1996. ix & 488 pages. ISBN 0-912632-57-7. Lists philosophers in the US and Canada by state or province under their respective university departments. The departments' full addresses, fax and telephone numbers are also listed. There is a separate listing of the names and addresses of philosophers. It also includes useful listings of assistantships, centers and institutes, societies, journals, and publishers. The directory is completed with indexes of universities, centers and institutes, societies, journals, and publishers. This latest edition includes e-mail addresses and philosophy web sites. Updated biennially.

International Directory of Philosophy and Philosophers: 1997-1998. Ramona Cormier and Richard H. Lineback, eds. Bowling Green, OH: 10th ed. Philosophy Documentation Center, 1997. 520 pages. ISBN 0-912632-69-0. Lists philosophers in countries outside the US and Canada by country under their respective university departments. The departments' full addresses, fax and telephone numbers are also listed. There is a separate listing of the names and addresses of philosophers. It also includes useful listings of assistantships, centers and institutes, societies, journals, and publishers. The directory is completed with indexes of universities, centers and institutes, societies, journals, and publishers. This latest edition includes e-mail addresses, ISSN numbers for journals, and entries for electronic journals. Updated biennially.

Electronic Sources and Handbooks

These were, at the time of preparation, the most current and useful paper resources for navigating in the developing field of electronic publication. New resources have almost certainly appeared in the interim.

Directory of Electronic Journals, Newsletters, and Academic Discussion Groups. 6th ed. Dru Mogge. Washington, DC: Association of Research Librarians, 1996. 770 pages. ISSN 1057-1337. Lists nearly 3,100 scholarly lists and 1,700 academic journals, newsletters, and related titles. The listings are prefaced by scholarly articles on the field of electronic publishing and their are instructions for electronic access to each publication. The directory is completed with an index of keywords, titles, and institutional affiliations. An abridged version is available at the Gopher site arl.cni.org under scholarly communications.

!%@:: A Directory of Electronic Mail Addressing and Networks. Donnalyn Frey and Rick Adams. Sebastopol, CA: O'Reilly and Associates, Inc., 1994. 500

pages. ISBN 1-56592-046-5. A directory of electronic mail addresses for all major Internet-based networks and the larger connecting commercial networks. It is a useful handbook for finding your way about.

Directory to Fulltext Online Resources 1992. Jack Kessler. Westport: Meckler, 1992. xviii & 138 pages. ISBN 0-88736833-6. Provides an introduction to and overview of text resources available through computer networks, including bulletin boards, conferences, journals, and libraries.

The Elements of E-Mail Style: Communicate Effectively via Electronic Mail. David Angell and Brent Heslop. Reading, MA: Addison-Wesley, 1994. xii & 157 pages. ISBN 0-201-62709-4. An E. B. White-style handbook for users of e-mail. The book applies the rules of grammar to the context of electronic mail and offers useful advice on network etiquette (netiquette).

The E-Mail Frontier: Emerging Markets and Evolving Technologies. Daniel J. Blum and David M. Litwack. Reading, MA: Addison-Wesley, 1995. 384 pages. ISBN 0-201-56860-8. An up-to-date guide on the developing place of new communications technology.

Everybody's Guide to the Internet. Adam Gaffin. Cambridge, MA: MIT Press, 1994. 200 pages. ISBN 9-780262-67105-7. One of the most complete and up-to-date guides, providing an excellent overview of the Internet. Also available online at **ftp.eff.org, gopher.eff.org**, and **http://www.eff.org** (and other directories).

Gale Directory of Databases. Kathleen Lopez Nolan, ed. 2 vols. New York: Gale Research, Inc., 1995. ISBN 0-8103-5748-8. An extensive listing of services and materials available online. Volume 1 contains a directory of online databases. Volume 2 contains directories of CD-ROM, Magnetic Tape, Handheld, and Batch Access Database Products.

The Internet Publishing Handbook: For World-Wide Web, Gopher, and WAIS. Mike Franks. Reading, MA: Addison-Wesley Publishing Co., 1995. xvii & 380 pages. ISBN 0-201-48317-3. Provides complete information for using the Internet in making information publicly available. Provides useful information and reference sources regarding copyright protection in electronic media. A helpful glossary and an extensive index complete the book.

Philosophy in Cyberspace: A Guide to Philosophy-Related Resources on the Internet. Dey Alexander, ed. Bowling Green: Philosophy Documentation Center, 1995. 200 pages. ISBN 0-912632-59-3. Travel guide to philosophy on the Internet. Designed to assist philosophers in finding philosophy and related resources.

The Student's Guide to Doing Research on the Internet. Dave and Mary Campbell. Reading, MA: Addison-Wesley, 1995. ix & 349 pages. ISBN 0-201-48916-3. A handbook directed at undergraduates in all disciplines. The book provides both a basic skills set for using the Internet and a set of resources for each of the major disciplines, philosophy included.

Biographies

Samuel Gorovitz is Professor of Philosophy and Professor of Public Administration at Syracuse University, where he was Dean of Arts and Sciences from 1986 to 1993. His most recent book is *Drawing the Line: Life, Death, and Ethical Choices in an American Hospital* (Temple University Press, 1993).

Nancy Simco has been actively involved in the Association of Philosophy Journal Editors since she became editor of *The Southern Journal of Philosophy* in 1974, and has served as president of the Association since 1990. She is Professor of Philosophy and Chair of the Department at The University of Memphis. Her areas of specialization are logic and philosophy of mathematics.

Thomas Magnell (D.Phil. Oxon) is Associate Professor and Chair of the Department of Philosophy at Drew University. He is Editor-in-Chief of the *Jounal of Value Inquiry*. He has written numerous papers, many of them having to do with ethics and, more broadly, matters of value, including "Evaluations as Assessments, Part I," and "Evaluations as Assessments, Part II," portions of which he presented as his Presidential Address to the American Society for Value Inquiry in 1990. He has also written an introduction to a re-issue of A. J. Ayer's *Metaphysics and Common Sense*. He is editing several books, including *Explorations of Value*, and is the immediate past President of the Conference of Philosophical Societies.

Francis P. Crawley is a lecturer at Vesalius College, University of Brussels. The majority of his publications are in the fields of philosophy of education and bioethics. For six years he taught Research and Composition in Philosophy at the Katholieke Universiteit Leuven. He is currently writing a handbook on *Composition in Philosophy: Elements of Rhetoric and Style.*

Marcia Yudkin received her Ph.D. from Cornell University in 1978. After publishing in *Mind, Philosophy and Feminist Studies*, she wrote fiction for *Yankee, Feldspar Prize Stories* and *Art Times* and nonfiction for *The New York Times, Boston Globe, Ms., Psychology Today, The Progressive, The Village Voice*, and others. Since co-authoring *The Guidebook for Publishing Philosophy* with Janice Moulton in 1986, she has written *Freelance Writing for Magazines and Newspapers: Breaking In Without Selling Out* (HarperCollins, Book of the Month Club selection), *Smart Speaking* (Henry Holt), *He and She Talk* (Plume), *Six Steps to Free Publicity* (Plume) and *Marketing Online: Low-Cost, High-Yield Tactics for Small Businesses and Professionals* (Plume).

Janice Moulton received her Ph.D. from the University of Chicago in 1971 and has been in the Philosophy Department at Smith College since 1981. She began *The Guidebook for Publishing Philosophy* twenty years ago, co-authored the 1986 version with Marcia Yudkin and put that version on the World Wide Web with Rachel Westmoreland (http://www.smith.edu/~jmoulton/guidebook). After writing *The Organization of Language* (with G. M. Robinson, Cambridge University Press) and *Ethical Problems in Higher Education* (with G. M. Robinson, Prentice Hall/Simon Schuster), and seeing her philosophy papers reprinted in anthologies that appealed to a wider audience, she wrote *Scaling the Dragon* (with G. M. Robinson, Cross Cultural Publications) about her adventures in China (page layout and cover designed by the authors) and is now working on adventure novels.

Listing of Philosophical Journals

The following listing of journals contains all the information in the *Directory of American Philosophers, 1996-97*, published by the Philosophy Documentation Center. This includes Canadian journals and journals from the United Kingdom, together with a few selected journals from other countries, as listed in the *International Directory of Philosophy and Philosophers, 1997-98.*

Although every effort has been made to ensure the accuracy of this information, in some cases no response has been received to our inquiries for updated information. In such cases, we have attempted to provide up-to-date information from other sources. These entries are marked with an asterisk to let the reader know that we were not able to confirm the information first-hand.

JOURNALS: UNITED STATES

ACORN: JOURNAL OF THE GANDHI-KING SOCIETY

Editor: Barry L. Gan

Box CB, St. Bonaventure University
St. Bonaventure, NY 14778

Tel. 716-375-2275
E-mail bgan@sbu.edu

Purpose: To examine various global issues of our time from the Gandhian standpoint of *Satyagraha.*

Sponsor: Gandhi-King Society

Manuscript info: Two articles per year are devoted to philosophy. Manuscripts about the philosophy of M. K. Gandhi, Martin Luther King, Jr., or related philosophical issues are preferred. There is no backlog. Manuscripts are not refereed. About 50% of manuscripts are accepted; none requires significant revision. Average evaluation time is 1 month. Thirty percent of articles are invited. Instructions for manuscript preparation are included in the journal. Manuscripts should be sent to the journal.

Book reviews: Included; 50% are invited. Unsolicited book reviews are welcome.

Frequency: 2 issues per year; Circulation: 50

Subscription rates: $10; Foreign $12

AGRICULTURE AND HUMAN VALUES

Editor: Richard P. Haynes

330 Griffin-Floyd Hall
University of Florida
Gainesville, FL 32611

Tel. 904-392-2084 Ext. 302
Fax 904-392-5577

ISSN 0889-048X

Date of founding: 1983

Purpose: To promote interdisciplinary research and scholarship in areas where the liberal arts and agricultural disciplines interface, especially the humanities and social sciences.

Sponsor: Agriculture, Food, and Human Values Society

Manuscript info: About 12 philosophy articles are published yearly; there is a small current backlog of accepted articles. Manuscripts with some relationship to agriculture, agricultural research, environmental considerations, land use and food systems, including distribution and consumption, are preferred. Manuscripts are refereed blind; referees' unsigned comments are given to authors. Acceptance rate is 15%; 80% of accepted papers require significant revision. Manuscript evaluation averages 90 days. Instructions for manuscript preparation are in the journal. Manuscripts should be submitted to the editor.

Book reviews: About 75% of the reviews are invited. Unsolicited book reviews are welcome.

Frequency: Quarterly; Circulation: 600

Publisher: Agriculture and Human Values, Inc., P.O. Box 14938 Gainesville, FL 32604, in affiliation with the Agriculture, Food, and Human Values Society

Subscription rates: $30, $38 Foreign; Institutions $40, $48 Foreign

AITIA: PHILOSOPHY-HUMANITIES MAGAZINE*

Editor: James P. Friel

Knapp Hall 15
SUNY College of Technology
Farmingdale, NY 11735

Tel. 516-420-2047
Fax 516-420-2698

ISSN 0731-5880

Date of founding: 1974

Purpose: To support the teaching of the humanities and the integration of philosophy with the other humanities.

Sponsor: SUNY Farmingdale

Manuscript info: 10 to 15 philosophy articles per year. Any area of philosophy welcome, preference given to those with a focus on teaching. Manuscripts are refereed blind; unsigned comments are given to authors on request. About 50% of manuscripts are accepted; 20% require significant revision. Average evaluation time is 18 months. About 50% of articles are invited. Instructions for manuscript preparation are included in the journal.

Book reviews: About 30% of book reviews are invited; unsolicited book reviews are welcome.

Frequency: 3 issues per year; Circulation: 2,000

Publisher: James P. Friel, SUNY, Farmingdale

Subscription rates: $14 (2 years), $16 (3 years); Institutions $16 (2 years), $20 (3 years)

ALASKA QUARTERLY REVIEW*

Editor: James J. Liszka

Phil. Editor
University of Alaska 3211
Providence Dr.
Anchorage, AK 99508

Tel. 907-786-4775
Fax 907-786-1688

ISSN 0737-268X

Purpose: A journal devoted to contemporary literary art. *AQR* includes a section on the philosophy of literature, which provides a unique format for communication between practicing artists and philosophers.

Manuscript info: One philosophy article per year (but some years we print more and some years philosophy is not included). Manuscripts in philosophy, contemporary literature, and semiotics are preferred. The backlog of accepted articles is 2 issues. Manuscripts are not refereed. Very few accepted manuscripts require significant revisions. Average evaluation time is 3 months. About 25% of articles are invited. Instructions for manuscript preparation are available through inquiry. Send manuscripts to the editor.

Book reviews: About 25% of the book reviews are invited; unsolicited book reviews are welcome.

Frequency: 2 double issues per year; Circulation: 1,000

Publisher: University of Alaska, Anchorage

Subscription rates: $8; Institutions $10

ALEXANDRIA

Editor: David Fideler

P.O. Box 6114
Grand Rapids, MI 49516

Tel. 616-456-5740
Fax 616-456-5740
E-mail phanes@cris.com

Purpose: To explore the relationships among cosmology, philosophy, myth, and culture in the Western world.

Sponsor: Alexandria Society

Manuscript info: About 5 articles per year are devoted to philosophy. Preference is given to manuscripts that explore the relationships among cosmology, philosophy, myth, and culture. Manuscripts are not refereed. Evaluation time averages 30 days. About 70% of articles are invited. Instructions for manuscript preparation are available from the editor.

Book reviews: Included; 50% are invited. Unsolicited book reviews are welcome.

Frequency: Annual; Circulation: 2,000

Publisher: Alexandria Foundation
P.O. Box 6114
Grand Rapids, MI 49516

Subscription rates: $35

63

AMERICAN CATHOLIC PHILOSOPHICAL QUARTERLY

Editor: Robert E. Wood

Institute of Philosophic Studies
University of Dallas
Irving, TX 75062

Tel. 214-721-5108
Fax 214-721-5052
E-mail cua-acpa@cua.edu

ISSN 1051-3558

Date of founding: 1927

Purpose: To promote philosophical research.

Sponsor: American Catholic Philosophical Association

Manuscript info: About 28-32 philosophy articles are published per year. Manuscripts are welcome in any area of philosophy. Backlog is 12 months. Manuscripts are refereed blind. Average evaluation time is 3 months. Instructions for manuscript preparation are included in the journal. Manuscripts should be sent to the editor.

Book reviews: About 90% of the book reviews are invited; unsolicited book reviews are welcome.

Frequency: Quarterly; Circulation: 1,400

Publisher: Capital City Press, Montpelier, VT 05601

Subscription rates: Single copy $10 (special issues $12) & 15% postage and handling; Yearly $34.50

AMERICAN JOURNAL OF PHILOLOGY

Editor: Philip A. Stadter

Classics Department
University of North Carolina
Chapel Hill, NC 27599-3145

Tel. 919-962-7191
Fax 919-962-4036
E-mail philip_stadter@unc.edu

ISSN 0002-9475

Date of founding: 1880

Purpose: We publish original research in Greek and Roman literature, classical linguistics, and Greek and Roman history, society, religion, and philosophy.

Sponsor: The Journal is owned by Johns Hopkins University.

Manuscript info: About 4 articles per year are devoted to philosophy. Preference is given to manuscripts in areas of Greek and Roman to late antiquity. In the case of articles on ancient philosophy we prefer discussion closely linked to the original texts. Backlog is 12 months. Manuscripts are refereed blind; unsigned comments are given to authors. About 30% of manuscripts are accepted; 80% require significant revision. Evaluation time averages 2 months. Only 1% of articles are invited. Instructions for manuscript preparation are included in the journal. Manuscripts should be sent to the editor.

Book reviews: Included; all are invited. Unsolicited book reviews are not welcome.

Frequency: Quarterly; Circulation: 1,281

Publisher: Johns Hopkins University Press

Subscription rates: Individuals $29; Institutions $72.50; Students (with student ID) $25; add $3.70 for postage to Canada or Mexico, $8.70 for air freight outside North America.

AMERICAN JOURNAL OF THEOLOGY AND PHILOSOPHY

Editor: Tyron Inbody

United Theological Seminary
1810 Harvard Blvd.
Dayton, OH 45406

Tel. 513-278-5817 Ext. 151
Fax 513-278-1218

ISSN 0194-3448

Date of founding: 1980

Purpose: Provides forum for discussion in 4 areas: 1) American theological efforts especially attentive to philosophical literature; 2) liberalism in

American religious thought; 3) themes of "Chicago School" of theology; 4) naturalism in American philosophy.

Sponsor: Highlands Institute for American Religious Thought

Manuscript info: 15 articles per year are devoted to philosophy. Manuscripts that deal with the purpose of the *Journal* are preferred. The backlog of accepted articles is 12 months. Manuscripts are refereed blind; referees' unsigned comments are given to authors. Instructions for manuscript preparation are included in the journal. Manuscripts should be sent to the editor.

Book reviews: Book reviews are requested.

Frequency: 3 issues per year; Circulation: 330

Subscription rates: Individuals $18; US Libraries $30; Foreign $30

AMERICAN PHILOSOPHICAL QUARTERLY

Editor: Gary Gutting

Dept. of Philosophy
University of Notre Dame
336 O'Shaughnessy
Notre Dame, IN 46556-0368

Tel. 412-624-5775
Fax 219-631-4268
E-mail gutting.1@nd.edu

ISSN 0003-0481

Date of founding: 1964

Purpose: To publish substantial papers.

Manuscript info: 30 philosophy articles are published per year. Any area of philosophy is welcome, except for historical studies. The journal does not publish discussion notes (regardless of length). Manuscripts are refereed. The refereeing is blind at the author's request; referees' unsigned comments are given to authors if the editor thinks they would be useful for the author. Fewer than 15% are accepted; 50% of accepted manuscripts require significant revisions. The average evaluation time is 8 weeks. Only critical literature reviews are invited. Instructions for manuscript preparation are in the journal.

Frequency: Quarterly; Circulation: 1,700

Publisher: North American Philosophical Publications; subscription agent: Philosophy Documentation Center

Subscription rates: $40; Institutions $160

ANCIENT PHILOSOPHY

Editor: Ronald Polansky

Dept. of Philosophy
Duquesne University
Pittsburgh, PA 15282-1705

Tel. 412-396-6500

ISSN 0740-2007

Date of founding: 1980

Purpose: To present articles, discussions, and reviews in classical philosophy and science.

Manuscript info: About 15 philosophy articles per year. Manuscripts in ancient philosophy are preferred. Manuscripts are refereed. The refereeing is blind, and the referees' unsigned comments are given to the authors. Fifteen to 20% of the manuscripts are accepted. About 50% of the accepted manuscripts require significant revision. Two to 4 months is the average time required to evaluate a manuscript. Instructions for manuscript preparation are included in Issue IV, I. Send manuscripts to the editor.

Frequency: Biannual; Circulation: 700

Publisher: Mathesis Publications, Dept. of Philosophy, Duquesne University, Pittsburgh, PA 15282

Subscription rates: Individuals $20; Institutions $45; Students $17

ANCIENT WISDOM FOR MODERN LIVING*

Daniel Fritz, Publisher

3910 Los Feliz Boulevard
Los Angeles, CA 90027

Tel. 213-663-2167
Fax 213-663-2051

Date of founding: 1941

Purpose: To present articles dealing with the nature of man and based upon the disciplines of philosophy, comparative religion, and psychology.

Sponsor: The Philosophical Research Society, Inc.

Manuscript info: Manuscripts in any area of philosophy are welcome. Evaluation time is publication cycles. Manuscripts should be sent to the publisher.

Book reviews: Unsolicited book reviews are welcome.

Frequency: Quarterly; Circulation: 13,000

Publisher: The Philosophical Research Society, Inc.

Subscription rates: $12; $14 Foreign

ANTIOCH REVIEW

Editor: Robert S. Fogarty

P.O. Box 148
Yellow Springs, OH 45387

Tel. 513-767-6389

ISSN 0003-5769

Date of founding: 1941

Purpose: A literary journal of interest to the liberal scholar and educated layperson, publishing articles of critical social and philosophical ideas; also fiction and poetry.

Manuscript info: About 2 philosophy articles are published per year; any area of philosophy is welcome as long as it is not technical or essentially academic. The average backlog is 6 months. Manuscripts are refereed, but not blind; comments are seldom returned. Acceptance rate is about 5%. The average evaluation time is 3 months. Instructions for manuscript preparation may be obtained by written request. Manuscripts should be sent to the editor.

Book reviews: Unsolicited book reviews are not welcome.

Frequency: Quarterly; Circulation: 4,900

Publisher: Antioch Review, Inc.

Subscription rates: 1996 rates: $35, Two years $63; Institutions $48; Foreign add $10.

ARION: A JOURNAL OF HUMANITIES AND THE CLASSICS

Editor: Herbert Golder

Arion, Boston University
10 Lenox St. 2nd Fl.
Brookline, MA 02146

Tel. 617-353-6480
Fax 617-353-5905

ISSN 0095-5809

Date of founding: 1962

Purpose: To publish articles on Greek and Roman literature and culture (as well as translations and book reviews) that will interest readers both inside and outside the academic profession.

Sponsor: Boston University

Manuscript info: About 5-10 philosophy articles are published per year. Manuscripts should have a definite tie to Greek and Roman culture. Preference is given to essays and book review-essays. Backlog is about 6 months. Manuscripts are refereed blind; referees' unsigned comments are given to authors. About 25% of manuscripts are accepted; 20% require significant revision. Average evaluation time is 6 months. About 70% of articles are invited. Manuscripts should be sent to the journal.

Book reviews: About 80% of book reviews are invited; unsolicted book reviews are welcome.

Frequency: 3 issues per year; Circulation: 800

Subscription rates: $19, Students $12; Institutions $35; add $3 outside US for surface mail.

AUGUSTINIAN STUDIES

Editor: Allan Fitzgerald

OSA, Tolentine Hall
Villanova University
Villanova, PA 19085

Tel. 610-645-7903
Fax 610-519-6306
E-mail fitzgeral@ucis.vill.edu

ISSN 0094-5323

Date of founding: 1970

Purpose: Devoted to scholarly studies on the life, teachings, and influence of Augustine through the ages.

Sponsor: Villanova University

Manuscript info: Manuscripts in any area of philosophy are welcome. Manuscripts are refereed blind; unsigned, edited comments are given to the authors. Average evaluation time is 4-5 months. Instructions for manuscript preparation are included in the journal.

Book reviews: Article-length book reviews. Book review editor: John Cavadini, Dept. of Theology, University of Notre Dame, South Bend, IN 46614.

Frequency: 2 issues per year; Circulation: 350

Publisher: Allan Fitzgerald, Villanova University

Subscription rates: $24 (or $12 each issue)

67

AUSLEGUNG: A JOURNAL OF PHILOSOPHY

Editor: Richard Michael Buck

Dept. of Philosophy
University of Kansas
Lawrence, KS 66045-2145

Tel. 913-864-3976
Fax 913-864-4298
E-mail rbuck@falcon.cc.ukans.edu

ISSN 0733-4311

Date of founding: 1973

Purpose: To provide a forum for the expression of any and all philosophical perspectives. Primarily interested in publishing the work of new Ph.D.s and students pursuing the Ph.D. degree, but all papers are considered.

Sponsor: Graduate Association of Students in Philosophy, University of Kansas

Manuscript info: Eight to 10 philosophy articles are published per year. Manuscripts are refereed blind, and the referees' unsigned comments are given to authors. The average time required to evaluate a manuscript is 3-4 months. 10 to 15% of manuscripts are accepted. About 60% of accepted manuscripts require significant revisions. Instructions for manuscript preparation are included in the journal. Manuscripts should be sent to the editor.

Book reviews: Book reviews are usually 4-6 pages in length; critical notices and review articles can be somewhat longer. Books may be selected from "Books Available" List or may be requested with prior approval of Book Review Editor.

Frequency: 2 issues per year; Circulation: 200

Publisher: University of Kansas

Subscription rates: $10; Students $8; Institutions $14; Sample copies $6

BEHAVIOR AND PHILOSOPHY

Editor: Max Hocutt

Dept. of Philosophy
P.O. Box 870218
University of Alabama
Tuscaloosa, AL 35487-0218

Tel. 205-339-9514
E-mail mhocutt@philos.as.ua.edu

Date of founding: 1972

Purpose: To publish articles on philosophical issues in behavioral psychology and related fields.

Manuscript info: About 20 philosophy articles are published per year. Manuscripts on philosophical issues relating to behavioral science are preferred. Backlog is 6 months. About 25% of manuscripts are accepted; 60% require significant revisions. Average evaluation time is 60 days. About 25% of articles are invited. Instructions for manuscript preparation are included in the journal.

Book reviews: About 75% of the book reviews are invited; unsolicited book reviews are welcome.

Frequency: Semi-annual; Circulation: 600

Publisher: Cambridge Center for Behavioral Studies, 675 Massachusetts Ave., Cambridge, MA 02139

Subscription rates: $15; Institutions $26; Students $10

BETWEEN THE SPECIES: A JOURNAL OF ETHICS

Editors: J. Stockwell & S. Sapontzis

P.O. Box 8496
Berkeley, CA 94707

Tel. 510-526-5346

Date of founding: 1984

Purpose: An interdisciplinary journal for discussion on ethical issues concerning non-human beings.

Manuscript info: Twelve philosophy articles are published yearly. Manuscripts in ethics are preferred. Manuscripts are refereed by the editors; unsigned comments are given to authors. About 75% of manuscripts are accepted; 50% require significant revision. Average evaluation time is 2 months. About 75% of manuscripts are invited. Contact editors for manuscript instructions. Manuscripts should be sent to the journal.

Book reviews: Substantive, extended critical studies. All reviews are invited. Short reviews may be submitted. Prospective reviewers should first contact the editors about their projects.

Frequency: Semi-annual; Circulation: 300

Publisher: Schweitzer Center, San Francisco Bay Institute, P.O. Box 254, Berkeley, CA 94701

Subscription rates: $16; Institutions $30; add $15 for overseas airmail.

BUCKNELL REVIEW

Editor: Pauline Fletcher

Bucknell University
Lewisburg, PA 17837

Tel. 717-524-1184

ISSN 0007-2869

Date of founding: 1941

Manuscript info: Up to 8 philosophy articles are published per year; occasional special issues are devoted entirely to philosophy. Manuscripts on literature and arts in relation to philosophy are given preference. Manuscripts are refereed; unsigned comments are sometimes given to authors. About 10% of manuscripts are accepted; 15% require significant revision. Average evaluation time is 4-8 weeks. About 80% of articles are invited. Manuscripts should be sent to the journal.

Frequency: Semi-annual; Circulation: 700

Publisher: Associated University Presses

Subscription rates: $22

BULLETIN DE LA SOCIÉTÉ AMERICAINE DE PHILOSOPHIE

Editor: Colette Michael

635 Joanne Lane
DeKalb, IL 60115

Tel. 815-753-6463
Fax 815-753-6302
E-mail tc0cvml@corn.cso.niu.edu

ISSN 1040-6833

Date of founding: 1989

Purpose: To facilitate international exchange of ideas among scholars interested not only in the French language but also in applications of philosophical theories (deconstruction, structuralism, hermeneutics, etc.) to literature.

Sponsor: Société Americaine de Philosophie de Langue Française

Manuscript info: All articles are devoted to philosophy. Articles relevant to French philosophy in a very broad sense are preferred. Manuscripts submitted on diskette, IBM-compatible software are most welcome. Backlog of accepted articles is 3-6 months. Manuscripts are refereed blind; referees' unsigned comments are given to authors. About 80% of manuscripts are accepted; 10-15% require significant revision. Evaluation time averages 2 months. About 30% of articles are invited. Articles are accepted only from members of the Société Americaine de Philosophie de Langue Française. Instuctions for manuscript preparation are included in the journal.

Book reviews: Reviews are included; 75% are invited. Unsolicited book reviews are welcome.

Frequency: 2 issues per year; Circulation: 300

Publisher: Société Americaine de Philosophie and Department of Foreign Languages and Literature, Northern Illinois University

Subscription rates: Individuals $18; Students $9; Institutions $23. Add $5 postage charges for foreign subscriptions.

BULLETIN OF SYMBOLIC LOGIC

Editor: Richard A. Shore

Managing Editor, Dept. of Mathematics White Hall, Cornell University Ithaca, NY 14853

E-mail shore@math.cornell.edu

ISSN 1079-8986

Purpose: To keep the logic community abreast of important developments in all aspects of the discipline.

Sponsor: Association for Symbolic Logic

Manuscript info: The Bulletin invites submission of articles and communications. Articles should be expository or survey papers of broad interest that are accessible to a wide audience of logicians. They may deal with any areas of logic, including mathematical or philosophical logic, logic in computer science or linguistics, the history or philosophy of logic, and applications of logic to other fields. Communications should be announcements of important new results and ideas in any aspect of logic. The communications will typically be preliminary announcements of longer, full papers that will be published elsewhere. In any case, they should, in addition to a description of the new results or ideas, include enough history, background, and explanation to make the significance of the work apparent to a wide audience. Articles should be submitted to Andreas R. Blass, Dept. of Mathematics, University of Michigan, Ann Arbor, MI 48190 (ablass@math.umich.edu). Communications can be submitted to any of the other editors: Alexander S. Kechris, Dept. of Mathematics,

Caltech, Pasadena, CA 91125 (kechris@caltech.edu); Daniel Lascar, UFR de Mathematique, Université de Paris VII, 2 pl Jussieu Tour 45-55, 75251 Paris cedex 05 France (lascar@logique.jussieu.fr); Charles D. Parsons, Dept. of Philosophy, Harvard University (parsons2@husc.harvard.edu); Andrew M. Pitts, University of Cambridge Computer Laboratory, New Museum Site, Pembroke St., Cambridge CB2 3QG, England (ap@cl.cam.ac.uk); Richard A. Shore, Dept. of Mathematics, Cornell University (shore@math.cornell.edu).

Frequency: 4 issues per year

Publisher: Association for Symbolic Logic

Subscription rates: $230 (combined with subscription for *The Journal of Symbolic Logic*)

BULLETIN OF THE SANTAYANA SOCIETY (OVERHEARD IN SEVILLE)

Editor: Herman J. Saatkamp, Jr.

Santayana Edition
Department of Philosophy
Texas A & M University
College Station, TX 77841-4237

Tel. 409-845-2003
Fax 409-845-0458
E-mail h-saatkamp@tamu.edu

ISSN 0846-8508

Date of founding: 1983

Purpose: To promote research and writing on the work of George Santayana and to support the publication of the works of George Santayana.

Sponsor: Santayana Society

Manuscript info: About 5 articles per year are devoted to philosophy. Manuscripts relating to George Santayana are preferred. Most articles (95%) are invited. Instructions for manuscript preparation are included in the journal. Manuscripts should be sent to the co-editor, Angus Kerr-Lawson, Department of Pure Mathematics, University of Waterloo, Waterloo, Ontario, Canada N2L 361.

Book reviews: Book reviews are included. Unsolicited book reviews are not welcome.

Frequency: Annual; Circulation: 500

Publisher: Angus Kerr-Lawson

Subscription rates: $25

BUSINESS AND PROFESSIONAL ETHICS JOURNAL

Editor: Robert J. Baum

Center for Applied Ethics
332 Griffin-Floyd Hall
University of Florida
Gainesville, FL 32611

Tel. 904-392-2084 Ext. 332
Fax 904-392-5577

ISSN 0277-2027

Date of founding: 1981

Purpose: A forum for the analysis of ethical issues that arise at the interface of business and the professions.

Manuscript info: All articles are devoted to business and professional ethics. Manuscripts are refereed blind; unsigned comments are usually given to authors. About 15-20% of manuscripts are accepted; 80% require significant revision. Average evaluation time is 3 months.

Instructions for manuscript preparation are in the journal. Manuscripts should be sent to the journal.

Book reviews: Unsolicited book reviews are welcome.

Frequency: Quarterly

Publisher: See the editors.

Subscription rates: $25; Institutions $75 (add $5 for Canada, $10 for surface mail to other countries).

BUSINESS ETHICS

Editor: Marjorie Kelly

52 S. 10th St., Suite 110
Minneapolis, MN 55403-2001

Tel. 612-962-4700
Fax 612-962-4810
E-mail bizethics@aol.com

ISSN 0894-6582

Date of founding: 1987

Purpose: To serve that growing number of business and professional people striving to live and work in socially responsible ways. To encourage ethical practices in corporate America and provide a forum where executives can think aloud together about issues.

Manuscript info: Manuscripts must be for a popular audience, not an academic one. Emphasis is on corporate programs, hands-on ideas, interviews, resources, case studies, and leading-edge thought. Some first-person musings and some well-written contemporary analyses are included. About 80% of accepted manuscripts require significant revision. The average time required to evaluate a manuscript is 2 months. About 90% of articles are invited. Please query the editor with article ideas before submission.

Book reviews: The magazine runs no traditional book reviews. A regular section called BookEnd features brief, one-paragraph excerpts/paraphrases from a significant recent book.

Frequency: 6 issues per year; Circulation: 20,000

Subscription rates: $29/year

BUSINESS ETHICS QUARTERLY

Editor: Patricia H. Werhane

Darden School
University of Virginia
P.O. Box 6550
Charlottesville, VA 22906

Tel. 804-924-4840
Fax 804-924-6378

ISSN 1052-150X

Date of founding: 1991

Purpose: To publish scholarly articles from a wide variety of disciplinary orientations on the general subject of the application of ethics to the business community.

Sponsor: Loyola University of Chicago, Olsson Center for Applied Ethics, University of Virginia

Manuscript info: About 60% of articles are devoted to philosophy. Manuscripts in ethics or applied ethics are preferred. Backlog is about 18 months. Manuscripts are refereed blind; unsigned comments are given to authors. About 50% of manuscripts require significant revision. Evaluation time averages 3 months. About 10% of articles are invited. Instructions for manuscript preparation are included in the journal. Manuscripts should be sent to the editor.

Book reviews: Included; 90% are invited. Unsolicited book reviews are welcome.

Frequency: Quarterly; Circulation: 900

Publisher: Society for Business Ethics

Subscription rates: Individuals $40; Institutions $98; Students $25

CHINESE STUDIES IN PHILOSOPHY*

Editor: Chung-Ying Cheng

Dept. of Philosophy
University of Hawaii
Honolulu, HI 96822

Tel. 808-956-6081
Fax 808-956-9228

ISSN 0023-8627

Date of founding: 1967

Purpose: To provide English translations from Chinese philosophical publications.

Manuscript info: Eighteen to 20 philosophy articles per year (all). All articles are based on translations of previously published material; therefore, we do not require the submission of manuscripts.

Frequency: Quarterly; Circulation: 400

Publisher: M. E. Sharpe, Inc.

Subscription rates: $37; Institutions $144

CLIO: A JOURNAL OF LITERATURE, HISTORY, AND THE PHILOSOPHY OF HISTORY

Editor: Lynette Felber & Clark Butler

Indiana U-Purdue U, Fort Wayne
Fort Wayne, IN 46805-1499

Tel. 219-481-6753
Fax 219-481-6985

ISSN 0884-2043

Date of founding: 1971

Purpose: To be a forum for the interplay of literature as informed by history, historiography, and the philosophy of history, with special attention to Hegel-related studies.

Manuscript info: About 6-9 philosophy articles are published yearly. Philosophy of history, either speculative or analytic, is preferred. Inderdisciplinary methodology is given preference. Average 6-month backlog. Manuscripts are refereed; referees' comments are sometimes given to authors. About 15% of manuscripts are accepted; most require significant revision. Average evaluation time is 4-6 months. About 10% of articles are invited. Instructions for manuscript preparation are in the journal. Manuscripts should be sent to the journal. Clark Butler is the philosophy editor.

Book reviews: All book reviews are invited; unsolicited book reviews are not welcome.

Frequency: 4 issues per year; Circulation: 650

Publisher: Purdue Research Foundation

Subscription rates: $16; Institutions $42; postage outside US $4/volume

73

CRIMINAL JUSTICE ETHICS

Editor: John Kleinig

Dept. of Law & Police Science
John Jay Col. of Crim. Just./CUNY
New York, NY 10019

Tel. 212-237-8033
Fax 212-237-8901
E-mail cjejj@cunyvm.cuny.edu

ISSN 0731-129X

Date of founding: 1982

Purpose: To focus greater attention on ethical issues by philosophers, criminal justice professionals, lawyers and judges, and the general public.

Sponsor: John Jay College of Criminal Justice, City University of New York

Manuscript info: About 70% of articles are devoted to philosophy. Preference is given to manuscripts in criminal justice ethics that are intelligible to a broader audience. There is very little backlog. Manuscripts are refereed blind; referees' unsigned comments are given to authors. About 15% of manuscripts are accepted; 80% require significant revision. Average evaluation time is 6 weeks. About 20% of articles are invited. Instructions for manuscript preparation are in the journal.

Book reviews: About 95% of book reviews are invited; unsolicited book reviews are not usually welcome.

Frequency: 2 issues per year; Circulation: 850

Publisher: John Jay College of Criminal Justice, CUNY

Subscription rates: $15; Institutions $30; Students $12.50; overseas rates higher.

CRITICAL INQUIRY

Editor: W. J. T. Mitchell

A. I. Davidson, University of Chicago
202 Wieboldt Hall, 1050 E. 59th St.
Chicago, IL 60637

Tel. 312-702-8477
Fax 312-702-3397
E-mail jww4@midway.uchicago.edu

ISSN 0093-1896

Date of founding: 1974

Manuscript info: About 15 philosophy articles are published per year. Manuscripts in any area of philosophy are welcome. Backlog is 6 months. Manuscripts are refereed; referees' unsigned comments are given to authors. About 3% of manuscripts are accepted; 50% require significant revision. Average evaluation time is 3-4 months. Instructions for manuscript preparation are included in the journal. Manuscripts should be sent to the editor. Home page URL: http://www2.uchicago.edu./jnl-crit-inq/

Book reviews: There are no book reviews, but a list of books received is included.

Frequency: Quarterly; Circulation: 4,500

Publisher: University of Chicago Press, Journals Division

Subscription rates: $37.50; Institutions $74; Students $23; add $4.50 for postage outside the US.

CRITICAL REVIEW

Editor: Jeffrey Friedman

Critical Review
275 West Park Avenue
New Haven, CT 06511

Tel. 203-387-1023
Fax 203-397-8170

ISSN 0891-3811

Date of founding: 1986

Purpose: To evaluate effects of various political, social, and economic orders on human well-being. Discussions of conceptions of the good, consequentialism, utilitarianism and critiques of liberalism, classical liberalism, and deontology especially welcome.

Sponsor: Critical Review Foundation, 275 W. Park Ave., New Haven, CT 06511

Manuscript info: About 8-10 philosophy articles are published per year. Articles should be in political philosophy, history of ideas, or social philosophy, but should avoid purely analytical or game-theoretical approaches or policy advocacy; preference is given to essays and review-essays of 6,000-10,000 words. Backlog is 6 months. After initial review, manuscripts are refereed blind; unsigned comments are given to authors. About 50% of manuscripts are accepted; 75% require significant revision. Average evaluation time is 2 months. About 50% of articles are invited.

Book reviews: About 75% of book reviews are invited; unsolicited book reviews are welcome, but one should check with the editors to make sure that a book has not already been sent out for review.

Frequency: Quarterly;
Circulation: 3,000

Publisher: Critical Review Foundation

Subscription rates: $29; Institutions $54; Students $15 with ID; Foreign: $35; Institutions $62; Students $15 with ID; add $15 per year for foreign airmail.

DIACRITICS

Editor: Richard Klein

Jonathan Culler, Romance Studies
278 Goldwin Smith Hall
Cornell University
Ithaca, NY 14853

Tel. 607-255-4155
Fax 607-255-6661
E-mail kb31@cornell.edu

ISSN 0300-7162

Date of founding: 1970

Purpose: To provide a forum for exchange among literary theorists, literary critics, and philosophers.

Sponsor: Cornell University

Manuscript info: About 25% of articles are devoted to philosophy. Preference is given to interdisciplinary articles and those in philosophy/literary theory. Backlog of accepted articles is 6 months. Manuscripts are refereed (not blind); referees' unsigned comments are sometimes given to authors. About 25% of manuscripts are accepted; 50% require significant revision. Evaluation time averages 3-6 months. About 30% of articles are invited. Manuscripts should follow *MLA Stylebook.*

Book reviews: Reviews are included; they are extended review essays with a theme. About 20% of book reviews are invited. Unsolicited book reviews are welcome.

Frequency: Quarterly; Circulation: 1,400

Publisher: Johns Hopkins University Press

Subscription rates: Individuals $25; Students $20; Institutions $63. Postage charges: $3.50 to Canada and Mexico, $8.40 elsewhere. Required currency: US dollars; Visa/MC accepted.

DIALOGOS

Editor: G. H. Fromm

G. E. Rosado Haddock
P.O. Box 21572, University Station
San Juan, PR 00931

Tel. 809-764-0000 Ext. 2072

ISSN 0012-2122

Date of founding: 1964

Manuscript info: Eighteen philosophy articles (all) are published per year. Manuscripts are welcome in any area of philosophy, provided they are written in Spanish or English. Backlog is 18-24 months. Manuscripts are refereed. About 40% of manuscripts are accepted. Average evaluation time is 4 months. About 20% of articles are invited. Instructions for manuscript preparation are included in the journal. Manuscripts should be sent to the editor.

Book reviews: About 80% of the book reviews are invited; unsolicited book reviews are welcome.

Frequency: Semi-annual; Circulation: 800

Publisher: University of Puerto Rico

Subscription rates: $12; Institutions $16; subscriptions should be ordered through EDUPR, P.O. Box 23322, San Juan, PR 00931-3322.

DIALOGUE

Editor: Thomas L. Prendergast

Dept. of Philosophy
Marquette University
Milwaukee, WI 53233-2289

Tel. 414-288-5975

ISSN 0012-2246

Date of founding: 1955

Purpose: To publish papers in all areas of philosophy by graduate and undergraduate students.

Sponsor: Phi Sigma Tau

Manuscript info: About 10 philosophy articles are published per year. Manuscripts are welcome in any area of philosophy. The backlog of accepted articles is 6 months. Manuscripts are usually refereed. About 25% of manuscripts are accepted; 20% require significant revisions. Average evaluation time is 3-4 months. No articles are invited. Send manuscripts to the editor.

Book reviews: Book reviews are rarely invited; unsolicited book reviews are welcome.

Frequency: Semi-annual; Circulation: 1,300

Publisher: Phi Sigma Tau

Subscription rates: $5; Foreign $5.50

EDUCATIONAL STUDIES*

Editor: Carlton H. Bowyer

303B Ball Education Building
Memphis State University
Memphis, TN 35812

Tel. 901-678-3417,
Fax 901-678-4778

ISSN 0013-1946

Date of founding: 1968

Sponsor: American Education
Studies Association

Manuscript info: Approximately 20%
of book reviews are devoted to philosophy per year. Reviews of books related to comparative, historical, philosophical, and social aspects of education are given preference. Instructions
for manuscript preparation are available from the editor. Manuscripts
should be sent to the editor.

Book reviews: About 90% of book
reviews are invited; unsolicited book
reviews are discouraged. About 99%
of the articles are invited.

Frequency: Quarterly

Subscription rates: $25, Institutions
$35, Foreign add $5

EDUCATIONAL THEORY

Editor: Nicholas Burbules

College of Education
University of Illinois
1310 S. Sixth Street
Champaign, IL 61820

Tel. 217-333-3003
Fax 217-244-3711

ISSN 0013-2004

Date of founding: 1950

Purpose: To foster the continuing
development of educational theory
and to encourage wide and effective
discussion of theoretical problems
within the educational profession.

Sponsor: Philosophy of Education
Society and the John Dewey Society

Manuscript info: About 25-30 philosophy articles are published yearly.
Any area of philosophy is welcome,
but should have relation to education.
Preference is given to articles of 7,500
words. Approximate backlog is 6
months. Manuscripts are refereed
blind; unsigned comments are sometimes given to authors. Acceptance
rate is 15%; 40% require significant
revision. The average evaluation time
is 2 months. Invitation rate is 20%.
Manuscript instructions may be
obtained from the editorial office.
Send manuscripts to the journal.

Book reviews: Most book reviews
are invited; unsolicited book reviews
are welcome.

Frequency: Quarterly;
Circulation: 2,100

Publisher: The University of Illinois

Subscription rates: Individuals $20,
Foreign $22; Institutions $30,
Foreign $32

ELECTRONIC JOURNAL OF ANALYTIC PHILOSOPHY

Editor: Craig DeLancey

Dept. of Philosophy
Sycamore Hall 026
Indiana University
Bloomington, IN 47405

Tel. 812-330-0743
E-mail ejap@tarski.phil.indiana.edu

ISSN 1071-5800

Date of founding: 1993

Purpose: To strengthen analytic philosophy by examining it at its most vulnerable points, drawing attention to areas of philosophical research previously neglected by analytic philosophy.

Sponsor: Indiana University Research and University Graduate School and other units at Indiana University

Manuscript info: The journal is at present publishing mostly topic issues with solicited papers. Each bi-yearly issue concentrates on topics of special concern to analytic philosophers. The journal is available on the WWW at http://www.phil.indiana.edu/ejap/ejap .html; via gopher: gopher://tarski.phil.indiana.edu:70/11 /ejap; and by anonymous ftp: file://phil.indiana.edu/ejap/ A listserv is available at listserv@iubvm.ucs.indiana.edu

Book reviews: Reviews are not included at this time.

Frequency: 2-3 issues per year

Subscription rates: The journal is free. See above for access information.

ENVIRONMENTAL ETHICS

Editor: Eugene C. Hargrove

Dept. of Phil. & Relig. Studies
Ctr. for Environmental Phil.
P.O. Box 13496, Univ. of N. Texas
Denton, TX 76203-6496

Tel. 817-565-2727,
Fax 817-565-4448,
E-mail ee@unt.edu

ISSN 0163-4275

Date of founding: 1979

Purpose: An analysis of environmental philosophy and ethics.

Manuscript info: About 20 to 22 philosophy articles are published per year. Manuscripts in any area of philosophy are welcome if they also apply to environmental philosophy and ethics. Manuscripts are refereed blind, and unsigned comments are given to authors. About 20% of manuscripts are accepted. About 50% of accepted manuscripts require significant revision. Average evaluation time is 3-4 months. Instructions for manuscript preparation are included in the journal. Send manuscripts to the editor.

Book reviews: All book reviews are invited; unsolicited book reviews are not welcome.

Frequency: Quarterly;
Circulation: 2,000

Publisher: Environmental Philosophy, Inc.

Subscription rates: $20; Institutions $40; Single copies $7/$10

ETHICS AND ADVOCACY*

Editor: Nina Cunningham

P.O. Box A-3595
Chicago, IL 60690

Tel. 312-664-4770
Fax 312-664-4779

Date of founding: 1985

Purpose: To provide a voice for those interested in problems of legal ethics from a philosophical, pedagogical, or practical point of view.

Sponsor: Center for Legal Ethics Education & Research

Manuscript info: About 10 philosophy articles per year. Ethics and law, teaching of ethics, problems of ethics in the legal system, a democracy, etc., are welcome. Manuscripts are refereed by the editor and 2 members of the editorial board. The refereeing is blind, and unsigned comments are given to the authors. About 10% of the manuscripts are accepted; about 50% of manuscripts require significant revision. Average evaluation time is 3 months. Invitation rate 50%. Instructions for manuscript preparation are included in the journal.

Book reviews: One-third of the reviews are invited. Unsolicited reviews are accepted.

Frequency: 3 issues per year

Publisher: Quidlibet Research, Inc. P.O. Box A-3595, Chicago, IL 60690

Subscription rates: $35; Institutions $42

ETHICS AND MEDICS

Editor: David Beauregard

OMV, Pope John XXIII Center
186 Forbes Rd.
Braintree, MA 02184-2612

Tel. 617-848-6965
Fax 617-849-1309
E-mail pjctr@tiac.net

ISSN 1071-3778

Date of founding: 1976

Purpose: To study ethics in health care.

Manuscript info: About 24 articles per year are devoted to philosophy.

Manuscripts in medical ethics are preferred. Normally, manuscripts are solicited and are 1,500 words in length. Backlog of accepted articles is 2 months. Manuscripts are refereed; referees' unsigned comments are given to authors. Evaluation time averages 2 weeks. About 98% of articles are invited. Instructions for manuscript preparation are available on request. Manuscripts should be sent to the editor.

Book reviews: Reviews are not included.

Frequency: 12 issues per year; Circulation: 25,500

Publisher: Pope John XXIII Medical-Moral Research and Education Center, and Russell E. Smith

Subscription rates: $18

ETHICS JOURNAL

Editor: William P. O'Brien

Ethics Resource Center
1120 G St. NW, Suite 200
Washington, DC 20005

Tel. 202-737-2258
Fax 202-737-2227

ISSN 1060-0698

Date of founding: 1984

Purpose: To increase public trust in education, business, government, and other American institutions by strengthening their ethical conduct; to keep readers up-to-date on news of ethics.

Manuscript info: Approximately 4 articles per year are devoted to philosophy. Manuscripts in any area of philosophy are welcome. About 50% of manuscripts are accepted; 50%

require significant revision.
Evaluation time averages 4-6 weeks.
About 50% of articles are invited. Call
before submitting manuscripts: 202-
434-8462. Manuscripts should be sent
to the editor. Managing editor: Ruth
E. Sellars.

Book reviews: Book reviews are
included; about 50% are invited.
Unsolicited book reviews are welcome.

Frequency: Quarterly

Publisher: Ethics Resource Center

Subscription rates: Contributions
are accepted.

ETHICS: AN INTERNATIONAL JOURNAL OF SOCIAL, POLITICAL AND LEGAL PHILOSOPHY

Editor: Gerald Dworkin

Univ. of Illinois at Chicago
601 S. Morgan St., Room 1424
Chicago, IL 60607-7114

Tel. 312-413-2087
Fax 312-413-2093
E-mail u62868@uicvm.uic.edu

ISSN 0014-1704

Date of founding: 1890

Purpose: To publish articles in moral,
social, political, and legal philosophy
devoted to the study of the ideas and
principles that form the basis for individual and collective action.

Manuscript info: About 40 philosophy articles are published yearly.
Moral, social, political, or legal philosophy is preferred, especially if interdisciplinary. About 50% of manuscripts are refereed. Refereeing is
blind, and unsigned comments are
given to authors. About 5% of manu-

scripts are accepted; 25% require significant revision. The average evaluation time is 3 months. Invitation rate
is 20%. Instructions for manuscript
preparation are in the journal.
Manuscripts should be sent to the editor.

Book reviews: All book reviews are
invited; unsolicited book reviews are
not welcome.

Frequency: Quarterly;
Circulation: 3,600

Publisher: University of Chicago
Press

Subscription rates: $32; Institutions
$75; Students $23; APA members
$27

FAITH AND PHILOSOPHY: JOURNAL OF THE SOCIETY OF CHRISTIAN PHILOSOPHERS

Editor: William J. Wainwright

Dept. of Philosophy
Univ. of Wisconsin-Milwaukee
Milwaukee, WI 53201

Tel. 414-229-4719

ISSN 0739-7046

Date of founding: 1981

Purpose: To serve as a forum for
articles that address philosophical
issues from a Christian perspective
and for discussions from any perspective of philosophical questions that
arise within the Christian faith.

Sponsor: The Society of Christian
Philosophers, Dept. of Philosophy,
Calvin College

Manuscript info: Manuscripts in any
area of philosophy are welcome. The
refereeing is blind if authors request it
and submit manuscripts in a suitable

format; referees' unsigned comments are given to the authors. The average time required to evaluate a manuscript is 2 months. Instructions for manuscript preparation are included in the journal. Manuscripts should be sent to the editor.

Book reviews: Most book reviews are invited. Unsolicited book reviews are welcome.

Frequency: Quarterly; Circulation: 1,600

Publisher: Society of Christian Philosophers

Subscription rates: $25; Students and unemployed philosophers $15; Institutions $40; add $4 for Canada and $6 for other non-US subscriptions.

FEMINIST STUDIES

Editor: Claire G. Moses

Women's Studies Program
University of Maryland
College Park, MD 20742

Tel. 301-405-7415
Fax 301-314-9190

ISSN 0046-3663

Date of founding: 1969

Purpose: To encourage analytic responses to feminist issues and to open new areas of research, criticism, and speculation.

Manuscript info: Two to 3 philosophy articles are published per year. Manuscripts are welcome in areas concerned with women or the question of gender. Manuscripts are refereed blind; unsigned comments are given to authors. About 7% of manuscripts are accepted; 85% require significant revi-

sion. Average evaluation time is 4-5 months. Instructions for manuscript preparation are in the journal. Manuscripts should be sent to the editor.

Book reviews: About 90% are invited. Ideas for review essays may be submitted to the editor.

Frequency: 3 issues per year; Circulation: 6,000

Publisher: Feminist Studies, Inc.

Subscription rates: Individuals $30/one year, $57/two years, $80/three years; Institutions $65/one year, $125/two years, $180/three years

FILM AND PHILOSOPHY

Editor: Kendall D'Andrade

Dept. of Philosophy
Shawnee State University
Portsmouth, OH 45662-4303

Tel. 614-355-2401

ISSN 1073-0427

Date of founding: 1993

Purpose: To publish work in the intersection of film and philosophy.

Sponsor: Society for the Philosophic Study of the Contemporary Visual Arts

Manuscript info: About 7 to 14 philosophy articles are published per issue. Manuscripts are blind refereed. Authors are given referees' comments if they seem helpful. The average time required to evaluate a manuscript is 3-4 months. Some works are invited. Manuscripts should be sent to the editor, with an accompanying disk if possible.

Book reviews: One or two review essays are published per issue; some are invited. Unsolicited review essays are welcome, but correspondence with an editor beforehand is recommended. Standard book reviews are published in the Society's newsletter.

Frequency: Annual; Circulation: 300

Publisher: Society for the Philosophic Study of the Contemporary Visual Arts

Subscription rates: $10 for members of the Society for the Philosophic Study of the Contemporary Visual Arts;
$15 for non-members

FOUNDATIONS OF SCIENCE

Editor: Paul Humphreys

Corcoran Dept. of Philosophy
521 Cabell Hall
University of Virginia
Charlottesville, VA 22903

Tel. 804-924-6921
Fax 804-924-6927
E-mail iandi@plearn.bitnet

ISSN 1233-1821

Date of founding: 1995

Purpose: To promote investigations into foundational issues of the sciences, to foster interaction between philosophers and scientists, to pursue objective truth across disciplines and national boundaries, and to make accessible research in developing fields.

Sponsor: Committee for Science Studies of the Polish Academy of Sciences

Manuscript info: About 15 to 20 articles per year are devoted to philosophy. Manuscripts in methodological and foundational issues in any science are welcome. Preference is given to nontechnical, substantive papers on contemporary research. Most (90%) are solicited. Manuscripts are refereed (not blind); unsigned comments are given to authors. About 5% of manuscripts are accepted; 90% require significant revision. Evaluation time averages 1 month. Instructions for manuscript preparation are included in the journal. Manuscripts should be sent to the editor.

Book reviews: Book reviews are not included.

Frequency: 2 issues per year; Circulation: 500

Publisher: Oficyna Akademicka, Foundations of Science, P.O. Box 32106, Raleigh, NC 27622-2106

Subscription rates: Members of AFOS and students $22; Others $35; Institutions $60

FRANCISCAN STUDIES

Editor: Conrad L. Harkins

Franciscan Institute
Saint Bonaventure University
Saint Bonaventure, NY 14778

Tel. 716-375-2105
Fax 716-375-2156
E-mail conrad@sbu.edu

ISSN 0080-5459

Date of founding: 1941

Purpose: To publish articles concerned with the Franciscan contribution to theological, philosophical, and scientific thought, and on the historical evolution of the Franciscan movement.

Manuscript info: About 6 philosophy articles are published yearly. Manuscripts on Franciscan thought that make a new contribution to knowledge are preferred. Editions of texts are also printed. There is no backlog. Manuscripts are refereed, but not blind; unsigned comments are given to authors. Acceptance rate is 40%; 80% require significant revision. Average evaluation time is 4 months. Invitation rate is 5%. Manuscript instructions are available from the editorial office. Manuscripts should be sent to the editor. (Editorial phone: 716-375-2159)

Book reviews: Unsolicited review articles and shorter reviews are accepted at the discretion of the editor.

Frequency: Annual; Circulation: 650

Publisher: Franciscan Institute

Subscription rates: $24

FREE INQUIRY

Editor: Paul Kurtz

Box 664
Buffalo, NY 14226-0664

Tel. 716-636-7571
Fax 716-636-1733

ISSN 0272-0701

Date of founding: 1980

Purpose: To deal with philosophical and intellectual issues concerned with secular humanism and freedom.

Sponsor: Council for Democratic and Secular Humanism

Manuscript info: About 16 to 20 philosophy articles are published per year. Manuscripts dealing with religion, ethics, and politics are welcome.

The backlog of accepted articles is 6 months. Manuscripts are refereed. About 10% of manuscripts are accepted; 30% require significant revision. The average time required to evaluate a manuscript is 2 months. About 80% of articles are invited. Manuscripts should be sent to the editor.

Book reviews: About 80% are invited. Unsolicited book reviews are welcome.

Frequency: Quarterly;
Circulation: 23,270

Subscription rates: $28.50; $47.50; $64.50

GRADUATE FACULTY PHILOSOPHY JOURNAL

Editor: The Editors

New School for Social Research
65 Fifth Avenue
New York, NY 10003

Tel. 212-229-5735
Fax 212-229-5315

ISSN 0093-4240

Purpose: To communicate ideas concerning continental philosophy and its tradition.

Manuscript info: About 10 to 15 philosophy articles are published yearly. Any area of philosophy is welcome, but history of philosophy and European philosophy are preferred. There is a 12-month backlog. Manuscripts are refereed blind; no comments returned. Acceptance rate is 30%; 5% require significant revision. Average evaluation time is 3-4 months. Invitation rate is 80%. Follow *Chicago Manual of Style.* Manuscripts should be sent to editors. Other editors: Aaron Garrett, Roger D. Hodge, Robert Del Principe, Charles Wolfe.

Book reviews: About 25% of book reviews are invited. Unsolicited book reviews are welcome.

Frequency: Biannual; Circulation: 1,000

Publisher: New School for Social Research

Subscription rates: $15; Institutions $35; Students $10

HASTINGS CENTER REPORT

Editor: Bette-Jane Crigger

255 Elm Road
Briarcliff, NY 10510

Tel. 914-762-8500
Fax 914-762-2124

ISSN 0093-0334

Date of founding: 1971

Purpose: To examine for an interdisciplinary audience the ethical issues in biology, medicine, the life sciences, social sciences, and the professions.

Manuscript info: Manuscripts are welcome in ethics, medicine, and the professions and sciences. Short, 2,000-3,000-word manuscripts are preferred. Backlog is 3 months. Manuscripts are refereed blind; unsigned comments are usually given to authors. Acceptance rate is 10%; 50% require significant revision. The average evaluation time is 2 months. Invitation rate is 30%. Instructions for manuscript preparation are in the journal. Manuscripts should be sent to the editor.

Book reviews: All book reviews are invited; there are no unsolicited book reviews.

Frequency: 6 issues per year; Circulation: 11,900

Publisher: The Hastings Center Report

Subscription rates: $55; Institutions and Libraries $70; Students $40 (applicable for 2 years only)

HEIDEGGER STUDIES

Editor: c/o Ken Maly

Dept. of Philosophy
Univ. of Wisconsin La Crosse
La Crosse, WI 54601

Tel. 608-785-8422
Fax 608-785-6918
E-mail kenneth_maly@uwlax.edu

ISSN 0885-4580

Date of founding: 1985

Purpose: The journal is dedicated to promoting the understanding of Heidegger's thought through the interpretation of his writings, i.e., his whole work including the volumes of his *Gesamtausgabe*.

Manuscript info: All articles are devoted to the philosophy of Heidegger. Preference is given to manuscripts in Heidegger's phenomenology. There is no backlog. Manuscripts are refereed blind; unsigned comments are given to authors. About 50% of articles are accepted; 30% require significant revision. Average evaluation time is 3 months. About 10% of articles are invited. Instructions for manuscript preparation are in the journal. Manuscripts should be sent to the editor.

Book reviews: About 50% of book reviews are invited; unsolicited book reviews are welcome.

Frequency: Annual

Publisher: Duncker & Humblot, Postfach 410329, D-12113 Berlin, Germany

Subscription rates: $28; add $2 for surface mail, $8 for airmail

---

HISTORY AND THEORY: STUDIES IN THE PHILOSOPHY OF HISTORY

Editor: Brian C. Fay

Wesleyan Station
Middletown, CT 06459-0507

Tel. 203-685-3292 Ext. 2069
Fax 203-685-2491
E-mail jperkins@wesleyan.edu

ISSN 0018-2656

Date of founding: 1960

Purpose: To publish in the theory of history, narrativism, historical method, and in the relationship of problems in historical method and theory to sociology, economics, psychology, anthropology, and the humanities.

Manuscript info: Eight philosophy articles are published per year. Definitive manuscripts in the philosophy of history are preferred. Backlog is 6 months. Manuscripts are refereed, but not blind, and unsigned comments are given to authors. Acceptance rate is about 15%; 50% require significant revision. The average evaluation time is 3 months. About 20% of articles are invited. Instructions for manuscript preparation are available from the editorial office. Manuscripts should be sent to the executive editor. World Wide Web site: http://www.wesleyan.edu/histjrnl/hthome.html

Book reviews: About 98% of the book reviews are invited; unsolicited book reviews are not welcome.

Frequency: Quarterly;
Circulation: 2,000

Publisher: Wesleyan University

Subscription rates: Individuals $30; Institutions $50

HISTORY OF PHILOSOPHY QUARTERLY

Editor: Andrew J. Reck

Dept. of Philosophy
Tulane University
105 Newcomb Hall
New Orleans, LA 70118

Tel. 504-862-3390
Fax 504-862-8714

ISSN 0740-0675

Date of founding: 1984

Purpose: To publish papers that cultivate philosophical history in the spirit of *philosophia perennis*.

Manuscript info: Twenty-six philosophy articles are published per year. Any aspect of the history of philosophy is welcome; only self-sufficient articles will be published. Backlog is 12 months. Manuscripts are refereed. The refereeing is blind; comments are given to the authors at their request. Acceptance rate is 15%; 50% require significant revision. The average evaluation time is 12 weeks. Instructions for manuscript preparation are in the journal. Manuscripts should be sent to the editor.

Frequency: Quarterly;
Circulation: 500

Publisher: North American Philosophical Publications; subscription agent: Philosophy Documentation Center

Subscription rates: $40; Institutions $160

HUMAN RIGHTS QUARTERLY

Editor: Bert B. Lockwood, Jr.

Morgan Inst. for Human Rights
College of Law
University of Cincinnati
Cincinnati, OH 45221

Tel. 513-556-0093
Fax 513-556-6265
E-mail nancy.ent@law.uc.edu

ISSN 0275-0392

Date of founding: 1979

Purpose: To offer scholars in law, philosophy, and the social sciences an interdisciplinary forum in which to present comparative and international research on public policy within the scope of the Universal Declaration of Human Rights.

Manuscript info: About 15% of articles are devoted to philosophy. Manuscripts in philosophy are welcome as applicable to the editorial purpose. Manuscripts are refereed blind; unsigned comments are shared with authors. About 10% of manuscripts are accepted. The average evaluation time is 6-8 weeks. Invitation rate 15%. Instructions for manuscript preparation are in the journal or available from the editor. Manuscripts should be sent to the editor.

Book reviews: All book reviews are presently invited; unsolicited book reviews are welcome.

Frequency: Quarterly

Publisher: Johns Hopkins University Press

Subscription rates: $28; Institutions $76.50; postage outside US $3.70 (Canada & Mexico); outside North America $10

HUMAN STUDIES: A JOURNAL FOR PHILOSOPHY AND THE SOCIAL SCIENCES

Editor: George Psathas

Dept. of Sociology
Boston University
100 Cummington St.
Boston, MA 02215

Tel. 617-353-2591
Fax 617-353-4837

ISSN 0163-8548

Date of founding: 1977

Purpose: Dedicated to advancing the dialogue between philosophy and the social sciences.

Manuscript info: Manuscripts from phenomenological and humanistic perspectives are preferred. Backlog is 8 to 12 months. Manuscripts are refereed blind, and the referees' unsigned comments are given to authors. Acceptance rate is 40%; 25% require significant revision. The average evaluation time is 3-5 months. About 10% of articles are invited. Instructions for manuscript preparation are in the journal. Manuscripts should be sent to the editor.

Book reviews: Unsolicited review articles are welcome and should be addressed to Review Editors.

Frequency: Quarterly;
Circulation: 500

Publisher: Kluwer Academic
Publishers, P.O. Box 17, 3300 AA
Dordrecht, The Netherlands

Subscription rates: $62.50;
Institutions $117

HUMANIST, THE*

Editor: Frederick Edwords

7 Harwood Drive
P.O. Box 1188
Amherst, NY 14226-7188

Tel. 716-839-5080
Fax 716-839-5079

ISSN 0018-7399

Date of founding: 1941

Purpose: To publish a journal of normative ethics and the philosophy of science that attempts to relate theoretical philosophy to practical moral and social issues.

Sponsor: American Humanist Association

Manuscript info: Twelve philosophy articles per year. Manuscripts in ethics, social philosophy, philosophical psychology, and frontiers of science are preferred. Backlog of 2 months. Manuscripts are refereed blind; referees' comments are not given to authors. About 2% of manuscripts are accepted. The average evaluation time is 2-5 months. About 80% of articles are invited. Instructions for manuscript preparation can be obtained from the editor.

Book reviews: About 80% of the book reviews are invited; unsolicited book reviews are welcome.

Frequency: 6 issues per year;
Circulation: 18,000

Publisher: American Humanist Association; toll-free telephone 800-743-6646

Subscription rates: $24.95

HUME STUDIES

Editors: Don Garrett &
William Morris

Dept. of Philosophy
341 Orson Spencer Hall
University of Utah
Salt Lake City, UT 84112

Tel. 801-581-3486
Fax 801-585-5195
E-mail hume@cc.utah.edu

ISSN 0319-7336

Date of founding: 1975

Purpose: To publish important work bearing on the thought of David Hume.

Sponsor: Univ. of Utah College of Humanities and Philosophy Department, and Univ. of Cincinnati

Manuscript info: Most articles are devoted to philosophy, but the journal is receptive to the widest variety of topics, methods, and approaches, so long as the work contributes to the understanding of Hume's thought (either philosophical or non-philosophical), meets the highest standards of scholarship, and demonstrates mastery of the relevant scholarly literature. Manuscripts are blind refereed. Approximately 12% of articles submitted are accepted; half of these require significant revision. Articles are invited only in unusual circumstances. Evaluation time averages 3 months;

87

the publication backlog is 6 months. Instructions for manuscript preparation are included in the journal. Articles may be submitted and published in English, French, or German. Manuscripts should be sent to the editors: Don Garrett, Univ. of Utah (address listed), or William Morris, Dept. of Philosophy University of Cincinnati, ML 374/McMicken Hall 206, Cincinnati, OH 45221-0374.

Book reviews: All book reviews are solicited. The Book Review Editor is Dorothy Coleman, Dept. of Philosophy, College of William and Mary, Williamsburg, VA 23185.

Frequency: 2 issues per year; Circulation: 650

Publisher: Hume Society

Subscription rates: $15; Institutions $30; add $2 for subscriptions outside North America. A subscription is included in Hume Society membership (annual dues $20; students $15). Back issues are available at $7.50 ($15 per volume).

HYPATIA: A JOURNAL OF FEMINIST PHILOSOPHY

Editor: L. L. McAlister

J. Waugh, C Hall
University of South Florida
SOC 107, 4202 E. Fowler Ave.
Tampa, FL 33620-8100

Tel. 813-974-5531
Fax 813-974-0336

ISSN 0887-5367

Date of founding: 1983

Purpose: *Hypatia* is the first journal in the United States devoted to the articulation and development of fundamental questions of feminist philosophy in all its many forms.

Manuscript info: Articles are devoted to feminist philosophy broadly defined; 8 articles are published per issue. Backlog is 4 months. Manuscripts are blind refereed; comments are given to authors. Acceptance rate is 16%; 95% require significant revision. Average evaluation time is 6 months. Some articles for special issues are invited. Instructions for manuscript preparation are in the journal. Manuscripts should be sent to the editor.

Book reviews: *Hypatia* does not accept unsolicited book reviews.

Frequency: Quarterly; Circulation: 2,000

Publisher: Indiana University Press

Subscription rates: $35; $60 Institutions; add $12.50 for overseas subscriptions.

IDEALISTIC STUDIES

Editor: Walter E. Wright

Dept. of Philosophy
Clark University
Worcester, MA 01610

Tel. 508-793-7414
E-mail wwright@vax.clarku.edu

ISSN 0046-8541

Date of founding: 1971

Purpose: To publish both historical and contemporary studies of idealistic themes and argumentation, and interdisciplinary studies in contemporary philosophy of science and mathematics.

Manuscript info: Manuscripts are welcome in any area of philosophy. Manuscripts are refereed. About 20-25% of manuscripts received are accepted; 5-10% require significant revision. The average evaluation time is 6-8 weeks. About 25% of articles are invited. Authors should follow the *MLA Style Sheet.* Manuscripts should be sent to the managing editor, Peter Longo; e-mail: plongo@vax.clarku.edu.

Frequency: 3 issues per year; Circulation: 650

Publisher: Clark University Press

Subscription rates: US individuals $25; US institutions $39.95; foreign individuals $29.95; foreign institutions $44.50

INTERNATIONAL JOURNAL FOR PHILOSOPHY OF RELIGION

Editor: Eugene Thomas Long

Dept. of Philosophy
University of South Carolina
Columbia, SC 29208

Tel. 803-777-4166

ISSN 0020-7047

Date of founding: 1970

Purpose: Provides a medium for the exposition, development, and criticism of philosophical insights and theories relevant to religion in any of its varied forms.

Sponsor: Society for the Philosophy of Religion

Manuscript info: About 20 philosophy articles are published per year. Manuscripts in philosophy of religion are preferred. Backlog is 9 months.

Manuscripts are refereed, but not blind, and unsigned comments are sometimes given to authors. About 15% of manuscripts are accepted; 33% require significant revision. Average evaluation time is 3-5 months. Occasional articles are invited. Instructions for manuscript preparation are in the journal. Manuscripts should be sent to the editor.

Book reviews: All book reviews are invited. Books for review should be sent to the book review editor.

Frequency: Bimonthly; Circulation: 800

Publisher: Kluwer Academic Publishers, P.O. Box 17, 3300 AA Dordrecht, The Netherlands

Subscription rates: 324 Dfl, Institutions 45 Dfl

INTERNATIONAL JOURNAL OF APPLIED PHILOSOPHY

Editor: Elliot D. Cohen

Dept. of Philosophy
Indian River College
Fort Pierce, FL 34981-5599

Tel. 407-462-4563

ISSN 0739-098X

Date of founding: 1981

Purpose: Dedicated to the thesis that philosophy, its theories and methods, can and should be brought to bear upon the clarification and solution of the practical issues of life. To publish works that exhibit the impact of philosophical thinking.

Manuscript info: Manuscripts in any area of philosophy are welcome so long as they fulfill the central aim of the journal. Manuscripts that apply philosophy to areas not usually given philosophical treatment or which apply philosophy in an original manner to more traditional areas of philosophical inquiry are preferred. Instructions for manuscript preparation are in the journal. Send manuscripts to Indian River Community College.

Book reviews: Book reviews are occasionally included; unsolicited book reviews are welcome.

Frequency: Semi-annual

Publisher: Pioneer Press, Indian River Community College

Subscription rates: $10; Institutions $12

INTERNATIONAL JOURNAL OF PHILOSOPHY AND PSYCHOTHERAPY: HSIN

Editor: Sandra A. Wawrytko

Dept. of Philosophy
San Diego State University
San Diego, CA 92181-0303

Tel. 619-566-1383
Fax 619-566-8083

Date of founding: 1985

Purpose: As a journal *HSIN*'s aim is the re-establishment of a dialogue among the multiple dimensions of human nature—mind, heart, and spirit—to overcome our self-induced alienation. All disciplines are encouraged to participate in this.

Sponsor: The International Society for Philosophy and Psychotherapy, San Diego State University

Manuscript info: Approximately half of yearly articles are devoted to philosophy. Any area of philosophy is welcome; those dealing with attempts to overcome dualistic trends of thought, and evaluating various means of re-integrating the human person are preferred. Backlog is 6 months. Manuscripts are blind refereed; comments are given to the authors. About 5% of the accepted manuscripts require significant revision. Average evaluation time is 3 months. Invitation rate is approximately 10%.

Book reviews: Book reviews are not included.

Frequency: Biannual

Publisher: HSIN Publications (in cooperation with Practitioner's Press)

Subscription rates: $25 US and Canada, $25 Overseas; Institution $30 US and Canada, $35 Overseas

INTERNATIONAL PHILOSOPHICAL QUARTERLY

Editor: Joseph W. Koterski

Canisius Hall, Fordham University
Bronx, NY 10458-5172

Tel. 718-817-4776
Fax 718-817-4785
E-mail ipq@murray.fordham.edu

ISSN 0019-0365

Date of founding: 1961

Purpose: To provide an international forum in English for the interchange of basic philosophical ideas. Its primary orientation is to encourage vital contemporary expression in the intercultural tradition of theistic and personalist humanism.

Manuscript info: About 24-30 philosophy articles per year. Any area of philosophy except formal logic is welcome. Backlog is 18 months. Manuscripts are refereed blind, and the comments are given to authors usually only if a revision is requested. Acceptance rate is 10%; 10% require significant revision. Average evaluation time is 2-3 months. Instructions for manuscript preparation are in the journal. Manuscripts should be sent to the editor.

Book reviews: All book reviews are invited; unsolicited book reviews are not accepted.

Frequency: Quarterly; Circulation: 1,600

Publisher: Foundation for International Philosophical Exchange, Fordham University

Subscription rates: $22; Students $15; Institutions $35

INTERNATIONAL STUDIES IN PHILOSOPHY

Editor: L. J. Goldstein & S. D. Ross

Dept. of Philosophy
SUNY Binghamton, Box 6000
Binghamton, NY 13902

Tel. 607-798-2735
Fax 607-777-2734
E-mail
sross@bingvaxa.cc.binghamton.edu

ISSN 0270-5664

Date of founding: 1969

Purpose: To publish important articles and to review books in all fields of philosophy, especially those of international interest.

Manuscript info: About 35 philosophy articles are published per year. There are 4 issues per year; 1 issue is devoted to papers delivered at meetings of the North American Nietzsche Society; 1 issue is devoted to papers from an annual conference in Philosophy, Interpretation, and Culture. Manuscripts are welcome in any area of philosophy. Backlog is 12 months. The refereeing is blind, and the comments are usually given to authors. Acceptance rate is about 25%; 50% require revision. No articles are invited. Instructions for manuscript preparation are in the journal. Manuscripts should be sent to the editors.

Book reviews: All book reviews are invited; unsolicited book reviews will be considered.

Frequency: 4 issues per year; Circulation: 450

Publisher: Scholars Press

Subscription rates: $35; Institutions $55

INTERPRETATION: A JOURNAL OF POLITICAL PHILOSOPHY

Editor: Hilail Gildin

Queens College
King Hall Room 101
Flushing, NY 11367-0904

Tel. 212-520-7099

ISSN 0020-9635

Date of founding: 1970

Purpose: To foster the study of political philosophy and the philosophic aspects of other disciplines.

Manuscript info: About 15 to 19 philosophy articles are published yearly. Manuscripts in political philosophy, theology, literature, and jurisprudence are preferred. Backlog is 11-15 months. Manuscripts are refereed. The refereeing is blind, and comments are usually given to authors. Acceptance rate is 10-12%; 40% require significant revision. The average evaluation time is 3 months. About 5% of articles are invited. Instructions for manuscript preparation are in the journal. Manuscripts should be sent to the editor.

Book reviews: All book reviews and review essays are invited; unsolicited reviews and review essays will be considered.

Frequency: 3 issues per year; Circulation: 1,000

Subscription rates: $25; Libraries and all other institutions $40; Students $16

JOURNAL FOR PEACE AND JUSTICE STUDIES

Editor: Barbara E. Wall

Ctr. for Peace & Justice Educ.
Villanova University
800 Lancaster Ave.
Villanova, PA 19085-1699

Tel. 610-519-4483
Fax 610-519-4496
E-mail bwall@email.vill.edu

Date of founding: 1988

Purpose: To publish work from a variety of disciplines, including, but not limited to, philosophy, theology, social and political theory, and public policy. We welcome submissions that seek the building of a just society and the promotion of peace.

Sponsor: Villanova University

Manuscript info: Three (of 8) articles per year are devoted to philosophy. Manuscripts in any area of philosophy are welcome. We especially encourage contributions arising out of the Judeo-Christian intellectual traditions, works from a variety of disciplines, including, but not limited to, philosophy, theology, social and political theory, and public policy. Manuscripts are refereed blind; referees' unsigned comments are given to authors. About 40% of manuscripts are accepted; 85% require significant revision. Evaluation time averages 4-6 months. About 5% of articles are invited. Instructions for manuscript prepared are included in the journal.

Book reviews: Reviews are included; all are invited.

Frequency: 2 issues per year; Circulation: 300

Publisher: Center for Peace and Justice Education

Subscription rates: Individuals $15; Institutions $35; Foreign postage charges: $5 surface, $10 airmail

JOURNAL FOR THE DEVELOPMENT OF PHILOSOPHY TEACHING

Editor: Bob Lichtenbert

1823 W. Barry Ave.
Chicago, IL 60657

Tel. 312-477-1744

Date of founding: 1991

Purpose: To develop philosophy teaching.

Sponsor: Association for the Development of Philosophy Teaching

Manuscript info: Two to 4 articles per year are devoted to philosophy. Brief articles on teaching philosophy are welcomed from any interested person. Articles that directly address how to teach better are preferred. There is no backlog. Articles are not refereed. About 70% of manuscripts require significant revision. Evaluation time averages 1-4 weeks. About 25% of articles are invited. Manuscripts should be sent to the editor.

Book reviews: Book reviews that relate to teaching philosophy are included. Unsolicited book reviews are welcome if they address the topic of teaching philosophy.

Frequency: 2 issues per year; Circulation: 200

Publisher: Bob Lichtenbert

JOURNAL FOR THE SCIENTIFIC STUDY OF RELIGION*

Editor: David G. Bromley

Dept. of Sociology
University of Virginia
Charlottesville, VA 22903

Tel. 804-367-6286
Fax 804-367-1027

ISSN 0021-8294

Date of founding: 1961

Purpose: To publish studies of religion using scientific methodology and to publish theories, critiques, etc., of scientific (objectively falsifiable) study of religion.

Sponsor: Society for the Scientific Study of Religion

Manuscript info: Only manuscripts bearing on the scientific study of religion are welcome. Disciplines most often represented are sociology, psychology, and anthropology. Backlog is 6 months. Manuscripts are refereed by 2 reviewers. The refereeing is blind; unsigned comments are given to authors. About 20% of manuscripts are accepted; 80% require significant revision. Average evaluation time is 1-2 months. Instructions for manuscript preparation are in the journal. Manuscripts should be sent to the editor.

Book reviews: All book reviews are invited; unsolicited book reviews are not welcome.

Frequency: Quarterly; Circulation: 3,000

Publisher: A & A Printing, 363 Stanton Ave., Akron, OH 44301-1440

Subscription rates: $28; Students $12

JOURNAL FOR THE THEORY OF SOCIAL BEHAVIOUR

Editor: Charles W. Smith

Dean of the Social Sciences
Queens College, CUNY
Flushing, NY 11367

Tel. 718-997-5210
Fax 718-995-5535
E-mail jtsb@qcuaxa.acc.gc.edu

ISSN 0021-8308

Date of founding: 1971

Purpose: To publish original papers bearing on the theory of social behavior, especially the mutuality of agency and social structure, from the disciplines of psychology, philosophy, sociology, and other social sciences.

Manuscript info: The journal publishes about one-third to one-half philosophy articles yearly. Theory emphasis is preferred. Manuscripts are refereed. The referees' comments, unsigned except by referee request, are given to authors. Acceptance rate is 10-25%; 75% require significant revision. Average evaluation time is 3 months. Instructions for manuscript preparation are in the journal. All manuscripts should be sent to the editor.

Book reviews: Occasional essay-type book reviews are published, usually by invitation. Authors should contact the editor before preparing a review.

Frequency: Quarterly; Circulation: 1,000

Publisher: Blackwell Publishers

Subscription rates: $59.90; Institutions $164

JOURNAL OF AESTHETIC EDUCATION

Editor: Ralph A. Smith

361 Education
1310 S. Sixth Street
Univ. of IL at Urbana-Champaign
Champaign, IL 61820

Tel. 217-333-7211
Fax 217-244-7064

ISSN 0021-8510

Date of founding: 1966

Purpose: To clarify issues of arts and aesthetic education in their broadest meanings.

Sponsor: University of Illinois Press

Manuscript info: Manuscripts relevant to arts and aesthetic education

are preferred. The backlog of accepted articles is sometimes up to 18 months. Some manuscripts are refereed. The average time required to evaluate a manuscript is 4 months. Instructions for manuscript preparation are included in the journal. Two copies of manuscripts, along with return postage, should be sent to the editor.

Book reviews: All book reviews are invited.

Frequency: Quarterly; Circulation: 1,000

Subscription rates: $28, Foreign $35; Institutions $42, Foreign $49; Single copy $11, Double issue $18; Book volume price $37

JOURNAL OF AESTHETICS AND ART CRITICISM

Editor: Philip A. Alperson

Dept. of Philosophy
University of Louisville
Louisville, KY 40292

Tel. 502-852-4768
Fax 502-852-0459
E-mail jaac@ulkyvm.louisville.edu

ISSN 0021-8529

Date of founding: 1941

Purpose: To promote study, research, discussion, and publication in aesthetics and the arts.

Sponsor: American Society for Aesthetics

Manuscript info: All articles are devoted to aesthetic theory and the philosophy of art. Manuscripts are refereed; the refereeing is blind. Information from the referees' reports is given to authors anonymously. About 10% of manuscripts are accepted. Instructions for manuscript preparation are included in the journal. Manuscripts should be sent to the editor.

Book reviews: All are invited.

Frequency: Quarterly; Circulation: 3,000

Publisher: American Society for Aesthetics

Subscription rates: Members $36; Non-members $40

JOURNAL OF BUDDHIST ETHICS

Editor: C. Prebish and Damien Keown

State Univ. of Pennsylvania
108 Weaver Building
University Park, PA 16802-5500

E-mail csp1@psuvm.ps.edu
http://www.psu.edu/jbe/jbe/html

ISSN 1076-9005

Date of founding: 1994

Purpose: To promote the study of Buddhist ethics through the publication of research articles.

JOURNAL OF CHINESE PHILOSOPHY

Editor: Chung-Ying Cheng

Dept. of Philosophy
University of Hawaii at Manoa
Honolulu, HI 96822

Tel. 808-956-6081
Fax 808-956-9228

ISSN 0301-8121

Date of founding: 1973

Purpose: The journal is devoted to the study of Chinese philosophy and Chinese thought in all stages of their development and all dimensions of their articulation.

Sponsor: International Society for Chinese Philosophy

Manuscript info: About 20 to 25 philosophy articles per year. Topics must be in Chinese philosophy or have topical or methodological relevance to Chinese philosophy. Backlog is 15 months. Manuscripts are refereed. The refereeing is not blind, and comments are not given to authors. Acceptance rate is 50%; 50% require significant revision. The average evaluation time is 6 months. About 50% of articles are invited. Instructions for manuscript preparation are in the journal. Manuscripts should be sent to the editor.

Book reviews: Most book reviews are invited; unsolicited book reviews are welcome.

Frequency: Quarterly; Circulation: 500

Publisher: Dialogue Publishing Company, P.O. 11071, Honolulu, HI 96828

Subscription rates: Individuals $45 plus postage; Institutions $114 plus postage

---

JOURNAL OF CHINESE STUDIES

Editor: Fred Gillette Sturm

555 Humanities
University of New Mexico
Albuquerque, NM 87131

Tel. 505-277-2405
Fax 505-277-6362

ISSN 0742-5929

Date of founding: 1984

Purpose: A multidisciplinary forum through which scholars of many disciplines who are engaged in research and teaching concerning China can communicate with each other and with a wider public.

Sponsor: American Association for Chinese Studies

Manuscript info: About 4 philosophy articles are published yearly. Any area of Chinese philosophy is welcome. There is no appreciable backlog. Manuscripts are refereed; signed comments are given to authors. Acceptance rate is 60%; 25% require significant revision. Evaluation time averages 1 month. Invitation rate is 30%. Instructions for manuscript preparation are available from the editor. Manuscripts should be sent to the editor.

Book reviews: About 90% of the book reviews are invited; unsolicited book reviews are welcome.

Frequency: 2 issues per year; Circulation: 300

Publisher: American Association for Chinese Studies, 300 Bricker Hall, Ohio State University, Columbus, OH 43210

Subscription rates: $12

JOURNAL OF ETHICAL STUDIES

Editor: David A. Mrovka

117 W. Harrison Bldg.
6th Floor, Suite I-104
Chicago, IL 60605-1709

ISSN 1010-7304

Date of founding: 1985

Purpose: To manifest the diversity of applications in ethics.

Sponsor: International Association of Ethicists, Inc.

Manuscript info: Manuscripts related to ethics are preferred. Backlog is 6 months. Manuscripts are not refereed. About 95% of manuscripts are accepted; 10% require significant revision. Average evaluation time is 3 months. About 5% of articles are invited. Instructions for manuscript preparation are available by requesting *IAE Information Handbook.*

Book reviews: Book reviews are included; unsolicited book reviews are welcome, but not necessarily accepted.

Frequency: 2 issues per year

Publisher: IAE Inc./IAE International

Subscription rates: $15; Institutions $50

JOURNAL OF ETHICS: AN INTERNATIONAL PHILOSOPHICAL REVIEW

Editor: J. Angelo Corlett

Dept. of Philosophy
Georgia State University
Atlanta, GA 30303

Tel. 404-651-2277
E-mail phljac@gsusgi2.gsu.edu

ISSN 1382-4554

Date of founding: 1995

Purpose: To provide a forum for philosophical research in ethics, both theoretical and practical.

Manuscript info: Manuscripts are welcome in any area of ethics. Manuscripts are refereed via a double-blind process. Some articles and reviews are solicited, although most are unsolicited. Instructions for manuscript preparation are included in the journal. Manuscripts should be sent to the publisher in triplicate. Articles, critical commentaries, and reviews are welcome.

Book reviews: Reviews are included. Unsolicited book reviews are welcome.

Frequency: Quarterly

Publisher: Kluwer Academic Publishers, c/o Anny Burer, P.O. Box 17, 3300 AA Dordrecht, The Netherlands; e-mail address anny.burer@wkap.nl

Subscription rates: $45 for members of the Society for Ethics. Information concerning institutional subscription rates may be obtained from the publisher.

JOURNAL OF LAW, MEDICINE AND ETHICS*

Editor: Michael Vasko

Managing Editor, ASLME
765 Commonwealth Ave., Suite 1634
Boston, MA 02215

Tel. 617-262-4990

ISSN 0277-8459

Purpose: To publish high-quality essays that critically examine major issues at the intersection of law, medicine, ethics, and policy in health care.

Sponsor: American Society of Law, Medicine & Ethics

Manuscript info: Submissions from lawyers, physicians, nurses, health care administrators and regulators, ethicists, and philosophers are welcome. All appropriate submissions are peer reviewed by at least 2 independent readers and are accepted or rejected on the basis of reviewers' recommendations. Reviews are conducted anonymously. Manuscripts should be typed and double spaced. Two copies are required. Length should not exceed 30 typewritten pages, including endnotes. Endnotes should also be typed, double spaced, and numbered consecutively. A short biographical statement (40-word maximum) should accompany the manuscript. Style sheets are available on request.

Frequency: Quarterly

JOURNAL OF MEDICAL HUMANITIES*

Editor: Charles R. Perakis

53 E. Grande Ave.
Scarborough, ME 04074

Tel. 207-883-3342
Fax 207-282-6379

ISSN 1041-3545

Date of founding: 1979

Purpose: Multidisciplinary consideration of medical and bioethical issues from humanistic rather than technical perspective.

Sponsor: University of New England

Manuscript info: Articles addressing issues in medicine from a humanistic discipline perspective welcome. Recent authors include philosophers, clergy, physicians, students, faculty in medical education, and geneticists.

Authors are encouraged to eschew technical jargon and write for a diverse, educated audience. Backlog of 6 months. Manuscripts are refereed. Assisted rewrites and improvements welcome. Instructions for manuscript preparation are in the journal. Manuscripts should be sent in triplicate to the editor.

Frequency: Quarterly; Circulation: 450

Publisher: Human Sciences Press, 233 Spring St., New York, NY 10013

Subscription rates: $32; Institutions $115

JOURNAL OF MEDICINE AND PHILOSOPHY

Editor: H. Tristram Engelhardt

Baylor College of Medicine
One Baylor Plaza
Houston, TX 77030

Tel. 713-798-3510
Fax 713-798-5678

ISSN 0360-5310

Date of founding: 1976

Purpose: An international forum for the discussion of issues in philosophy of medicine and bioethics.

Sponsor: Center for Medical Ethics and Health Policy

Manuscript info: Manuscripts are refereed blind; comments are given to authors. About 10% of manuscripts are accepted; 90% require significant revision. Average time to evaluate a manuscript is 8 weeks. About 70% of articles are invited. Instructions for manuscript preparation are in the journal. Manuscripts should be sent to the managing editor.

Book reviews: Book reviews are sometimes included.

Frequency: 6 issues per year; Circulation: 2,000

Publisher: Kluwer Academic Publishers, P.O. Box 17, 3300 AA Dordrecht, The Netherlands

Subscription rates: $48; Institutions $225; Special $42

JOURNAL OF MEDIEVAL AND EARLY MODERN STUDIES

Editors: Annabel Wharton & David Aers

Box 90764
Durham, NC 27708

Tel. 919-684-2495
Fax 919-688-4574
E-mail wharton@acpub.duke.edu

ISSN 0047-2573

Date of founding: 1970

Sponsor: Duke University

Manuscript info: About 3-4 articles per year are devoted to philosophy. Manuscripts in medieval to early modern philosophy are preferred. Most issues are devoted to a particular theme; upcoming themes are announced in the journal. Manuscripts are refereed (not blind); signed or unsigned comments are given to authors. About 25% of manuscripts are accepted; 25% require significant revision. Evaluation time averages 3-4 months. About 50% of articles are invited. Instructions for manuscript preparation are available from the editors or from Duke University Press. Manuscripts that fit a specific anounced theme should be sent to Editor Annabel Wharton.

Book reviews: Reviews are not included.

Frequency: 3 issues per year

Publisher: Duke University Press

Subscription rates: Individuals $32; Institutions $78

JOURNAL OF MIND AND BEHAVIOR

Editor: Raymond C. Russ

Dept. of Psychology
Room 301
5742 Little Hall
University of Maine
Orono, ME 04469-5742

Tel. 207-581-2057

ISSN 0271-0137

Date of founding: 1980

Purpose: Dedicated to the interdisciplinary approach within psychology, philosophy and related fields, building upon the assumption of a unified science.

Sponsor: Institute of Mind and Behavior, University of Maine

Manuscript info: About 18-20 philosophy articles are published per year. Manuscripts in any area of philosophy are welcome. Backlog is 10 months. Manuscripts are refereed, but not blind; unsigned comments are given to authors. About 8-12% of manuscripts are accepted; 50% require significant revision. Average evaluation time is 6-10 weeks. About 3% of articles are invited. Optional $13 fee for postage and handling; authors unwilling or unable to pay this fee should write to the editor. Subscribers are exempt from this fee.

Book reviews: About 20% of book reviews are invited; unsolicited book reviews are welcome.

Frequency: Quarterly; Circulation: 1,072

Publisher: Institute of Mind and Behavior, P.O. Box 522, Village Station, New York, NY 10014

Subscription rates: $42; Institutions $73; Students $32; add $15 for airmail to Canada, $24 for airmail to Europe, Asia, Africa, etc.

JOURNAL OF NEOPLATONIC STUDIES

Editor: James T. H. Martin

Philosophy Department
St. John's University
Jamaica, NY 11439

Tel. 718-990-6378
Fax 718-380-0353

ISSN 1065-5840

Date of founding: 1985

Purpose: To promote the study of the Neoplatonic tradition–philosophical, literary, and artistic–in its Greek, Christian, Islamic, and Hebraic developments.

Sponsor: International Society for Neoplatonic Studies

Manuscript info: All articles are devoted to philosophy. Only manuscripts in Neoplatonism and related areas are welcome. Manuscripts are refereed blind; unsigned comments are given to the authors. Instructions for manuscript preparation are included in the journal. Manuscripts should be sent to the editor.

Book reviews: Book reviews are included; unsolicited book reviews are not welcome.

Frequency: 2 issues per year

Publisher: The Institute of Global Cultural Studies, Binghamton University, Binghamton, NY

Subscription rates: $15; Institutions $25; Students $10

Book reviews: Most book reviews are invited; sometimes unsolicited book reviews are welcome.

Frequency: Biannual; Circulation: 750

Publisher: Humanities Press International

Subscription rates: $35; Institutions $50

JOURNAL OF PHENOMENOLOGICAL PSYCHOLOGY

Editor: Frederick J. Wertz

c/o Div. of Social Science
LL916
Fordham University
113 W. 60th St.
New York, NY 10023

Tel. 212-636-6396

ISSN 0047-2662

Date of founding: 1970

Purpose: Articles demonstrating and developing the idea of phenomenological psychology.

Manuscript info: Manuscripts that are devoted to the relationship of phenomenology and psychology are preferred. The backlog of accepted articles is about 1 year. Manuscripts are refereed; the refereeing is not blind. The referees' unsigned comments are given to the author. About 25% of manuscripts are accepted; about 50% require significant revision. The average evaluation time is 6 months. About 10% of articles are invited. Manuscripts should be sent (4 copies, APA style) to the editor.

JOURNAL OF PHILOSOPHICAL LOGIC

Editor: J. M. Dunn & Krister Segerberg

Dept. of Philosophy
Indiana University
Bloomington, IN 47405

Tel. 812-855-9403
Fax 812-855-3777
E-mail jpl@phil.indiana.edu

ISSN 0022-3611

Date of founding: 1971

Purpose: Philosophical studies utilizing formal methods or dealing with topics in logical theory; discussions of philosophical issues relating to logic and the logical structure of language; philosophical work relating to special sciences.

Sponsor: Association for Symbolic Logic

Manuscript info: Manuscripts are welcome in any of the areas mentioned previously. The backlog of accepted articles is less than a year. Manuscripts are refereed. The refereeing is blind; unsigned comments are given to authors. About 10% of manuscripts are accepted; 50% of accepted manuscripts require signifi-

100

cant revision. The average time required to evaluate a manuscript is 12 weeks. No articles are invited. Manuscripts should be sent to editor J. M. Dunn or to Krister Segerberg, Dept. of Philosophy, Uppsala University, Villavägan 5, S-752 36 Uppsala, Sweden.

Frequency: 6 issues per year; Circulation: 730

Publisher: Kluwer Academic Publishers, P.O. Box 17, 3300 AA Dordrecht, The Netherlands

Subscription rates: $36; ASL members $26; Institutions $117.50

JOURNAL OF PHILOSOPHICAL RESEARCH

Editor: Panayot Butchvarov

Dept. of Philosophy
University of Iowa
Iowa City, IA 52242-1408

Tel. 319-335-0495
Fax 319-335-2535

ISSN 0153-8364

Date of founding: 1975

Purpose: To provide a publication that is free of many of the disadvantages and constraints of standard journal publications.

Sponsor: American Philosophical Assoc., Canadian Philosophical Assoc., Philosophy Documentation Ctr.

Manuscript info: Manuscripts, annotated bibliographies, and translations in any area of philosophy are eligible, in French as well as English. Manuscript refereeing is blind; comments are given to authors. Acceptance rate is 20-30%; 60% require significant revision.

Average evaluation time is 2-3 months. Instructions for manuscript preparation are in back issues. Manuscripts should be sent to *Journal of Philosophical Research,* 269 EPB, University of Iowa, Iowa City, IA 52242.

Frequency: Annual

Publisher: Philosophy Documentation Center

Subscription rates: $20.50; Institutions $46; add $2 for subscriptions outside the US.

JOURNAL OF PHILOSOPHY*

Editor: Michael Kelly

Managing Editor
709 Philosophy Hall
Columbia University
New York, NY 10027

Tel. 212-866-1742
Fax 212-932-3721

ISSN 0022-362X

Date of founding: 1904

Purpose: To publish distinguished philosophical articles of current interest and encourage the interchange of ideas, especially the exploration of the borderline between philosophy and the special disciplines.

Manuscript info: About 30-40 philosophy articles per year. Any area of philosophy welcome. Manuscripts under 5,000 words are given preference. Backlog: 6-9 months. Manuscripts are refereed only by the editorial board listed in the journal; the editorial process is not blind. About 5-8% of manuscripts are accepted; 10-15% require revision. Average evaluation time is 5 months. Almost no articles are invited.

101

Instructions for manuscript preparation are available on request. Manuscripts should be sent to the managing editor.

Book reviews: About 15 to 20 book reviews published yearly by invitation. Unsolicited book reviews are not accepted.

Frequency: 12 issues per year; Circulation: 4,375

Publisher: Journal of Philosophy, Inc.

Subscription rates: $35; Students and Professors Emeriti $20; Institutions $65

JOURNAL OF RELIGIOUS ETHICS

Editor: D. M. Yeager

Theology Department
Georgetown University
Washington, DC 20057-0998

Tel. 202-687-1647
Fax 202-687-8000

ISSN 0384-9694

Date of founding: 1973

Purpose: To publish scholarly articles in religious ethics that contribute to a fuller understanding of theoretical foundations, comparisons between philosophical and theological treatments of ethical issues, and historical issues.

Manuscript info: Only articles in ethics are welcome. Preference is given to articles that compare philosophical and religious perspectives and arguments, or that bring philosophical tools and resources to bear on issues in religious ethics. Backlog is 8-12 months. Manuscripts are refereed blind; unsigned comments are

given to authors. About 20% of manuscripts are accepted; 40% require significant revision. Evaluation time is 3 months. About 30% of articles are invited. Manuscripts should be sent to the editor.

Book reviews: All book reviews are invited; unsolicited book reviews are not welcome.

Frequency: 2 issues per year; Circulation: 1,145

Publisher: Scholars Press handles subscriptions and distribution.

Subscription rates: $18; Institutions $24

JOURNAL OF SOCIAL AND EVOLUTIONARY SYSTEMS

Editor: Paul Levinson

65 Shirley Lane
White Plains, NY 10607

Tel. 914-428-8766
Fax 914-428-8775
E-mail plevinson@cinti.com

ISSN 1061-7361

Date of founding: 1978

Purpose: To explore the unity, analogy, and relationships, theoretical and practical, between biological dynamics and mechanisms such as evolution and natural selection, and social activities including technology, politics, ideology, and culture.

Manuscript info: About 10 philosophy articles are published yearly. Articles should be in philosophy of science and technology; preference is given to those that make connections between philosophy and the sciences, culture, technology. Backlog is 3 months. Manuscripts are refereed if author requests; unsigned comments are given to authors. About 50% of manuscripts are accepted; 80% require significant revision. Evaluation time is 3-6 months. About 20% of articles are invited. Send manuscripts to the editor on computer disk.

Book reviews: About 50% of book reviews are invited. Unsolicited book reviews are welcome.

Frequency: Quarterly; Circulation: 500

Publisher: JAI Press, Inc.

Subscription rates: $90; Institutions $225

JOURNAL OF SOCIAL PHILOSOPHY

Editor: Peter A. French

Ethics Center
Univ. of S. Florida-St. Petersburg
100 Fifth Avenue South
St. Petersburg, FL 33701-5016

Tel. 813-553-3172
Fax 813-553-3169
E-mail french@bayflash.stpt.usf.edu

ISSN 0047-2786

Date of founding: 1970

Purpose: To facilitate communication among philosophers on important social, political, legal, and moral issues.

Manuscript info: Thirty philosophy articles are published per year. The backlog of accepted articles is 24 months. Unsolicited manuscripts are refereed. The refereeing is blind. About 10% of manuscripts are accepted. The average time required to

evaluate a manuscript is 3 months. Articles are often invited by the editor. Instructions for manuscript preparation are included in the journal. Manuscripts should be sent to the editor.

Book reviews: We do not currently run book reviews.

Frequency: 3 issues per year; Circulation: 600

Subscription rates: Individuals $25; US libraries $75; Foreign individuals $30; Canadian and foreign libraries $80

JOURNAL OF SPECULATIVE PHILOSOPHY, THE

Editors: Douglas Anderson & Carl Hausman

Pennsylvania State Univ.
240 Sparks Bldg.
University Park, PA 16802-5201

Tel. 814-865-1512
Fax 814-865-0119

ISSN 0891-625X

Date of founding: 1987

Purpose: To publish systematic and interpretive, but not merely historical, essays about philosophical questions that relate to American philosophy and its interaction with Continental thought.

Manuscript info: About 16 philosophy articles are published yearly. Manuscripts about art, religion, and literature that are not strictly or narrowly philosophical will also be considered for occasional publication. Backlog is one year. Manuscript refereeing is blind; unsigned comments are given to the authors. About 20%

of manuscripts are accepted; 50% require significant revision. Average evaluation time is 3 months. About 10% of the articles are invited. Instructions for manuscript preparation are in the journal. Manuscripts should be sent to the editors.

Book reviews: About 95% of book reviews are invited. Unsolicited book reviews are welcome.

Frequency: Quarterly

Publisher: The Pennsylvania State University Press

Subscription rates: $40; Institutions $27.50

JOURNAL OF SYMBOLIC LOGIC

Editor: Herbert B. Enderton

UCLA
Los Angeles, CA 90095-1566

Tel. 310-825-1878
Fax 310-206-6673
E-mail hbe@math.ucla.edu

ISSN 0022-4812

Date of founding: 1936

Purpose: To promote research and critical studies in the field of mathematical logic and immediately related fields.

Sponsor: Association for Symbolic Logic

Manuscript info: About 80 articles are published yearly. Original technical papers in symbolic logic, expository papers, and studies in the history of logic are welcome. Manuscripts are refereed. The refereeing is not blind, and comments are given to authors. Acceptance rate is 65%; 50% require significant revision. Average evalua-

tion time is 6-8 months. Very few articles are invited. Instructions for manuscript preparation are in the journal. Manuscripts should be sent to the appropriate editor.

Book reviews: All book reviews are invited; unsolicited book reviews are not welcome.

Frequency: Quarterly; Circulation: 2,700

Publisher: Association for Symbolic Logic

Subscription rates: Non-members $260; Members $52; Students $26. All subscribers also receive the new *Bulletin of Symbolic Logic.*

JOURNAL OF THE AMERICAN ACADEMY OF RELIGION

Editor: Glenn Yocum

Dept. of Religious Studies
Whittier College
Whittier, CA 90608

Tel. 310-907-4200 Ext. 4302
Fax 310-907-4910
E-mail gyocum@whittier.edu

ISSN 0002-7189

Date of founding: 1933

Purpose: To publish scholarly articles in academic religious studies.

Sponsor: American Academy of Religion

Manuscript info: The number of philosophy articles varies with the submissions. Backlog is 9 months. Manuscripts are refereed. The refereeing is blind, and the comments are almost always given to authors. Acceptance rate is about 10%; about 70% require significant revision. The average evaluation time is 3 months. Instructions for manuscript preparation are in the issue of March 1980 or from the editor. Manuscripts should be sent to the editor.

Book reviews: About 95% of the book reviews are invited.

Frequency: Quarterly; Circulation: 7,900

Publisher: American Academy of Religion

Subscription rates: $60

Instructions for manuscript preparation are in the journal. Send manuscripts in triplicate to the editor.

Book reviews: All book reviews are invited; unsolicited book reviews are not welcome.

Frequency: Quarterly; Circulation: 3,200

Publisher: Rutgers, The State University of New Jersey

Subscription rates: $23; Institutions $49; Foreign add $11 air freight.

JOURNAL OF THE HISTORY OF IDEAS

Editor: Donald R. Kelley

88 College Ave.
Rutgers, The State Univ. of NJ
New Brunswick, NJ 08903

Tel. 908-932-1227
Fax 908-932-8708
E-mail dkelley@gandalf.rutgers.edu

ISSN 0022-5037

Date of founding: 1940

Purpose: To show the development of ideas of cross-cultural and interdisciplinary significance in the history of philosophy and religion, natural and social sciences, literature and the arts.

Manuscript info: Interdisciplinary manuscripts in the history of philosophic ideas are welcome. Historical relations of philosophy to the sciences, arts, and literature are given preference. Backlog is 6 months. Refereeing is blind; comments are given to the author. Acceptance rate is 10%; 75% require significant revision. The average evaluation time is 2 to 3 months. A small number of articles are invited.

JOURNAL OF THE HISTORY OF PHILOSOPHY

Editor: Rudolf A. Makkreel

Dept. of Philosophy
Emory University
Atlanta, GA 30322

Tel. 404-329-6412
E-mail philrm@emoryu1.cc.emory.edu

ISSN 0022-5053

Date of founding: 1963

Purpose: To advance the history of philosophy through the publication of original articles, notes, discussions, and book reviews.

Manuscript info: About 20 to 24 philosophy articles and about 4 notes and discussions are published yearly. History of Western philosophy is welcome, from the Greeks to twentieth century (excluding work on living authors). Backlog is 12 to 18 months. Manuscript refereeing is blind; comments are returned if they seem helpful. Acceptance rate is 10%; 85% require revision. The average evaluation time is 3 months. Instructions for manuscript preparation are in the journal. Manuscripts should be sent to the editor.

Book reviews: About 60 book reviews are published per year; nearly all reviews are invited; unsolicited reviews will be considered. Book review office: Hunter College; e-mail: jhphc@cunyvm.cuny.edu

Frequency: Quarterly; Circulation: 1,600

Publisher: Journal of the History of Philosophy, Inc., Business Office, Dept. of Philosophy, Washington University, St. Louis, MO 63130, 314-889-6670

Subscription rates: $25; Students $18; Institutions $65

JOURNAL OF THE PHILOSOPHY OF SPORT

Editor: William J. Morgan

Cultural Studies Unit
1914 Andy Holt Blvd.
University of Tennessee
Knoxville, TN 37996-2700

Tel. 615-974-1273
Fax 615-974-8981
E-mail wjmorgan@utkvx.utkedu

ISSN 0094-8705

Date of founding: 1974

Purpose: To foster philosophic interchange among scholars interested in better understanding sport; to stimulate and further scholarship and research in the philosophy of sport, games, and play; and to explore their cultural aspects.

Sponsor: Philosophic Society for the Study of Sport

Manuscript info: About 10 to 12 philosophy articles are published per year. Areas preferred are philosophy of sport, games, play, movement, and dance. Backlog is 3 months. Manuscripts are refereed blind; unsigned comments are given to the author. Acceptance rate 30%; 25% require significant revision. The average time required to evaluate a manuscript is 8 weeks. About 20% of articles are invited. Instructions for manuscript preparation are in the journal. Send manuscripts to the editor.

Book reviews: About 50% are invited; unsolicited book reviews are welcome.

Frequency: Annual; Circulation: 800

Publisher: H. K. P., Box 5706, Champaign, IL 61820

Subscription rates: Free with Society membership, or $19/volume (US)

JOURNAL OF THOUGHT

Editors: D. Musial, F. O'Neill, & W. Miranda

LEPS
Northern Illinois University
Dekalb, IL 60115-2866

Tel. 815-753-1561
Fax 815-753-8750
E-mail foneill@aol.com

ISSN 0022-5231

Date of founding: 1966

Purpose: The journal is a quarterly publication devoted to the reflexive examination of educational issues and problems from the perspective of diverse disciplines.

Manuscript info: Most of the articles per year are philosophy. Editorial preference is for articles that present arguments, analysis, or a fresh interpretation. Backlog is 3 months. Manuscript refereeing is blind; comments are given to authors on request. Acceptance rate is about 50%; average evaluation time is 2-3 months. Instructions for manuscript preparation are in the journal. Send manuscripts to the editors.

Book reviews: Review essays are welcome but are not solicited.

Frequency: Quarterly; Circulation: 1,000

Publisher: Caddo Gap Press
3145 Geary Blvd., Suite 275
San Francisco, CA 94118

Subscription rates: $40; Institutions $50; Foreign $60

JOURNAL OF VALUE INQUIRY

Editor: Robert Ginsberg

Pennsylvania State University
Delaware County Campus
Media, PA 19063-5596

Tel. 610-892-1424
Fax 610-892-1357

ISSN 0022-5363

Date of founding: 1967

Purpose: An illustrated international philosophical quarterly devoted to the stimulation and communication of current research in value studies.

Sponsor: American Society for Value Inquiry

Manuscript info: About 40 philosophy articles are published. Any area of philosophy is welcome. Backlog is 18 months. Refereeing is often blind; referees' comments are often given to authors. About 10% of manuscripts are accepted; 95% require significant revision. Average evaluation time is 4 months. Articles are occasionally invited. Manuscript preparation instructions are in the journal. Manuscripts should be sent to the publishers, P.O. Box 17, 3300 Dordrecht, The Netherlands.

Book reviews: All book reviews are invited; unsolicited book reviews are welcome.

Frequency: Quarterly; Circulation: 650

Publisher: Kluwer Academic Publishers, P.O. Box 17, 3300 AA Dordrecht, The Netherlands

Subscription rates: Institutions $242, including postage and handling; American Society for Value Inquiry members, included in dues of $49.

KENNEDY INSTITUTE OF ETHICS JOURNAL

Editor: Carol Mason Spicer

Kennedy Institute of Ethics
Georgetown University
Washington, DC 20057-1065

Tel. 202-687-6774
Fax 202-687-8089
E-mail spicer@guvax.georgetown.edu

ISSN 1054-6863

Date of founding: 1991

Purpose: To publish opinion and analysis dealing with social, ethical, and public policy aspects of bioethics and related areas of applied ethics, and to present varied points of view and encourage open debate on critical issues.

Manuscript info: All articles are devoted to philosophy. Opinion and analysis dealing with social, ethical, and public policy aspects of bioethics and related areas of applied ethics are preferred. Manuscripts are refereed blind; comments are given to authors by request. Average evaluation time is about 6 weeks. Manuscripts should be sent to the editor.

Book reviews: Book reviews are not included.

Frequency: Quarterly; Circulation: 2,100

Publisher: Johns Hopkins University Press

Subscription rates: $50; Institutions $73; Students $26; Canada and Mexico add $7; all other countries outside North America add $7.30 air freight.

KINESIS: GRADUATE JOURNAL IN PHILOSOPHY

Editor: Katherine Resmondo Tietge

Dept. of Philosophy
Southern Illinois University
Carbondale, IL 62901

Tel. 618-453-7447
Fax 618-453-4290
E-mail kinesis@siuc.edu

ISSN 0023-1568

Date of founding: 1968

Purpose: To offer a forum for graduate students in all fields to express their philosophical views in a critical yet open-ended context.

Manuscript info: Six philosophy articles are published per year. Any area of philosophy is welcome. Backlog is 8 months. Manuscript refereeing is blind; comments are given to authors upon request. About 25-50% of manuscripts received are accepted; 50% require significant revision. The average evaluation time is 3 months. No articles are invited. Instructions for manuscript preparation are in the journal. Manuscripts should be sent to the Editor-In-Chief, Katherine Resmondo Tietge.

Book reviews: About 50% of the book reviews are invited; unsolicited book reviews are welcome.

Frequency: Semi-annual; Circulation: 200

Publisher: Southern Illinois University at Carbondale

Subscription rates: Students $10; General subscribers $15

LAW AND PHILOSOPHY

Editor: Alan Mabe

Dept. of Philosophy
153 Dodd Hall
Florida State University
Tallahassee, FL 32306

Tel. 904-644-0224
Fax 904-644-3832
E-mail rfletche@mailer.fsu.edu

ISSN 0167-5249

Date of founding: 1982

Purpose: To publish work in legal philosophy and jurisprudence and to encourage exchange between philosophers and lawyers.

Manuscript info: Eighteen articles per year are devoted to philosophy. Manuscripts dealing with legal philosophy are preferred. Manuscripts are refereed anonymously; unsigned comments are given to the author. The average time required to evaluate a manuscript is 4-6 months. About one-third of the articles are invited. Instructions for manuscript preparation are included in the journal. Manuscripts should be sent to Editorial Office, P.O. Box 17, 3300 AA Dordrecht, The Netherlands; or to Roxane M. Fletcher, Managing Editor, Dept. of Philosophy, 153 Dodd Hall, Florida State University, Tallahassee, FL 32306.

Book reviews: Most book reviews are invited; unsolicited book reviews are invited with an inquiry first.

Frequency: 4 issues per year

Publisher: Kluwer Academic Publishers, P.O. Box 17, 3300 AA Dordrecht, The Netherlands

Subscription rates: $89; Institutions $214

LEIBNIZ SOCIETY REVIEW

Editor: Glenn A. Hartz

Philosophy Dept.
Ohio State University
1680 University Dr.
Mansfield, OH 44906-1599

Tel. 419-755-4354
Fax 419-755-4367
E-mail hartz.1@osu.edu

ISSN 1069-5192

Date of founding: 1991

Purpose: To publish reviews of recent works on the philosophy of Leibniz, and to inform philosophers of the status of Leibniz studies around the world.

Sponsor: Leibniz Society of North America

Manuscript info: Reviews (written in English) of recent books (in any language) on the philosophy of Leibniz, and of critical editions of Leibniz's works, are considered. Submissions should be in standard manuscript format: double spaced, standard type size, maximum of 5 pages. Occasionally longer reviews are accepted. If possible, typescript should be accompanied by a disk with the review on an ASCII file for, or convertible to, Macintosh. Deadline is September 30 of the year the review will appear. (The *Review* is published in December of each year.) Authors of works that are reviewed are given a chance to respond to the reviews before they are published when possible.

Book reviews: Reviews are included.

Frequency: Annual; Circulation: 150

Publisher: Ohio State University

Subscription rates: Currently there is no fee for members of the Leibniz Society. Institutional Libraries subscribe for $20/issue. Supplemental funding is provided by Ohio State University.

LINGUISTICS AND PHILOSOPHY

Editor: Greg N. Carlson

Dept. of Linguistics
Lattimore Hall
University of Rochester
Rochester, NY 14627

Tel. 716-275-1560
Fax 716-273-1088
E-mail lap@ling.rochester.edu

ISSN 0165-0157

Date of founding: 1976

Purpose: To publish high-quality manuscripts representing original research in areas of common interest to linguists and philosophers.

Manuscript info: About 25 philosophy articles are published per year. Areas of philosophy that are of substantial linguistic interest are preferred. Backlog is 9 months. Manuscript refereeing is not blind; unsigned comments are given to authors. About 15% of manuscripts are accepted; 80% require significant revision. The average evaluation time is 3 months. About 5% of articles are invited. Instructions for manuscript preparation are in the journal. Manuscripts should be sent to the editor.

Book reviews: Major works are given extended reviews, and all are invited. Suggestions for reviews and reviewers should be sent to the editor.

Frequency: 6 issues per year; Circulation: 1,000

Publisher: Kluwer Academic Publishers

Subscription rates: $54

LISTENING: JOURNAL OF RELIGION AND CULTURE*

Editor: Victor S. LaMotte

Lewis University
Box 1108
Romeoville, IL 60441-2298

Tel. 815-838-0500 Ext. 324
Fax 815-838-9456

ISSN 0024-4414

Date of founding: 1965

Purpose: To explore issues of enduring importance regarding the mutual influences on each other of religion and culture.

Sponsor: Central Province of Dominicans; Lewis University

Manuscript info: About 6-10 philosophy articles per year. Manuscripts are refereed, but not blind; comments are sometimes given to authors. All of articles are invited; it is very rare that an unsolicited manuscript is published by the journal.

Book reviews: Book reviews are not included.

Frequency: 3 issues per year; Circulation: 800

Publisher: Victor S. LaMotte

Subscription rates: $10; Institutions $13

MAN AND WORLD: AN INTERNATIONAL PHILOSOPHICAL REVIEW

Editor: Robert C. Scharff

Dept. of Philosophy
University of New Hampshire
Hamilton Smith Hall
Durham, NH 03824-3574

Tel. 603-862-1040
Fax 603-862-1488
E-mail robert.scharff@unh.edu

ISSN 0025-1534

Date of founding: 1968

Purpose: To foster international dialog on expressly theoretical topics and their implications for the wider socio-political world, with special concern for keeping abreast of developments in contemporary Continental philosophy.

Manuscript info: Encompassing in its focus and gender inclusive by editorial policy despite its now problematic title, the journal invites essays on fundamental philosophical problems and original approaches to them, as well as explorations in art, morality, science, and religion insofar as they relate to specific philosophical issues. Its concern for contemporary Continental philosophy does not reflect a commitment to any one trend or school. Most articles are in English, but very occasionally, a manuscript in French or German may be accepted. 20 to 25 articles are published per year. Backlog is 3-6 months. Manuscript refereeing is usually blind; reviewers' comments, or paraphrases, are sometimes given to authors. Acceptance rate is approximately 8-10%; some articles require significant revision. The average evaluation time is 3 months.

About 5% of articles are invited; occasional special issues are published. Instructions for manuscript publication are in the journal. Manuscripts, in triplicate, should be sent to the editor.

Book reviews: All books to be reviewed as well as reviewers are selected by the book review editor: Thomas Flynn, Department of Philosophy, Emory University, Atlanta, GA 30322.

Frequency: Quarterly;
Circulation: 500

Publisher: Kluwer Academic Publishers

Subscription rates: Institutions $172

MEANING OF LIFE, THE

Editor: Bob Lichtenbert

1823 W. Barry
Chicago, IL 60657
312-477-1744

Date of founding: 1987

Purpose: To develop fully the concept of the meaning of life in its most basic dimensions (metaphysical, religious, and aesthetic); to apply the concept to everyday life; to engage in dialogue about living the most meaningful life.

Manuscript info: About 12 to 15 articles, plus 4 sections of "Nuggets," or aphorisms about the meaning of life, are published each year. Each article (and "Nugget") must refer explicitly to the meaning of life, although they can be on any branch of philosophy. Submissions are refereed by the editor. Evaluation time averages 1-2 months. Backlog is approximately 3-6 months.

Frequency: Quarterly;
Circulation: 3,450

Publisher: Bob Lichtenbert

Subscription rates: $15;
Libraries $10

MEDICAL HUMANITIES REVIEW

Editor: Ronald A. Carson

Director
Institute for Medical Humanities
Univ. of Texas Medical Branch
Ashbel Smith Bldg. Rm. 2.208
Galveston, TX 77550-2764

Tel. 409-772-2376
Fax 409-772-5640

ISSN 0892-2772

Date of founding: 1987

Purpose: To publish authoritative reviews of books dealing with medicine and the humanities, as well as essay reviews that help analyze and define the medical humanities, thematic reviews, and comparative reviews of one author's work over time.

Manuscript info: About 4-5 philosophy articles are published yearly. Extended book reviews and essays in the areas of philosophy of medicine and medical ethics are preferred. Most articles are commissioned. They are edited and returned to the author for comments.

Book reviews: About 95% of book reviews are invited. Unsolicited book reviews are welcome.

Frequency: 2 issues per year

Publisher: Institute for the Medical Humanities, University of Texas Medical Branch

Subscription rates: $20;
Institutions $40; add $5 for addresses outside the US.

METAPHILOSOPHY

Editor: Armen T. Marsoobian

Dept. of Philosophy
Southern Connecticut State Univ.
New Haven, CT 06515

Tel. 203-392-6792
Fax 203-392-6338
E-mail metaphil@scsu.ctstateu.edu

ISSN 0026-1068

Date of founding: 1970

Purpose: To publish articles about philosophy, branches of philosophy, philosophy's relation to other disciplines, or teaching philosophy.

Sponsor: The Metaphilosophy Foundation

Manuscript info: About 25 philosophy articles are published per year.

Book reviews: Book reviews are included.

Frequency: Quarterly;
Circulation: 800

Publisher: Blackwell Publishers, 108 Cowley Rd., Oxford OX4 1JF England

Subscription rates: $61 North America, UK/Europe £39, Overseas £48; Institutions $169 North America, UK/Europe £82, rest of world £100.50

METHOD: JOURNAL OF LONERGAN STUDIES

Editors: M. Morelli, P. Byrne & C. Hefling

Philosophy Dept.
Boston College
Chestnut Hill, MA 02167-9928

Tel. 617-552-8095

ISSN 0736-7392

Date of founding: 1983

Purpose: To promote original research into the methodological foundations of the sciences and disciplines; to further interpretive, historical, and critical study of the philosophical, theological, and methodological writings of Bernard Lonergan.

Manuscript info: Eight articles per year are devoted to philosophy. Any area of philosophy is welcome, but Lonergan studies are given preference. Backlog is 6 months. Manuscript refereeing is blind; comments are given to the author. About 20% of the manuscripts are accepted; 25% require significant revision. Average evaluation time is 2 months. About 5% of the articles are invited. Instructions for manuscript preparation are in the journal. Manuscripts should be sent to the editor.

Book reviews: About 50% of the reviews are invited; unsolicited reviews are welcome.

Frequency: Biannual; Circulation: 250

Publisher: Institute for Integrative Studies

Subscription rates: $14; Institutions $25

MIDWEST STUDIES IN PHILOSOPHY

Editor: Peter A. French

Ethics Center
Univ. of S. Florida-St. Petersburg
100 Fifth Avenue South
St. Petersburg, FL 33701-5016

Tel. 813-553-3172
Fax 813-553-3169
E-mail french@bayflash.stpt.usf.edu

Manuscript info: Most papers are invited and previously unpublished. The editors will, however, consider unsolicited manuscripts that are received by January of the year preceding the appearance of a volume. All manuscripts must be pertinent to the topic area of the volume for which they are submitted. Manuscripts may be sent to any one of the three editors: Peter French, University of South Florida-St. Petersburg; Theodore E. Uehling, Jr., University of Minnesota, Morris; or Howard K. Wettstein, University of California, Riverside.

Frequency: Annual

Publisher: University of Notre Dame Press

Subscription rates: Subscription and price information is available from the publisher.

MODERN SCHOOLMAN: A QUARTERLY JOURNAL OF PHILOSOPHY

Editor: William C. Charron

Dept. of Philosophy
Saint Louis University
St. Louis, MO 63103

Tel. 314-977-3149

ISSN 0026-8402

Date of founding: 1925

Purpose: To promote historical and analytically critical research in all periods of philosophy: ancient, medieval, Renaissance, and modern.

Manuscript info: About 16 to 20 philosophy articles are published yearly. Manuscripts are welcome for any period of the history of philosophy. Backlog is 6-12 months. Manuscript refereeing is blind; unsigned comments are given to authors. About 15% of manuscripts are accepted; 25% require significant revision. Average evaluation time is 3-4 months. Follow *Chicago Manual of Style*. Manuscripts should be sent to the editor.

Book reviews: Most book reviews are invited.

Frequency: Quarterly; Circulation: 650

Publisher: The Modern Schoolman

Subscription rates: $26; Back issues $6.50 each

MODERN THEOLOGY

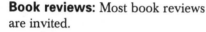

Editor: L. Gregory Jones or James Buckley

Dept. of Theology
Loyola College
4501 N. Charles St.
Baltimore, MD 21210

Tel. 410-617-2217
Fax 410-617-2628
E-mail
jones@loyola.edu/buckley@loyola.edu

ISSN 0266-7177

Date of founding: 1984

Purpose: To publish articles in contemporary theology and theology's relationship to other disciplines.

Manuscript info: Manuscripts in philosophical theology of religion, hermeneutics, and cultural criticism are preferred. Backlog is 12-14 months. Manuscripts are refereed blind; unsigned comments are given to authors. About 15% of manuscripts are accepted; 50% require significant revision. Average evaluation time is 8-10 weeks. About 10% of articles are invited. Instructions for manuscript preparation are in the journal. Manuscripts should be sent to the editors.

Book reviews: About 99% of book reviews are invited. Unsolicited book reviews are not welcome.

Frequency: Quarterly; Circulation: 650

Publisher: Blackwell Publishers 108 Cowley Rd., Oxford OX4 1JP England

Subscription rates: $67; Institutions $170.50

MONIST, THE

Editor: Barry Smith

Dept. of Philosophy
SUNY Buffalo
Buffalo, NY 14260-1010

Tel. 716-645-2444
Fax 716-645-3825
E-mail
phismith@ubvms.cc.buffalo.edu

ISSN 0026-9662

Date of founding: 1888

Purpose: To publish an international quarterly journal of general philosophical inquiry devoted to problems arising in any area of philosophy and to interdisciplinary problems arising out of the philosophical issues considered in related disciplines.

Manuscript info: About 30 to 40 philosophy articles are published yearly. Each issue is devoted to a single, previously announced topic, often of a controversial nature. Half of the articles are invited, and the other half are selected on a competitive basis. Blind refereeing of submitted papers is done by the editor in conjunction with advisory editors. Deadlines are 9 months prior to issue publication date. 8 issues at a time are worked on, each with its own closing date. Some instructions for manuscript preparation are in the journal, and others are given on request. Manuscripts should be sent to the editor.

Book reviews: Abstracts of books are accepted only from their authors. There are no other book reviews.

Frequency: Quarterly; Circulation: 1,600

Publisher: The Hegeler Institute, Box 600, LaSalle, IL 61301

Subscription rates: $25; Institutions $48; Single copy $9; back issues are available.

MONTHLY REVIEW: AN INDEPENDENT SOCIALIST MAGAZINE*

Editors: Paul M. Sweezy & Harry Magdoff

122 West 27th St.
New York, NY 10001

Tel. 212-691-2555
Fax 212-727-3676

Date of founding: 1949

Frequency: Monthly

Subscription rates: $25

NEW LITERARY HISTORY: A JOURNAL OF THEORY AND INTERPRETATION

Editor: Ralph Cohen

Bryan Hall
University of Virginia
Charlottesville, VA 22903

Tel. 804-982-2712
Fax 804-924-1478

ISSN 0028-6087

Date of founding: 1969

Manuscript info: Any area of philosophy is welcome; theoretical essays are preferred. Backlog is 24 months. Manuscript refereeing is not blind, and comments are not given to authors; 15% of manuscripts are accepted. The average evaluation time is 6 months. About 85% of articles are invited. Manuscripts should follow the *Chicago Manual of Style*. Manuscripts should be sent to the editor.

Book reviews: "Books Received" are listed.

Frequency: Quarterly; Circulation: 2,300

Publisher: Johns Hopkins University Press

Subscription rates: Individuals $25; Institutions $75

NEW PHILOSOPHY, THE

Editor: Erland J. Brock

Box 717
Bryn Athyn, PA 19009

Tel. 215-938-2658
Fax 215-938-2658

ISSN 0028-6443

Date of founding: 1898

Purpose: To expose and promote philosophic principles contained in works of Emanuel Swedenborg.

Sponsor: Swedenborg Scientific Association

Manuscript info: About 7 to 10 philosophy articles are published yearly; those with relation to Swedenborg's religious or philosophical systems are preferred. Backlog is 6 months. Manuscript refereeing is not blind; comments are given to authors if affecting substance. Acceptance rate is 80-85%; 10-15% require substantial revision and 50-60% require revision of form. Average evaluation time is 6 weeks. Invitation rate is 15%. Instructions for manuscript preparation are in the journal. Manuscripts should be sent to the editor.

Book reviews: About 85 to 90% of the book reviews are invited; unsolicited book reviews are welcome if within the scope of the magazine.

Frequency: Quarterly;
Circulation: 425

Publisher: Swedenborg Scientific Association

Subscription rates: $25

NEW VICO STUDIES

Editors: G. Tagliacozzo
& D. P. Verene

69 Fifth Ave., Suite 17A
New York, NY 10003

Tel. 212-989-2909

ISSN 0733-9542

Date of founding: 1983

Purpose: *New Vico Studies* is an annual publication of essays, notes, reviews, and bibliography reflecting the state of work on Vico's thought.

Manuscript info: About 7 philosophy articles are published yearly; articles and book reviews relating to Vico are preferred. Manuscripts are refereed; unsigned comments are given to authors. About 40% of manuscripts are accepted; 75% require significant revision. Average evaluation time is 3 months. About 50% of articles are invited. See *Chicago Manual of Style* for manuscript preparation instructions. Manuscripts should be sent to co-editor Giorgio Tagliacozzo at the address above, or to co-editor Donald Phillip Verene, Dept. of Philosophy, Emory University, Atlanta, GA 30322; phone: 404-727-4340; fax: 404-727-4959.

Book reviews: About 50% of the book reviews are invited. Unsolicited book reviews are welcome.

Frequency: Annual

Publisher: Institute for Vico Studies/Humanities Press International

Subscription rates: $35 per issue

NOTRE DAME JOURNAL OF FORMAL LOGIC

Editors: M. Detlefsen & A. Pillay

P.O. Box 5
Notre Dame, IN 46556-0005

Tel. 219-631-6157
Fax 219-631-8609
E-mail ndjfl@nd.edu

ISSN 0029-4527

Date of founding: 1960

Purpose: To provide common ground for philosophers and mathematicians to read and publish work in all areas of logic, philosophy of language, formal semantics, and foundations of logic and mathematics.

Manuscript info: Philosophical articles are 50% of annual publication. Manuscripts are published in philosophy of logic, philosophy of math, philosophy of language, formal semantics, logical areas of computer science, and logical areas of linguistics. Those accessible and of interest to both mathematicians and philosophers are preferred. Backlog is 9 months. Manuscript refereeing is blind; comments are given to authors. Acceptance rate is 15-20%; 85-90% require revision. Average evaluation time is 3-4 months. Invitation rate varies. Instructions for manuscript preparation are in the journal. Send manuscripts to Martha Van Overberghe, Production & Business Manager, Notre Dame Journal of Formal Logic, P.O. Box 5, Notre Dame, IN 46556-0005.

Book reviews: Book reviews are included.

Frequency: Quarterly;
Circulation: 800

Publisher: University of Notre Dame

Subscription rates: $25;
Institutions $45

NOTRE DAME JOURNAL OF LAW, ETHICS AND PUBLIC POLICY

Editor: Matthew Schecter

T. J. White Center on Law & Gov't.
Notre Dame Law School
Notre Dame, IN 46556

Tel. 219-631-4888
Fax 219-631-6371

ISSN 0883-3648

Date of founding: 1984

Purpose: To analyze legal and public policy issues from an ethical perspective. The journal examines policy issues using various methods and seeks to build on Notre Dame's religious tradition by translating Judeo-Christian principles into practical proposals.

Sponsor: Thomas J. White Center on Law and Government

Manuscript info: Most articles concern philosophy to some degree. Each issue centers around a specific symposia topic (such as civil disobedience, media, women and the law, legal ethics); manuscripts must fall within the categories chosen for a specific year. About 90% of articles are invited. About 20% of unsolicited manuscripts are accepted; 25% require significant revision. Average evaluation time is 1 month. Instructions for manuscript preparation are in the journal.

Book reviews: Book reviews are not included.

Frequency: 2 issues per year;
Circulation: 300

Publisher: Joe Christensen, Inc.,
1540 Adams St., Lincoln, NE 68521

Subscription rates: $16 ($8/issue)

NOÛS

Editor: James Tomberlin

Dept. of Philosophy
C. S. U.-Northridge
Northridge, CA 91330

Tel. 818-885-2757 Ext. 2751
E-mail nouscsun@huey.csun.edu

ISSN 0029-4624

Date of founding: 1966

Purpose: To publish papers that
report important results of philosophical research, high-quality critical studies, and reviews of important books.
Publication of discussion notes has
been discontinued.

Sponsor: Blackwell Publishers

Manuscript info: About 20 philosophy articles are published per year.
Any area of analytic philosophy is welcome. Backlog is 15 months.
Manuscript refereeing is blind if contributor requests; unsigned comments
are given to authors. Acceptance rate
is 7%; 30% require significant revision.
Average evaluation time is 4-5 months.
Instructions for manuscript preparation are in the journal. Manuscripts
should be sent, in triplicate, to the editor listed above. Co-editors are
Geoffrey Sayre-McCord and William
G Lycan, UNC Chapel Hill.

Book reviews: All book reviews are
invited.

Frequency: Quarterly;
Circulation: 1,100

Publisher: Blackwell Publishers
350 Main Street, Malden, MA 02148

Tel. 617-388-8200
Fax 617-388-8210

Please direct subscription inquiries to
this office.

Subscription rates: $30, two years
$57, three years $80; Institutions $60,
two years $120, three years, $180

OPINION

Editor: James E. Kurtz

P.O. Box 681
Cape May Court House
NJ 08210-0681

Date of founding: 1956

Purpose: To share thoughts, ideas,
and opinions on philosophical, sociological, and theological subjects.

Manuscript info: About 12 philosophy articles are published per year.
Manuscripts are welcome in any area
of philosophy. There is no backlog of
accepted articles. About 10% of manuscripts are accepted; no accepted
manuscripts require significant revisions. The average time required to
evaluate a manuscript is 6 to 8 weeks.
Instructions for manuscript preparation are not included in the journal.
Manuscripts should be sent to the
editor.

Book reviews: Reviews are included;
unsolicited book reviews are welcome.

Frequency: Monthly;
Circulation: 3,000

Publisher: Opinion Publications

Subscription rates: Subscription is by donation.

OWL OF MINERVA

Editor: Ardis B. Collins

Dept. of Philosophy
Loyola University of Chicago
Chicago, IL 60626

Tel. 312-508-3477
E-mail acollin@wpo.it.luc.edu

ISSN 0030-7580

Date of founding: 1969

Purpose: To promote the study of Hegelian philosophy; to act as a vehicle for The Hegel Society of America.

Sponsor: Hegel Society of America

Manuscript info: Manuscripts dealing with Hegel, Hegelianism, or 19th century German-related thought (Fichte, Schelling, Schleiermacher, etc.) are preferred. Manuscripts are blind refereed; the referees' comments are returned if the manuscript is not accepted. Uninvited articles are welcome. Instructions for manuscript preparation are included in the journal. Manuscripts should be sent to the editor.

Book reviews: All book reviews are invited. Contact Professor William Maker, Book Review Editor, Dept. of Philosophy, Clemson University, Clemson, SC 29631.

Frequency: Biannual;
Circulation: 650

Publisher: Hegel Society of America

Subscription rates: $15; Students $6; Libraries $25

PACIFIC PHILOSOPHICAL QUARTERLY*

Editors: J. Dreher, S. Lloyd, & E. McCann

University of S. California
University Park, CA 90089-0451

Tel. 213-743-5630
Fax 213-747-4176

ISSN 0279-0750

Date of founding: 1920

Purpose: To explore philosophical problems.

Manuscript info: Manuscripts are welcome in any area of philosophy. The average time required to evaluate a manuscript is 3 months. Instructions for manuscripts should be sent to the managing editor, *Pacific Philosophical Quarterly*, University of Southern California.

Frequency: Quarterly;
Circulation: 930

Publisher: Blackwell Publishers for the University of Southern California

Subscription rates: $21;
Institutions $38.50

PERSONALIST FORUM, THE

Editor: Thomas O. Buford

Department of Philosophy
Furman University
Greenville, SC 29613

Tel. 803-294-3139
Fax 803-294-3001
E-mail buford_tom/furman@furman.edu

ISSN 0889-065X

Date of founding: 1984

Purpose: A biannual journal devoted to publishing scholarly work that takes personal categories seriously and addresses issues of being persons in this world. Each issue includes articles and a review of recent philosophical works.

Manuscript info: Six philosophy articles are published yearly. Any area of philosophy is welcome; sometimes an issue is organized under a theme. Manuscript refereeing is blind; comments are given to the authors. About 10% of manuscripts are accepted, though some revision is required. Average evaluation time is 3 months. Some articles are invited. Manuscript instructions are available from the editor, and all manuscripts should be sent to the editor.

Book reviews: Though book reviews are invited, unsolicited reviews are welcome.

Frequency: Biannual; Circulation: 200

Publisher: Thomas O. Buford

Subscription rates: $10; Institutions $15

PHENOMENOLOGICAL INQUIRY: A REVIEW OF PHILOSOPHICAL IDEAS AND TRENDS

Editor: Anna-Teresa Tymieniecka

348 Payson Road
Belmont, MA 02178

Tel. 617-489-3696

Date of founding: 1977

Purpose: Offers exchange of ideas and information of the phenomenological work around the world to scholars and philosophers working in phenomenology.

Sponsor: World Phenomenology Institute with its 3 societies

Manuscript info: All articles are devoted to philosophy and interdisciplinary phenomenology. Only manuscripts in phenomenology are welcome. Original ideas, book reviews, research instruments and information are given preference. Manuscripts should be sent to the managing editor, Robert Wise, at address above.

Book reviews: Unsolicited book reviews are welcome.

Frequency: Annual; Circulation: 1,000

Publisher: World Phenomenology Institute

Subscription rates: $25-$45

PHILOSOPHER'S INDEX, THE: AN INTERNATIONAL INDEX TO PHILOSOPHICAL PERIODICALS AND BOOKS

Editor: Richard H. Lineback

Philosopher's Information Ctr.
1616 E. Wooster St., Box P
Bowling Green, OH 43402

Tel. 419-353-8830
Fax 419-353-8920
E-mail 102574.1737@compuserve.com

ISSN 0031-7993

Date of founding: 1967

Purpose: To provide an up-to-date subject and author index of articles in more than 350 international philosophy and interdisciplinary journals, as well as philosophy books.

Manuscript info: Professional philosophers index all articles and books, which are listed alphabetically by subject and author. Abstracts of the articles and books are published in each issue and are generally written by the authors. There is an annual cumulative edition of the *Index* in addition to the 4 quarterly issues. It is also available on CD-ROM and online from DIALOG and CompuServe.

Frequency: Quarterly; Circulation: 2,000

Publisher: Philosopher's Information Center

Subscription rates: For 1996: $55; Institutions $179; Annual Cumulative Edition (Vol 29, 1995) $65; Institutions $189

PHILOSOPHIC EXCHANGE

Editor: Joseph Gilbert

Ctr. for Philosophic Exchange
SUNY College at Brockport
Brockport, NY 14420

Tel. 716-395-2493

ISSN 0193-5046

Date of founding: 1969

Purpose: Primarily to publish the lectures invited by the Center for Philosophic Exchange.

Sponsor: Center for Philosophic Exchange

Manuscript info: About 4 to 6 philosophy articles are published per year. Only research sponsored by the Center is published. There is no backlog of accepted articles. One hundred percent of articles are invited.

Book reviews: Book reviews are not included.

Frequency: Annual; Circulation: 500

Publisher: Center for Philosophic Exchange

Subscription rates: $6; Institutions $15

PHILOSOPHICAL BOOKS

Editor: Anthony Ellis

Dept. of Phil. & Relig. Studies
Virginia Commonwealth Univ.
915 W. Franklin St.
Richmond, VA 23284

E-mail aellis@gems.vcu.edu

ISSN 0031-8051

Date of founding: 1960

Purpose: Prompt and scholarly reviews of professional books in philosophy, including regular articles reviewing recent works in specific areas.

Sponsor: The Analysis Committee

Manuscript info: Approximately 130 articles per year are devoted to philosophy.

Book reviews: Reviews are included.

Frequency: Quarterly; Circulation: 600

Publisher: Blackwell Publishers

PHILOSOPHICAL FORUM

Editor: Marx W. Wartofsky

Box G-1437
Baruch College of CUNY
111 E. 18 St.
New York, NY 10010

Tel. 212-387-1682
Fax 212-614-9410

ISSN 0031-806X

Date of founding: 1943

Purpose: To provide open-minded discussions that aim not so much at agreement as at lively response.

Manuscript info: About 25 philosophy articles are published per year. Any area of philosophy is welcome; original work is preferred. Backlog is about 12 months. Manuscript refereeing is blind; comments are given to authors. About 10% of manuscripts are accepted; 30% of accepted manuscripts require significant revision. The average evaluation time is 3 months. No articles are invited except for special issues, in which case 90% are invited. Instructions for manuscript preparation are in the journal. Send manuscripts to the editor.

Frequency: Quarterly;
Circulation: 2,000

Publisher: The Philosophical Forum, Inc.

Subscription rates: $15; Institutions $60; add $4 for foreign subscriptions.

PHILOSOPHICAL PSYCHOLOGY

Editor: William Bechtel

Phil.-Neuroscience-Psych. Prog.
Washington University
Campus Box 1075/1 Brookings Dr.
St. Louis, MO 63130-4899

Tel. 314-935-6873
Fax 314-935-7349
E-mail pp@twinearth.wustl.edu

ISSN 0951-5089

Date of founding: 1988

Purpose: To promote interaction of philosophers and psychologists by publishing high-quality articles of interest to both professions.

Manuscript info: About 20 philosophy articles are published per year. Only manuscripts relevant to the intersection of philosophy and psychology are welcome. Manuscripts are refereed. The refereeing is blind, and unsigned comments are given to the authors. About 15% of manuscripts are accepted; 80% require significant revision. About 4 months is the average evaluation time. About 10% of articles are invited. Instructions for manuscript preparation are included in the journal. Manuscripts should be sent to the editor.

Book reviews: About 90% of the book reviews are invited; unsolicited book reviews are welcome.

Frequency: Quarterly;
Circulation: 500

Publisher: Carfax Publishing Company, P.O. Box 25, Abingdon Oxfordshire OX14 3UE United Kingdom

Subscription rates: $98;
Institutions $268

PHILOSOPHICAL REVIEW

Editor: Faculty

Cornell University
Sage School of Philosophy
327 Goldwin Smith Hall
Ithaca, NY 14853-3201

Tel. 607-255-6817
Fax 607-255-8177
E-mail phil_review@cornell.edu

ISSN 0031-8108

Date of founding: 1892

Purpose: To publish philosophical articles and book reviews.

Manuscript info: About 16 to 20 philosophy articles are published per year. Any area of philosophy is welcome. Refereeing of manuscripts is blind; comments are not usually given to authors. About 4% of manuscripts are accepted; about 80% of accepted manuscripts have been significantly revised before acceptance. The average evaluation time is 2 months. Instructions for manuscript preparation are in the journal. Manuscripts should be sent to *The Philosophical Review*, Cornell University, 327 Goldwin Smith, Ithaca, NY 14853-3201.

Book reviews: All book reviews are invited; unsolicited book reviews are not welcome.

Frequency: Quarterly;
Circulation: 3,200

Publisher: Sage School of Philosophy, 327 Goldwin Smith, Cornell University

Subscription rates: $33; Institutions $54; Students, retired, unemployed $20; postage outside of US $6

PHILOSOPHICAL STUDIES IN EDUCATION*

Editor: Susan R. Martin

Indiana State University
Terre Haute, IN 47809

Tel. 812-237-2930

ISSN 0160-7561

Date of founding: 1968

Purpose: To foster and to engage in philosophical studies in philosophy and education.

Sponsor: Indiana State University

Manuscript info: All articles are in philosophy; those on education issues and problems are preferred. No backlog. Manuscript refereeing is not blind; unsigned comments are given to authors upon request. About 40% of manuscripts are accepted; 20% require significant revision. About 20% of articles are invited. Instructions for manuscript preparation are included in the journal. Manuscripts should be sent to the Program Committee or editor.

Book reviews: Are not included.

Frequency: Annual;
Circulation: 210

Subscription rates: Members $15; Students $5; Libraries $13.50

PHILOSOPHICAL STUDIES: AN INTERNATIONAL JOURNAL FOR PHILOSOPHY IN THE ANALYTIC TRADITION*

Editor: Stewart Cohen

Arizona State University
Tempe, AZ 85287-2004

Tel. 602-965-9365

ISSN 0031-8116

Date of founding: 1950

Purpose: To provide a forum for discussion of philosophical issues in the analytical tradition.

Manuscript info: Any area of philosophy welcome. Backlog of 1 year. Manuscript refereeing is mostly blind; unsigned comments are given to authors when appropriate. About 15% of manuscripts are accepted; 40% require significant revision. Average evaluation time is 2 months. Less than 20% invitation rate. Instructions for manuscript preparation in the journal. Manuscripts should be sent to the editor in triplicate.

Book reviews: Ordinary (short) book reviews are not published, but occasional critical review articles are published.

Frequency: 12 issues per year; Circulation: 1,000

Publisher: Kluwer Academic Publishers

Subscription rates: $153.50 per volume

PHILOSOPHICAL TOPICS

Editor: Christopher S. Hill

Dept. of Philosophy
318 Old Main
University of Arkansas
Fayetteville, AR 72701

Tel. 501-575-3551

ISSN 0276-2080

Date of founding: 1970

Purpose: To publish contributions to all fields of philosophy.

Manuscript info: About 18 to 25 philosophy articles are published per year. Each issue is devoted to problems in one area of philosophy. All papers are invited.

Book reviews: Reviews are not included.

Frequency: Biannual;
Circulation: 350

Publisher: University of Arkansas Press (address inquiries to journal's manager).

Subscription rates: $25, Institutions $45 (US and Canada); $30, Institutions $50 (outside US and Canada)

PHILOSOPHY AND GEOGRAPHY

Editors: Andrew Light
& Jonathan Smith

Dept. of Philosophy
University of Montana
Missoula, MT 59812-1038

Tel. 406-243-0211
Fax 403-492-0364

ISSN 0-8476-8221-8

Date of founding: 1995

Purpose: To promote the exchange of ideas between philosophers and geographers on areas of mutual interest, and to promote philosophical work on space, place, and the environment.

Sponsor: Society for Philosophy and Geography

Manuscript info: About 11-15 articles per year are devoted to philosophy. Each volume of the journal focuses on a specific theme. Preference is given to papers that will be of interest to both philosophers and geographers.

Preference is also given to clearly written, analytic manuscripts. Manuscripts are refereed blind; unsigned comments are given to authors. About 15% of manuscripts are accepted; 25% require significant revision. Evaluation time averages 3 months. No articles are invited. Instructions for manuscript preparation are included in the journal. Manuscripts should be sent to Andrew Light, University of Montana. Co-editor is Jonathan M. Smith, Department of Geography, Texas A & M University, College Station, TX 77843-3147.

Book reviews: Not included.

Frequency: Annual

Publisher: Rowman & Littlefield Publishers, Inc.

Subscription rates: Variable, usually $23 per issue, plus $3 postage

PHILOSOPHY AND LITERATURE

Editor: Patrick Henry, Co-Editor

Whitman College
Walla Walla, WA 99362

Tel. 509-527-5254
Fax 509-527-5039

ISSN 0190-0013

Date of founding: 1976

Purpose: To provide a forum for scholars who wish to explore the relationship between philosophy and literary arts.

Sponsor: Whitman College

Manuscript info: Manuscripts are refereed, blind if detachable title/author page is included. Unsigned comments are given to authors when possible. Fewer than 10% of manuscripts are accepted; fewer than 20% require significant revision.

Average evaluation time is 3 months. Instructions for manuscript preparation are included in the journal. Manuscripts should be sent to the co-editor listed above or to the editor, Denis Dutton, University of Canterbury, Christchurch, New Zealand.

Book reviews: About 80% of book reviews are invited. Unsolicited book reviews are welcome.

Frequency: 2 issues per year; Circulation: 1,200

Publisher: Johns Hopkins University Press

Subscription rates: $22; Institutions $43; Students $17

PHILOSOPHY AND PHENOMENOLOGICAL RESEARCH

Editor: Ernest Sosa

Box 1947
Brown University
Providence, RI 02912

Tel. 401-863-3215
Fax 401-863-2719
E-mail ppr@brownvm.brown.edu

ISSN 0031-8205

Date of founding: 1939

Purpose: The journal is international in content and is not restricted to the doctrines of any particular philosophical school.

Sponsor: International Phenomenological Society

Manuscript info: There are 10 to 15 contributions in each issue, all devoted to philosophy. Any area of philosophy is welcome. Backlog is 1 year.

Manuscript refereeing is blind if requested by the author; unsigned comments are given to authors. Average evaluation time is 2 months. A very small percentage of articles are invited. Instructions for manuscript preparation are included in the journal. Manuscripts should be sent to the editor.

Book reviews: All book reviews are invited; unsolicited book reviews are not welcome.

Frequency: Quarterly; Circulation: 1,500

Publisher: International Phenomenological Society

Subscription rates: $20, Foreign $24; Libraries and Institutions $55, Foreign $59

PHILOSOPHY AND PUBLIC AFFAIRS

Editor: Marshall Cohen

Princeton University Press
41 William Street
Princeton, NJ 08540

Tel. 609-258-4900
Fax 609-258-6305
E-mail papa@pupress.princeton.edu

ISSN 0048-3915

Date of founding: 1971

Purpose: Founded in the belief that a philosophical examination of issues of public concern can contribute to their clarification and resolution. It welcomes philosophical discussion of abstract and substantive legal, social, and political problems.

Manuscript info: Only philosophy articles are published each year. Manuscripts are occasionally refereed

but not blind; comments are not generally given to authors. About 5% of manuscripts are accepted; 30% require significant revision. Average evaluation time is 2-3 months. Fewer than 5% of articles are invited. Instructions for manuscript preparation are in the journal. Manuscripts should be sent to Robert E. Brown, Managing Editor, Princeton University Press.

Frequency: Quarterly; Circulation: 3,000

Publisher: Princeton University Press

Subscription rates: $34; Institutions $60; Students $17

PHILOSOPHY AND RHETORIC

Editors: H. Johnstone, M. Secor & S. Browne

Pennsylvania State University
240 Sparks Bldg.
University Park, PA 16802-5201

Tel. 814-865-1512
Fax 814-865-0119

ISSN 0031-8213

Date of founding: 1968

Purpose: To publish articles on theoretical issues involving the relationship between philosophy and rhetoric, philosophical aspects of argumentation, studies of rhetorical views of history, and the relationship of rhetoric to other areas of human thought.

Manuscript info: About 75% of articles per year are devoted to philosophy. Backlog is 1 year. Manuscript refereeing is blind; unsigned comments are given to authors if necessary or needed. About 12% of manuscripts are accepted; 30% require significant revision. The average evaluation time is 3 months.

About 10% of articles are invited. Instructions for manuscript preparation are included in the journal. Manuscripts should be sent to the editors.

Book reviews: More than 90% of the book reviews are invited; unsolicited book reviews are welcome.

Frequency: Quarterly; Circulation: 850

Publisher: The Pennsylvania State University Press

Subscription rates: $27.50, Foreign $35; Institutions $40, Foreign $48

PHILOSOPHY AND SOCIAL CRITICISM*

Editor: David Rasmussen

Dept. of Philosophy
Boston College
Chestnut Hill, MA 02167

Tel. 617-552-3860
Fax 913-843-1274

ISSN 0191-4537

Date of founding: 1978

Purpose: To publish essays in continental and American thought, politics, ethics, law, literature, economics, and related areas. The journal provides a forum for scholarly discussion, debate and interchange of ideas.

Manuscript info: About 20 philosophy articles per year. Manuscripts in continental philosophy, critical theory, and phenomenology are given preference, but others are welcome. Backlog of 3 months. Manuscripts are refereed blind; unsigned comments are given to authors. About 10-20% of manuscripts are accepted; 10% require significant revision. Average evaluation time is 3

months. About 5-10% of articles are invited. Instructions for manuscript preparation are in the journal. Manuscripts should be sent to the editor.

Book reviews: About 5-10% of book reviews are invited; unsolicited book reviews are welcome.

Frequency: Quarterly; Circulation: 800

Publisher: Allen Press, 1041 New Hampshire St., P.O. Box 368, Lawrence, KS 66044

Subscription rates: $30 (US and Canada); Institutions $80 (US and Canada); Students $25 (US and Canada); $33 (Foreign); Institutions $88 (Foreign); Students $28 (Foreign)

PHILOSOPHY AND THEOLOGY

Editor: Philip Rossi

Theology Dept.
Coughlin Hall 100
Marquette University
P.O. Box 1881
Milwaukee, WI 53201-1881

Tel. 414-288-3738
Fax 414-288-5548

ISSN 0-87462-559-9

Date of founding: 1986

Purpose: To address all issues of philosophical and theological interest.

Sponsor: Marquette University

Manuscript info: About 20-25 philosophy articles are published per year. Manuscripts in any area of philosophy are welcome; preference is given to those that focus on areas of common interest to philosophy and theology. Backlog is 6 months. Manuscripts are refereed blind; referees' unsigned comments are given to authors. About 30% of manuscripts are accepted; 20% require significant revision. Average evaluation time is 3 months. About 15% of articles are invited. Manuscripts should be sent to the editor on computer disk and in hard copy.

Book reviews: Book reviews are not included.

Frequency: Quarterly; Circulation: 230

Publisher: Marquette University Press; subscription agents: Philosophy Documentation Center

Subscription rates: $25; $15 for subscription on computer disk

---

PHILOSOPHY EAST AND WEST

Editor: Roger T. Ames

2530 Dole Street
Honolulu, HI 96822

Tel. 808-956-8410
Fax 808-956-9228

ISSN 0031-8221

Date of founding: 1951

Purpose: To publish specialized articles in Asian philosophy and articles that seek to illuminate, in a comparative manner, the distinctive characteristics of the various philosophical traditions in the East and West.

Sponsor: University of Hawaii

Manuscript info: About 28 philosophy articles are published yearly. Any area of philosophy is welcome, but original philosophy from a multicultural background is preferred. Backlog is 9 months. Manuscript

independent refereeing is blind; comments are sometimes given to authors. Acceptance rate is 15%; 25% require significant revision. Average evaluation time is 2 to 3 months. Invitation rate 10%. Instructions for manuscript preparation are in the journal. Manuscripts should be sent to the editor.

Book reviews: About 95% of the book reviews are invited; unsolicited book reviews are welcome.

Frequency: Quarterly; Circulation: 1,500

Publisher: University Press of Hawaii

Subscription rates: $26

PHILOSOPHY IN SCIENCE

Editor: W. R. Stoeger

Stenard Observatory
University of Arizona
Tucson, AZ 85721

Fax 602-297-4797

ISSN 0277-2434

Date of founding: 1983

Purpose: A forum for the articulation and discussion of philosophical issues arising within the sciences.

Manuscript info: About 10 philosophy articles are published per year. Manuscripts from all schools of philosophy but related to sciences are welcome. The refereeing is blind, and the referees' signed comments are given to the authors. Instructions for manuscript preparation are available from the editors or the publisher. Manuscripts should be sent to the editors.

Book reviews: Reviews are included.

Frequency: Irregular

Publisher: A. G. Pacholczyk
Pachart Publishing House

Subscription rates: $48

PHILOSOPHY IN THE CONTEMPORARY WORLD

Editor: Jack Weir

Morehead State University
U.P.O. 662
Morehead, KY 40351-1689

Tel. 606-783-2785
Fax 606-783-2678
E-mail
j.weir@msuacad.morehead-st.edu

ISSN 1077-1999

Date of founding: 1993

Purpose: To engage issues and problems of the contemporary world through a philosophical dialogue informed by diverse modes of inquiry.

Sponsor: Society for Philosophy in the Contemporary World

Manuscript info: About 24 to 28 articles per year are devoted to philosophy. Manuscripts may be from any area of philosophy, but should have contemporary relevance to an issue or problem. Backlog of accepted articles is 3-6 months. Manuscripts are refereed blind; unsigned comments are given to authors. About 60% of articles are accepted; 50% require significant revision. Evaluation time averages 6-8 weeks. About 10% of articles are invited. Instructions for manuscript preparation are included in the journal and will be sent if requested. Manuscripts should be sent to the editor.

Book reviews: Reviews are not included.

Frequency: Quarterly;
Circulation: 120

Publisher: Society for Philosophy in the Contemporary World

Subscription rates: Individuals and institutions $40; Students $20; Postage charges $10 foreign (airmail only); required currency: US dollars

PHILOSOPHY OF EDUCATION: CURRENT ISSUES

Editor: Diana Dummitt

Managing Editor
University of Illinois
College of Education
1310 South Sixth St.
Champaign, IL 61820

Tel. 217-333-3003
Fax 217-244-3711
E-mail edtheory@ux1.cso.uiuc.edu

ISSN 8756-6575

Date of founding: 1941

Purpose: To publish papers presented at the annual meeting of the Philosophy of Education Society (hardcover).

Sponsor: Philosophy of Education Society

Manuscript info: About 30-35 philosophy articles are published yearly. Education bearing is required; 15-page maximum is preferred. There is no backlog. Annual dates for acceptance are November 1-15. Manuscript refereeing is blind; unsigned comments are given to authors on request. About 15-25% of manuscripts are accepted; 10% require significant revision. Average evaluation time is 2-3 months. Invitation rate is 10%. Instructions for manuscript preparation are in back issues. Manuscripts should be sent to the editor.

Frequency: Annual; Circulation: 800

Publisher: Philosophy of Education Society

Subscription rates: Free to members of the Philosophy of Education Society; all others, $35 plus postage.

PHILOSOPHY OF SCIENCE

Editor: Philip Kitcher

Department of Philosophy
Univ. of California, San Diego
9500 Gilman Dr.
La Jolla, CA 92093-0302

Tel. 619-534-6607

ISSN 0031-8248

Date of founding: 1934

Purpose: To publish articles of merit or significant interest in philosophy of science, broadly construed.

Sponsor: Philosophy of Science Association

Manuscript info: About 25% of the journal's articles are philosophy. Manuscripts in philosophy of science are preferred. Backlog of accepted articles is 1 year. The referees' unsigned comments are given to authors. Blind refereeing is the usual practice. About 15% of manuscripts are accepted; 65% of accepted manuscripts require significant revision. The average evaluatuation time is 2-3 months. Instructions for manuscript preparation are included in the journal. Send manuscripts to the editor.

Book reviews: About 80% of book reviews are invited; unsolicited book reviews are occasionally welcome, depending on the topic and previous requests.

Frequency: Quarterly; Circulation: 2,150

Publisher: Philosophy of Science Association

Subscription rates: Members $40-$60; Non-members $60; Students $20; Single copies $15; Institutions $60 (outside US $65)

PHILOSOPHY TODAY

Editor: David Pellauer

DePaul University
2320 N. Kenmore Ave.
Chicago, IL 60614-3298

Tel. 312-325-7267
Fax 312-325-7268
E-mail phltoday@condor.depaul.edu

ISSN 0031-8256

Date of founding: 1957

Purpose: To publish articles in contemporary philosophy, with an emphasis on issues arising out of the continental and American traditions.

Sponsor: DePaul University Philosophy Department

Manuscript info: About 30-40 philosophy articles yearly. Any area of philosophy is welcome, but continental tradition from existentialism to postmodernism and cross-disciplinary studies are preferred. Acceptance rate is 20%. Average evaluation time is 2 months. Accepted articles do not usually require significant revision. Instructions for manuscript preparation are available from the editorial office; generally we follow *Chicago Manual of Style*. Manuscripts suitable for blind reviewing should be sent to the editorial office.

Book reviews: Article-length reviews and long surveys of literature in a particular area or by and about an individual thinker are published on a regular basis; unsolicited review-articles are welcome.

Frequency: Quarterly; Circulation: 1,200

Publisher: DePaul University

Subscription rates: $24; Outside US $30

POLITICAL THEORY

Editor: Tracy B. Strong

Dept. of Political Science
Univ. of California, San Diego
La Jolla, CA 92093-0521

Tel. 619-534-7370
Fax 619-534-7130
E-mail tstrong@weber.ucsd.edu

ISSN 0090-5917

Date of founding: 1972

Purpose: To serve the political theory and philosophy community with essays on historical political topics and modern political theory, normative and analytic philosophy, history of ideas, and philosophical examination of current political and social issues.

Manuscript info: About 20 philosophy articles are published per year. Manuscripts in any area of philosophy are welcome; preference is given to those in political philosophy. Manuscripts are refereed blind; unsigned comments are given to authors. About 10% of manuscripts

are accepted; 85% require significant revision. Average evaluation time is 3 months. Fewer than 5% of articles are invited. Instructions for manuscript preparation are in the journal.

Book reviews: All book reviews are invited; unsolicited book reviews are not welcome.

Frequency: Quarterly; Circulation: 2,400

Publisher: Sage Publications, Inc.

Subscription rates: $56; Institutions $175; add $8 for postage outside US. Orders from the UK, Europe, the Middle East, and Africa should be sent to Sage Publications, 6 Bonhill St., London EC2A 4PU, UK.

POSTMODERN JEWISH PHILOSOPHY NETWORK

Editor: Peter Ochs

Program in Jewish Studies
Drew University
Madison, NJ 07940

Tel. 201-408-3222
Fax 201-408-3939
E-mail pochs@drew.edu

Date of founding: 1991

Purpose: An electronic journal devoted to discussions of Postmodern Judaism, philosophically considered.

Sponsor: Drew University

Manuscript info: The journal style falls between a Listserv network and a standard newsletter-journal. Manuscript submissions are made only by subscribers, who are listed in each journal issue as members of the network. Manuscripts of 15 or fewer typescript pages may be sent to the editor via e-mail, or hardcopy accompanied by IBM or Mac disk. It is best to discuss the essay first with the editor, since each journal issue is integrated thematically. The Network considers manuscripts only on postmodern Jewish philosophy, including theoretical discussions (applications of semiotics, pragmatics, deconstruction, critical theory and so on to issues in Jewish philosophy) or text studies (postmodern approaches to Talmud, Bible, Kabbalah, Jewish philosophy, or literature). Backlog of accepted articles is 4-6 months. Some manuscripts are refereed (not blind); referees' signed comments are given to authors. About 40% of manuscripts are accepted; 30% require significant revision. Evaluation time averages 1.5 months. About 50% of articles are invited.

Book reviews: A review section is included in each issue. Unsolicited book reviews are welcome.

Frequency: Quarterly; Circulation: 230

Publisher: Program in Jewish Studies, Drew University

Subscription rates: $12/volume for hardcopy (send check, made out to Drew University Network, to Peter Ochs); e-mail subscription is free of charge (to subscribe, send a brief bio to pochs@drew.edu). Back issues may be accessed via WWW address: http://www.drew.edu/~pmjp

PROCEEDINGS AND ADDRESSES OF THE AMERICAN PHILOSOPHICAL ASSOCIATION

Editor: Eric Hoffman, Exec. Dir.

APA
University of Delaware
Newark, DE 19716

Tel. 302-831-1112
Fax 302-831-8690

ISSN 0065-972X

Date of founding: 1928

Purpose: Principal publication of The American Philosophical Association, serves as a means of communication among philosophers and a forum for reflection on the philosophical profession.

Sponsor: The American Philosophical Association

Manuscript info: Regular features include the annual addresses of divisional presidents, programs of the divisional meetings, committee and special reports, essays on issues in the profession, information concerning grants and fellowships, announcements of prizes, conferences, forthcoming events, and publications in philosophy. Brief essays on the practice of philosophical teaching and research on the changing needs of the profession are also invited.

Frequency: 5 issues per year; Circulation: 8,300

Publisher: American Philosophical Association

Subscription rates: $50 per year (included in APA membership dues, $30-$115 per year)

PROCEEDINGS OF THE AMERICAN CATHOLIC PHILOSOPHICAL ASSOCIATION

Editor: Robert E. Wood

University of Dallas
1845 E. Northgate Dr.
Irving, TX 75062

E-mail cua-acpa@cua.edu

ISSN 0065-7638

Date of founding: 1926

Purpose: To promote philosophical scholarship.

Sponsor: American Catholic Philosophical Association

Manuscript info: The *Proceedings* consist of the approximately 21 papers delivered at the ACPA annual meeting, along with the official records of the Association.

Frequency: Annual;
Circulation: 1,200

Publisher: American Catholic Philosophical Association; for claims and other correspondence contact Mark Rasevic, ACPA, Room 403 Administration Bldg., The Catholic University of America, Washington, DC 20064-0001; telephone and fax: 202-319-5518.

Subscription rates: $20; Back issues $20; 15% shipping fee added to all subscriptions and back issue orders.

PROCEEDINGS OF THE BOSTON AREA COLLOQUIUM IN ANCIENT PHILOSOPHY

Editor: John J. Cleary

Dept. of Philosophy
Boston College
Chestnut Hill, MA 02167-3806

Tel. 617-552-3869

Date of founding: 1985

Purpose: To publish revised versions of the lectures and commentaries presented to the Boston Area Colloquium during each academic year, so as to make available to a more general academic audience some of the latest research in ancient philosophy.

Sponsor: Boston College

Manuscript info: About 8-10 philosophy articles are published per year. The journal publishes invited papers only in ancient philosophy, classics, ancient religion, and history. Manuscripts are refereed blind; unsigned comments are given to authors. About 90% of manuscripts are accepted; 10% require significant revision. Average evaluation time is 2-3 months. 100% of articles are invited.

Book reviews: Book reviews are not included.

Frequency: Annual

Publisher: University Press of America

Subscription rates: Rates are set by co-publisher for each volume.

PROCESS STUDIES

Editor: Lewis S. Ford

Dept. of Philosophy
Old Dominion University
Norfolk, VA 23508

Tel. 804-627-1396
Fax 804-683-5345

ISSN 0360-6503

Date of founding: 1971

Purpose: Exploration of the process thought of Whitehead and Hartshorne, related philosophies and theologies, and application to other fields.

Manuscript info: About 10-20 philosophy articles are published per year. Manuscripts in process thought are preferred. There is some backlog of accepted articles. Manuscript refereeing, if necessary, is usually not blind; unsigned comments are given to authors. About 30% of manuscripts are accepted; 40% of accepted manuscripts require significant revision. Average evaluation time is 1-3 months. Very few articles are invited. Partial instructions for manuscript preparation are in the journal.

Book reviews: Most book reviews are invited; unsolicited book reviews are welcome.

Frequency: Quarterly;
Circulation: 700

Publisher: Center for Process Studies

Subscription rates: $20;
Institutions $30

PROFESSIONAL ETHICS: A MULTIDISCIPLINARY JOURNAL

Editor: Robert J. Baum

Center for Applied Ethics
332 Griffin-Floyd Hall
University of Florida
Gainesville, FL 32611

Tel. 904-392-2084 Ext. 332
Fax 904-392-5577

ISSN 1063-6579

Date of founding: 1992

Purpose: A forum for the analysis of ethical issues that arise in practicing a profession and in professional organizations.

Manuscript info: All articles are devoted to professional ethics. Manuscripts are refereed blind; unsigned comments are usually given to authors. About 15-20% of manuscripts are accepted; 80% require significant revision. Average evaluation time is 3 months. Instructions for manuscript preparation are in the journal. Manuscripts should be sent to the journal. Approximately 50% of authors are philosophers.

Book reviews: Unsolicited book reviews are welcome.

Frequency: Quarterly;
Circulation: 800

Subscription rates: $25; Institutions $50 (add $5 for Canada; $10 for surface mail to other countries).

PUBLIC AFFAIRS QUARTERLY

Editor: Robert L. Holmes

Dept. of Philosophy
University of Tulsa
600 South College Ave.
Tulsa, OK 74104-3189

Tel. 412-624-5704

ISSN 0887-0373

Date of founding: 1987

Purpose: To enhance the quality of our understanding of public issues by publishing essays that bring philosophical depth and sophistication to the consideration of matters on the agenda of public debate.

Manuscript info: About 28-30 philosophy articles are published per year. Manuscripts will be accepted only in "applied philosophy" topics relating to public issues. Backlog is 8-9 months. Manuscript refereeing is blind at the author's request; comments are given to authors. Acceptance rate is 15-20%; 50% require significant revision. The average evaluation time is 8 weeks. No articles are invited. Some instructions for manuscript preparation are in the journal. Manuscripts should be sent to the editor.

Frequency: Quarterly;
Circulation: 450

Publisher: North American Philosophical Publications; Subscription agent: Philosophy Documentation Center

Subscription rates: $40;
Institutions $160

QUEST, THE*

Editor: William Metzger

P.O. Box 270
Wheaton, IL 60189-0270

Tel. 708-668-1571
Fax 708-665-8791

ISSN 1040-533X

Date of founding: 1988

Purpose: Comparative study of philosophy, science, religion, and the arts, based on a worldview embracing wholeness and compassion.

Sponsor: Theosophical Society in America

Manuscript info: About 12-15 philosophy articles per year. Manuscripts in the areas of perennial (holistic) philosophy and spiritual practice (meditation, etc.) are welcome. Backlog is 6 months. Manuscripts are not refereed. Acceptance rate for manuscripts is 5%; 20% of these require significant revision. Average evaluation time is 2 months. About 25% of articles are invited. Manuscripts should be sent to William Metzger, Editor.

Book reviews: About 50% of the book reviews are invited; unsolicited book reviews are welcome.

Frequency: Quarterly;
Circulation: 27,000

Publisher: Theosophical Society in America

Subscription rates: $13.97

RACE, GENDER AND CLASS

Editor: Jean Belkhir

Inst. for Teach. & Res. on Women
Towson State University
Towson, MD 21204-7097

Tel. 410-830-2580
Fax 410-830-3469
E-mail e7a8bel@toe.towson

ISSN 1082-8354

Purpose: To provide a forum for promoting the integration of multicultural education focusing on race, gender, and class in higher education.

Manuscript info: The journal publishes articles of 10-20 pages, notes of 5-10 pages, review essays on books or films, autobiographies, essays, brief summaries of teacher-related experiences with other journals, data sets, theories, stories, field work studies, and letters to the journal. Papers should have practical implications, direct or indirect, for education. It is preferred that manuscripts be submitted in WordPerfect 5.X or 6.0 IBM-compatible word-processor format, along with 3 hard copies of the manuscript. The journal is interested in papers without footnotes, and which cut through the technical jargon commonly used in academic writing. Papers are blind refereed.

Frequency: 3 issues per year

Subscription rates: $20; Institutions $30

REASON PAPERS: A JOURNAL OF INTERDISCIPLINARY NORMATIVE STUDIES

Editor: Tibor R. Machan

Dept. of Philosophy
Auburn University
Auburn, AL 36849

Tel. 205-826-4344

ISSN 0363-1893

Date of founding: 1974

Purpose: To explore the scope and content of normative rational thought across the various humane and social disciplines.

Manuscript info: About 3-5 philosophy articles are published per year. Manuscripts on normative matters, in political theory, ethics, philosophy of social science, aesthetics, meta-economics, history of thought, and legal philosophy are preferred. Backlog is 1 year. Manuscript refereeing is blind; comments are given to authors. Acceptance rate is 15%; 50% require significant revision. The average evaluation time is 3 months. About 10% of articles are invited. Instructions are in the journal.

Book reviews: About 90% of book reviews are invited; unsolicited book reviews are not welcome.

Frequency: Annual;
Circulation: 350

Publisher: Patrington Press Ltd. Enholmes Hall, Patrington, Hull HU12 OPR, UK

Subscription rates: $15 per copy (special issues $17)

RELIGIOUS HUMANISM

Editor: Mason Olds

Dept. of Religion & Philosophy
Springfield College
Springfield, MA 01109

Tel. 413-788-3260
Fax 413-748-3854

ISSN 0034-4095

Date of founding: 1963

Purpose: To print articles that promote and encourage the religious,
ethical, and philosophical thought
and life of its subscribers.

Sponsor: Fellowship of Religious
Humanists

Manuscript info: About 35 philosophy articles are published per year.
Manuscripts are welcome in any area
of philosophy. Religious manuscripts
are given preference. Manuscripts are
not refereed. The average time
required to evaluate a manuscript is 4
months. About 50% of the articles are
invited. Instructions for manuscript
preparation are included in the journal. Manuscripts should be sent to the
editor.

Book reviews: About 50% of book
reviews are invited; unsolicited book
reviews are welcome.

Frequency: Quarterly;
Circulation: 1,100

Publisher: Fellowship of Religious
Humanists

Subscription rates: $22/year

REPORT FROM THE INSTITUTE FOR PHILOSOPHY AND PUBLIC POLICY

Editor: Arthur Evenchik

Inst. for Phil. & Public Policy
3111D Van Munching Hall
University of Maryland
College Park, MD 20742

Tel. 301-405-4766
Fax 301-314-9346
E-mail ae24@umail.umd.edu

ISSN 1067-2478

Date of founding: 1981

Purpose: To make the Institute's
research available to a broad audience, and to provide a forum for outside contributors whose work
addresses philosophical issues in law,
medicine, education, politics, and
environmental protection.

Sponsor: Institute for Philosophy
and Public Policy

Manuscript info: Sixteen articles per
year are devoted to philosophy.
Preference is given to manuscripts in
legal, medical, and environmental
ethics; civic and moral education;
political theory and morality; discrim-
ination and cultural identity. Essays of
about 3,300 words that are accessible
to a broad audience are preferred.
There is no backlog. Manuscripts are
not refereed. Evaluation time averages 3 weeks. About 95% of articles
are invited. Instructions for manuscript preparation are included in the
journal.

Book reviews: Reviews are not
included.

Frequency: Quarterly;
Circulation: 10,145

Publisher: Institute for Philosophy and Public Policy

Subscription rates: Free

RESEARCH IN PHENOMENOLOGY

Editor: John Sallis

Dept. of Philosophy
Pennsylvania State University
University Park, PA 16802

Tel. 814-863-7986

ISSN 0085-5553

Date of founding: 1971

Purpose: To publish original research and interpretive studies in continental philosophy, including phenomenology, hermeneutics, and deconstruction.

Manuscript info: All articles are devoted to philosophy; continental philosophy is preferred. Manuscript refereeing is not blind; comments are given to authors upon request. The acceptance rate is about 20%; 10% require significant revision. The average evaluation time is 2 months. About 30% of articles are invited. Instructions for manuscript preparation are available from the editor. Manuscripts should be sent to the editor.

Book reviews: About 80% of the book reviews are invited; unsolicited book reviews are not encouraged.

Publisher: Humanities Press International

Subscription rates: Individuals $39.95; Institutions $49.95

RESEARCH IN PHILOSOPHY AND TECHNOLOGY

Editor: Carl Mitcham

Science, Technology, & Society Prog.
Willard 133
Penn State University
University Park, PA 16802

Tel. 814-865-9951
Fax 814-865-3047

Date of founding: 1978

Purpose: To provide readers a healthy pluralism in philosophical approaches in published articles along with bibliographical information on works in philosophy and technology.

Manuscript info: About 15-20 philosophy articles are published per year. Submission deadline is September 1 each year for publication the following year, but manuscripts are accepted at any time. Manuscripts must be in English. Backlog is 12 months. Manuscript refereeing is blind. About 20% of the manuscripts are accepted; 50% require significant revision. Average evaluation time is 2 months. About 10% of articles are invited. Manuscript preparation information is available from the editor. Manuscripts should be sent to the editor.

Book reviews: All book reviews are invited.

Frequency: Annual

Publisher: JAI Press, Inc.

Subscription rates: $43.95; Institutions $73.25; Single copy $43.95; Postal charges: $2.50 US, $4 outside of the US.

REVIEW JOURNAL OF PHILOSOPHY AND SOCIAL SCIENCE

Editor: Michael V. Belok

1003 Soledad Way
Lady Lake, FL 32159

Tel. 904-750-4402

Date of founding: 1976

Purpose: To promote research and writing in philosophy and social science, including education.

Manuscript info: Manuscripts dealing with any area of philosophy are welcome. Backlog is 6 months. Manuscript refereeing is blind if article is unsolicited; comments are given to the author. About 78% of manuscripts are accepted; 20% require significant revision. Average evaluation time is 3 months. About 70% of articles are invited. Manuscript preparation information is available from the editor. Manuscripts should be sent to the editor.

Book reviews: About 50% are invited.

Frequency: Biannual;
Circulation: 400

Publisher: Anu Prakashan, Shivaji Road, Meerut 250 001, India

Subscription rates: $10

REVIEW OF EXISTENTIAL PSYCHOLOGY AND PSYCHIATRY*

Editor: Keith Hoeller

P.O. Box 23220
Seattle, WA 98102

ISSN 0361-1531

Purpose: To bring an existential and phenomenological approach to the understanding of human experience, with a special focus on the psychotherapeutic endeavor.

Manuscript info: Manuscripts should be typewritten and doublespaced (including block quotations and notes), submitted in duplicate, and accompanied by a stamped, self-addressed envelope. Footnotes should be numbered consecutively on a separate page. One copy of the journal will be provided for the author. Mail manuscripts directly to the editor.

Frequency: 3 issues per year

Publisher: Humanities Press International

REVIEW OF METAPHYSICS

Editor: Jude P. Dougherty

School of Philosophy
The Catholic Univ. of America
Washington, DC 20064

Tel. 202-319-5259
Fax 202-319-4731

ISSN 0034-6632

Date of founding: 1947

Purpose: Devoted to the promotion of technically competent, definitive contributions to all areas of philosophy. As an independent journal, it is interested in persistent, resolute inquiries into root questions, regardless of the writer's affiliations.

Manuscript info: About 20-25 philosophy articles are published per year. Manuscripts are welcome in any area of philosophy. The backlog of accepted articles is 3 months. About 7% of manuscripts are accepted.

Average evaluation time is 2 weeks. About 10% of articles are invited. Instructions for manuscript preparation are included in the journal. Manuscripts should be sent to the editor.

Book reviews: All book reviews are invited.

Frequency: Quarterly; Circulation: 3,000

Publisher: Philosophy Education Society, Inc.

Subscription rates: $28; Students and Retirees $18; Institutions $45

ROLL, THE

Editor: James Somerville

Schola Contemplationis
3425 Forest Ln.
Pfafftown, NC 27040-9545

Tel. 910-924-4980

ISSN 1072-9380

Date of founding: 1984

Purpose: Philosophy of religion for college or post-graduate readers and writers.

Sponsor: Schola Contemplationis

Frequency: 4 issues per year; Circulation: 550

Publisher: Schola Contemplationis, 3425 Forest Lane, Pfafftown, NC 27040-9545

Subscription rates: $15

RUSSIAN STUDIES IN PHILOSOPHY

Editor: James P. Scanlan

Dept. of Philosophy
The Ohio State University
Columbus, OH 43210

Tel. 614-481-0419
Fax 614-481-0270
E-mail scanlan.1@osu.edu

ISSN 1061-1967

Date of founding: 1962

Purpose: To publish unabridged translations, with editorial introduction, of material from leading Russian journals and publications, in order to reflect developments in Russian philosophy. Continues *Soviet Studies in Philosophy.*

Manuscript info: About 20 philosophy articles are published per year. Articles selected for translation are from all areas of philosophy. Current Russian journals are followed. The editor has responsibility for selecting material to be translated.

Book reviews: Book reviews are occasionally selected.

Frequency: Quarterly; Circulation: 293

Publisher: M. E. Sharpe, Inc.

Subscription rates: US Institutions $381, Foreign Institutions $421

SOCIAL JUSTICE*

Editor: Gregory Shank

Managing Editor
P.O. Box 40601
San Francisco, CA 94140

ISSN 0094-7571

Purpose: To discuss the world as it really is, while suggesting alternatives that could promote human dignity, equality, and peace, by delving into issues ranging from the causes of crime and conflict to the workings of the world order.

Book reviews: Included; book review editor: Christina Johns

Frequency: Quarterly

SOCIAL PHILOSOPHY AND POLICY

Editor: Ellen Frankel Paul

Social Philosophy & Policy Ctr.
Bowling Green State University
Bowling Green, OH 43403

Tel. 419-372-2536
Fax 419-372-8738

ISSN 0265-0525

Date of founding: 1983

Purpose: Each issue addresses a single topic, examined from an ethical perspective. Eminent thinkers in philosophy, economics, law, political science, and other relevant disciplines apply their special skills in considering the designated topics.

Manuscript info: About 25 philosophy articles are published per year.

Book reviews: Reviews are not included.

Frequency: 2 issues per year

Publisher: Cambridge University Press

Subscription rates: $30; Institutions $75

SOCIAL THEORY AND PRACTICE

Editor: Russell Dancy

Dept. of Philosophy
Florida State University
Tallahassee, FL 32306-1054

Tel. 904-644-0224
Fax 904-644-3832
E-mail journals@mailer.fsu.edu

ISSN 0037-802X

Date of founding: 1970

Purpose: A forum for the discussion of important and controversial issues in social, political, legal, economic, educational, and moral philosophy.

Manuscript info: Approximately 18 articles are published yearly. Manuscripts in social, political, legal, economic, educational, and moral philosophy are preferred. Backlog is 6 months. Manuscript refereeing is anonymous; comments are given to authors. About 20% of manuscripts are accepted; 30% of those require significant revision. The average evaluation time is 4 months. Instructions for manuscript preparation are in the journal. Send manuscripts to the editor.

Book reviews: About 80% of book reviews are invited; unsolicited book reviews are welcome.

Frequency: 3 issues per year; Circulation: 700

Publisher: Dept. of Philosophy, Florida State University

Subscription rates: Individuals $12; Institutions $33; Foreign postage $4

SOUTH ATLANTIC PHILOSOPHY OF EDUCATION SOCIETY YEARBOOK

Editor: Evelyn M. Powers

School of Education
East Carolina University
Greenville, NC 27858

Tel. 919-328-6830

Purpose: To explore philosophical issues related to the study of education.

Sponsor: South Atlantic Philosophy of Education Society

Manuscript info: All articles are devoted to philosophy. Those related to education and dealing with the announced topic are given preference. Manuscripts are refereed blind; unsigned comments are given to authors. About 50% of manuscripts are accepted; a few require significant revision. Average evaluation time is 3 months. About 10% of articles are invited. Manuscripts should be sent to the Program Chair, South Atlantic Philosophy of Education Society.

Book reviews: Book reviews are not included.

Frequency: Annual;
Circulation: 75

Publisher: Evelyn M. Powers
East Carolina University

Subscription rates: $7;
Institutions $10

SOUTHERN JOURNAL OF PHILOSOPHY

Editor: Nancy D. Simco

Dept. of Philosophy
University of Memphis
Memphis, TN 38152-0017

Tel. 901-678-2669
Fax 901-678-4365
E-mail
simcond@msuvxl.memphis.edu

ISSN 0038-4283

Date of founding: 1963

Purpose: To serve as a forum for the expression of philosophical ideas.

Manuscript info: Any area of philosophy is welcome. Backlog is 5 months. Manuscript refereeing is blind if possible; comments are almost always given to the author. Acceptance rate is 5%; 21% require significant revision. Average evaluation time is 5-7 weeks, if 2 copies of the manuscript are sent. No articles are invited. Manuscripts should be sent to the editor.

Book reviews: Book reviews are not included.

Frequency: Quarterly + supplement;
Circulation: 1,250

Publisher: Dept. of Philosophy, Memphis State University

Subscription rates: $20; Students $10; Institutions $30

SOUTHWEST PHILOSOPHY REVIEW

Editor: J. K. Swindler

Department of Philosophy
Wittenberg University
P.O. Box 720
Springfield, OH 45501-0720

Tel. 513-327-7836
Fax 513-327-6340
E-mail swindler@wittenberg.edu

ISSN 0897-2346

Date of founding: 1986

Purpose: To publish the proceedings of the annual meetings of the Southwestern Philosophical Society and other papers of philosophical merit and interest.

Sponsor: The Southwestern Philosophical Society

Manuscript info: About 25-30 philosophy articles are published per year. Manuscripts in any area of philosophy are welcome; preference is given to those with fewer than 30 pages. There is no backlog. Manuscripts are refereed blind; unsigned comments are given to authors. About 20% of manuscripts are accepted; 20% of those accepted require significant revision. Average evaluation time is 2 months. There are no invited articles. Instructions for manuscript preparation are included in the journal. Manuscripts should be sent to the editor.

Book reviews: Unsolicited book reviews are welcome; most are accepted.

Frequency: 2 issues per year;
Circulation: 300

Publisher: Southwestern Philosophical Society and Wittenberg University

Subscription rates: $30 per year individual and institutional; includes membership in Southwestern Philosophical Society

STUDIES IN PHILOSOPHY AND THE HISTORY OF PHILOSOPHY

Editor: Jude P. Dougherty

School of Philosophy
The Catholic Univ. of America
Washington, DC 20064

Tel. 202-319-5259
Fax 202-319-4731

Date of founding: 1960

Purpose: To publish scholarly articles on philosophical subjects and on philosophers, schools, works, and problems in philosophy.

Sponsor: The Catholic University of America

Manuscript info: *Studies in Philosophy and the History of Philosophy* is published as an occasional volume on a theme selected by the general editor. The editor of a specific volume is likewise selected by the general editor. Manuscripts for a specific volume are solicited by the editor of that volume.

Frequency: 1 or 2 volumes per year

Publisher: The Catholic University of America Press

Subscription rates: $35 to $45 (Price varies with volume.)

SYNTHESE: AN INTERNATIONAL JOURNAL FOR EPISTEMOLOGY, METHODOLOGY, AND PHILOSOPHY OF SCIENCE

Editor: Jaakko Hintikka

Dept. of Philosophy
Boston University
745 Commonwealth Ave.
Boston, MA 02215

Tel. 617-353-6806
Fax 617-353-6805

ISSN 0039-7857

Date of founding: 1936

Purpose: An international journal for epistemology, methodology, and philosophy of science; publishes articles in all fields covered by the subtitle.

Manuscript info: All articles are devoted to philosophy. Manuscripts in epistemology, methodology, and philosophy of science are preferred. Manuscripts are refereed blind; unsigned comments usually are given to authors. Evaluation time averages 4 months. Instructions for manuscript preparation are included in the journal. Manuscripts should be sent to the journal.

Book reviews: Book reviews are included. Please contact the review editor, Paul Humphreys, University of Virginia.

Frequency: Monthly

Publisher: Kluwer Academic Publishers

Subscription rates: Institutions: vol. Dfl 306, $191.50; yearly Dfl 1,224, $766

TEACHING PHILOSOPHY

Editor: Michael Goldman

Department of Philosophy
Hall Auditorium
Miami University
Oxford, OH 45056

Tel. 513-529-2427
Fax 513-529-4731
E-mail goldmam@muohio.edu

ISSN 0145-5788

Date of founding: 1975

Purpose: To explore ideas about teaching and learning philosophy by publishing articles on aims of philosophy education, new courses, methods, materials and their impact on philosophy. Textbook and audio-visual reviews are regular features.

Manuscript info: About 24 philosophy articles are published per year. Manuscripts dealing with teaching and philosophy education are preferred. Backlog is 4 months. Manuscript refereeing is blind; comments are usually given to authors. About 15% of manuscripts are accepted; 50% require significant revision. The average evaluation time is 2 months. No articles are invited. Instructions for manuscript preparation are in the journal. Manuscripts should be sent to the editor.

Book reviews: About 95% of all book reviews are invited by the book review editor, Shannon Sullivan, Miami University; the editor prefers query.

Frequency: Quarterly;
Circulation: 1,200

Publisher: Philosophy Documentation Center

Subscription rates: $26;
Institutions $63; outside US add $4.

TECHNOLOGY AND CULTURE

Editor: John Standenmaier

Henry Ford Museum
P.O. Box 1970
Dearborn, MI 48121

Tel. 313-271-1620 Ext. 402
Fax 313-271-3630
E-mail jmpschultz@aol.com

ISSN 0040-165X

Date of founding: 1959

Purpose: To study the development
of technology and its relations with
society and culture.

Sponsor: Society for the History of
Technology

Manuscript info: Manuscripts in
philosophy of technology are welcome. Manuscript refereeing is blind;
comments are given to authors.
About 30% of manuscripts are accepted; 90% require significant revision.
The average evaluation time is 12-16
weeks. Instructions for manuscript
preparation are in the journal. Three
copies of the manuscript should be
sent to the editor.

Book reviews: Almost all book
reviews are invited.

Frequency: Quarterly;
Circulation: 3,000

Publisher: University of Chicago
Press

Subscription rates: $32;
Institutions $71

TELOS: A QUARTERLY JOURNAL OF CRITICAL THOUGHT*

Editor: Paul Piccone
431 E. 12th St.
New York, NY 10009

Tel. 212-228-6479
Fax 212-228-6379

Date of founding: 1968

Purpose: To address philosophical
problems in radical social and political theory.

Manuscript info: Twenty philosophical articles per year. Manuscripts on
radical social and political philosophy,
existentialism, continental philosophy,
and critical theory are preferred.
Manuscript refereeing is blind, and
the referees' unsigned comments are
given to authors. About 10% of manuscripts are accepted; almost all require
significant revision. The average evaluation time is 6 months. No articles
are invited. Brief instructions for manuscript preparation are in the journal.
Send manuscripts to the editor.

Book reviews: About 70% of the
book reviews are invited; unsolicited
book reviews are welcome.

Frequency: Quarterly;
Circulation: 3,000

Publisher: Telos Press

Subscription rates: $30;
Institutions $75, Foreign add 15%.

THINKING: THE JOURNAL OF PHILOSOPHY FOR CHILDREN*

Editor: Matthew Lipman

40 Park St.
Montclair, NJ 07042

Tel. 201-893-4277

145

Fax 201-893-5455

ISSN 0190-3330

Date of founding: 1979

Purpose: To publish scholarly articles relevant to philosophy for children, as well as reports of experimental research, news from school districts using philosophy in their classrooms, and statements by educators who have taught children or teachers.

Manuscript info: About 10% to 20 philosophy articles yearly. Only manuscripts relevant to philosophy of children and learning welcome; those on reports of classroom and experimental use, theoretical papers, and reflective education preferred. Backlog of 6-12 months. Manuscripts are not refereed. Acceptance rate is 30%. Invitation rate is 75-90%. Instructions for manuscript preparation upon request. Manuscripts should be sent to *Thinking*, IAPC, Montclair State College, Upper Monclair, NJ 07043.

Frequency: Quarterly; Circulation: 650

Publisher: IAPC, Montclair State College; Subscription agent: Philosophy Documentation Center

Subscription rates: $25; Institutions $40

THOMIST

Editor: J. A. DiNoia

487 Michigan Avenue, NE
Washington, DC 20017

Tel. 202-529-5300
Fax 202-636-4460

ISSN 0040-6325

Date of founding: 1939

Purpose: To clarify and foster contemporary relevance of Thomistic thought.

Manuscript info: About 40-50% of articles per year are philosophical. Manuscripts are welcome in any area of Thomistic philosophy; those with the thought of St. Thomas are preferred. Backlog is 6 months. Acceptance rate is 12%; 30% require significant revision. The average evaluation time is 6 months. About 20% of articles are invited. Instructions for manuscript preparation are in the journal. Manuscripts should be sent to the editor.

Book reviews: Almost all book reviews are invited; unsolicited book reviews are welcome.

Frequency: Quarterly; Circulation: 1,050

Publisher: Thomist Press

Subscription rates: $25; Institutions $45; Foreign $35

TOPOI

Editor: Ermanno Bencivenga

Dept. of Philosophy
University of California
Irvine, CA 92717

Tel. 714-824-6527
Fax 714-824-2379
E-mail ebencive@uci.edu

Date of founding: 1982

Purpose: To publish high-quality articles in all areas of philosophy. Each issue is devoted to a specific topic.

Manuscript info: Manuscripts in any area of philosophy are welcome. Backlog is 2 years. Manuscript refereeing is blind; unsigned comments are given to the authors when useful. About 5% of manuscripts are accepted. About 50% of accepted manuscripts require significant revision. The average time to evaluate a manuscript is 2 months. About 80% of the articles are invited. Manuscript instructions are in the journal. Manuscripts should be sent to the editor.

Book reviews: All reviews are invited; unsolicited reviews are not welcome.

Frequency: Biannual; Circulation: 200

Publisher: Kluwer Academic Publishers

Subscription rates: $180

TRADITIO: STUDIES IN ANCIENT AND MEDIEVAL HISTORY, THOUGHT, AND RELIGION

Editor: Elizabeth Parker

c/o Fordham University Press
University Box L
Bronx, NY 10458-5172

Tel. 718-817-4780
Fax 718-817-4785

Date of founding: 1943

Manuscript info: About 2-3 philosophy articles are published per year. Manuscripts intended for publication should be submitted between the beginning of January and the beginning of July and may be sent to the editor: Elizabeth Parker, Arts Dept., Fordham University, Lincoln Center, 432-B, New York, NY 10023.

Frequency: Annual; Circulation: 1,000

Publisher: Fordham University Press

Subscription rates: $52

TRANSACTIONS OF THE CHARLES S. PEIRCE SOCIETY: A QUARTERLY JOURNAL IN AMERICAN PHILOSOPHY

Editor: Peter H. Hare

Philosophy Dept.
Baldy Hall
SUNY Buffalo
Buffalo, NY 14260

Tel. 716-645-2444
Fax 716-645-3825

ISSN 0009-1774

Date of founding: 1965

Purpose: Publication of scholarly articles and reviews concerning the philosophy of Charles S. Peirce and other American philosophers.

Sponsor: Charles S. Peirce Society

Manuscript info: About 25 philosophy articles are published per year. Manuscripts on Peirce and other American philosophers, but not on American philosophers still living, are welcome. Backlog is more than 12 months. Manuscript refereeing is not blind; comments are usually given to authors. Acceptance rate is 20-30%; 50% require significant revision. Average evaluation time is 2-3 months. About 10% of articles are invited. Manuscripts concerned with Peirce should be sent to Richard Robin, others to Peter Hare.

Book reviews: All book reviews are invited.

Frequency: Quarterly;
Circulation: 500

Subscription rates: $35;
Institutions $60

VERA LEX: AN INTERNATIONAL REVIEW ON A GLOBAL ISSUE

Editor: Virginia Black

Philosophy & Religious Studies
Pace University
Pleasantville, NY 10570-2799

Tel. 914-773-3309
Fax 914-773-3541

ISSN 0893-4851

Date of founding: 1979

Purpose: To communicate and dialogue on the subject of natural law and natural right, to clarify its supporting ideas, and to strengthen the current interest in the discussion of morals and law and advance its historical research.

Sponsor: Pace University: The Dyson College of Arts and Sciences

Manuscript info: About 15 philosophy articles are published yearly. Articles must demonstrate some relationship to the ethics of natural law or positive law; timely articles are given preference. Backlog is 2 years. Most manuscripts are refereed blind; comments are not given to authors. About 90% of manuscripts are accepted; 20% require significant revision. Evaluation time ranges from 1 week to 2 months. About 50% of articles are invited. Instructions for manuscript preparation are in the journal; send manuscripts to the editor.

Book reviews: About 70% of book reviews are invited; unsolicited book reviews are welcome.

Frequency: 2 issues per year;
Circulation: 350

Publisher: Pace University

Subscription rates: $15;
Institutions $30

ZYGON: JOURNAL OF RELIGION AND SCIENCE

Editor: Philip Hefner

Chicago Ctr. for Relig. and Sci.
1100 E. 55th St.
Chicago, IL 60615-5199

Tel. 312-753-0671
Fax 312-753-0682

ISSN 0591-2385

Date of founding: 1966

Purpose: To provide a forum for scholarly papers by natural and social scientists, philosophers, and religious thinkers who attempt to integrate contemporary scientific knowledge and basic human values.

Sponsor: Joint Publication Board of *Zygon*

Manuscript info: Articles in philosophy of biology, epistemology in religion and science, and naturalistic metaethics are preferred, especially if contemporary scientific theory is applied to human values, moral motivation, and religion. Manuscript refereeing is blind; comments are available. Acceptance rate is 20%; 30% require significant revision. Average evaluation time is 12 months. About 50% of articles are based on planned conferences. Instructions for manuscripts are in the journal. Send to the editor.

Book reviews: About 95% of book reviews are invited. Unsolicited book reviews are sometimes accepted.

Frequency: Quarterly; Circulation: 2,100

Publisher: Joint Publication Board of *Zygon*, c/o Editors, Chicago Center for Religion and Science

Subscription rates: Individuals $39.50; Institutions $62.50; Students (when verified by professor) $29. Send payment and inquiries to Blackwell Publishers, 350 Main Street, Malden, MA 02148.

JOURNALS: CANADIAN

APEIRON: A JOURNAL FOR ANCIENT PHILOSOPHY AND SCIENCE

Editor: Roger A. Shiner

Dept. of Philosophy
4-108 Humanities Centre
University of Alberta
Edmonton, AB T6G 2E5

Tel. 403-492-3307
Fax 403-492-9160
E-mail rshiner@gpu.srv.ualberta.ca

ISSN 0003-6390

Date of founding: 1966

Purpose: To publish high-quality interpretive, philosophical, and textual scholarship in ancient philosophy and science.

Manuscript info: All articles are devoted to philosophy. Manuscripts in ancient philosophy and science are preferred. Backlog is 6 months. Manuscripts are refereed blind; unsigned comments are given to authors. About 10% of manuscripts are accepted; 30% require significant revision. Average evaluation time is 3-4 months. About 25% of articles are invited. Instructions for manuscript preparation are included in the journal. Manuscripts should be sent to the editor.

Book reviews: Very few book reviews are published, and all are invited.

Frequency: Quarterly; Circulation: 350

Publisher: Academic Printing and Publishing

Subscription rates: Canadian $42, Non-Canadian $65, US $47; Institutions: Canadian $78, Non-Canadian $103, US $78

BIBLIOGRAPHIE DE LA PHILOSOPHIE/BIBLIOGRAPHY OF PHILOSOPHY

Editor: R. Klibansky

Director, Department of Philosophy
McGill University
855 Sherbrooke St. West
Montréal, PQ H3A 2T7

Tel. 514-398-6060

ISSN 0006-1352

Date of founding: 1937

Purpose: Recension de la production philosophique mondiale.

Sponsor: Institut International de Philosophie, 8 rue Jean-Calvin, 75005 Paris, France

Manuscript info: About 1,500 abstracts of books per year are devoted to philosophy. Manuscripts in any area of philosophy are welcome, but the manuscripts must be book descriptions. Backlog of accepted articles is about 3 months. Manuscripts are refereed (not blind). About 99% percent of articles are accepted; 30% require significant revision. Average time to publish a manuscript is 15 months. Instructions for manuscript preparation are sent to each new bibliographical center.

Book reviews: Only book descriptions are included. All book descriptions must come through the national center established in each country. Unsolicited book descriptions are not welcome.

Frequency: Quarterly; Circulation: 943

Publisher: Librarie Philosophique J. Vrin, 6 place de la Sorbonne, 75006 Paris, France

Subscription rates: $65; Institutions $53; Single copies $20; Required currency is dollars.

BIOLOGY AND PHILOSOPHY

Editor: Michael Ruse

Department of Philosophy
University of Guelph
Guelph, ON N1G 2W1

Tel. 519-824-4120 Ext. 3232
Fax 519-837-8634
E-mail mruse@arts.uoguelph.ca

ISSN 0169-3867

Date of founding: 1986

Purpose: To promote the interaction between biology and philosophy.

Manuscript info: All articles are devoted to philosophy. Manuscripts

in the area of philosophy of biology are preferred. Backlog is 6 months. Manuscripts are refereed, but not blind; unsigned comments are given to authors. About 20% of manuscripts are accepted; 80% require significant revision. Evaluation time averages 3 months. No articles are invited. Instructions for manuscript preparation are included in the journal. Manuscripts should be sent to the editor.

Book reviews: All book reviews are invited; unsolicited book reviews are welcome.

Frequency: Quarterly; Circulation: 600

Publisher: Kluwer Academic Publishers, P.O. Box 17, 3300 AA Dordrecht, The Netherlands

Subscription rates: $43; Institutions $200

CANADIAN JOURNAL OF PHILOSOPHY

CJP Editorial Office

Dept. of Philosophy
University of Lethbridge
Lethbridge, AB T1K 3M4

Tel. 403-329-2545
Fax 403-329-5109

ISSN 0045-5091

Date of founding: 1971

Purpose: To publish, in English or French, works in any field of philosophy.

Manuscript info: About 40 philosophy articles are published each year. Manuscripts are welcome in any area of philosophy. Backlog is 18 months. Manuscripts that stand a reasonable chance of being accepted are refereed. The refereeing is blind; unsigned comments are given to authors when helpful. About 10% of unsolicited manuscripts are accepted; 40% require significant revision. The average evaluation time is 4 months. About 5% of articles are invited. Instructions for manuscript preparation are included in the journal. Send manuscripts to Anne Williams, University of Lethbridge.

Book reviews: Longer critical notices are published, not book reviews; most critical notices are invited; unsolicited critical notices are not usually published.

Frequency: Quarterly; Circulation: 1,150

Publisher: University of Calgary Press

Subscription rates: $25; Students $15; Institutions $40; Single issues $9. A joint subscription to the *CJP* and the *Australasian Journal of Philosophy* is available to individuals at $40/year, students $25.

CANADIAN PHILOSOPHICAL REVIEWS

Editors: Roger A. Shiner & Andrew Light

Dept. of Philosophy
4-108 Human Center
University of Alberta
Edmonton, AB T6G 2E5

Tel. 403-492-3307
Fax 403-492-9160
E-mail cprs@ualtamts.bitnet

ISSN 0228-491X

Date of founding: 1981

Purpose: To provide an up-to-date and comprehensive reviewing service of books in philosophy and related fields of interest to philosophers.

Manuscript info: Almost all articles are invited; all are reviews of books. Manuscripts under 1,000 words are preferred. Backlog is 4 months. Manuscripts are refereed by the editor; comments are given to authors if applicable. About 90% of manuscripts are accepted; 10% require significant revision. Evaluation time averages 3-4 weeks. Manuscripts should be sent to the editor.

Frequency: 6 issues per year; Circulation: 275

Publisher: Academic Printing and Publishing

Subscription rates: Per volume: Institutions: $95 (Canadian), $93 (US); Individuals: $45 (Canadian), $48 (US); Students: $34 (Canadian), $33 (US)

151

CARLETON UNIVERSITY STUDENT JOURNAL OF PHILOSOPHY

Editor: Dept. of Philosophy

Carleton University
Ottawa, ON K1S 5B6

Tel. 613-788-2110

Date of founding: 1974

Purpose: To encourage individual, original research on topics of philosophical interest; to make available to the academic community high-level research by students.

Manuscript info: About 4-8 philosophy articles are published per year. Manuscripts are welcome in any area of philosophy. Backlog of accepted articles is 5-6 months; manuscripts are refereed. The refereeing is blind. About 75% percent of manuscripts are accepted; 10% of accepted manuscripts require significant revisions. The percentage of invited articles varies. Instructions for manuscript preparation are included in the journal. Manuscripts should be sent to the editor.

Book reviews: The number of invited book reviews varies; unsolicited book reviews are welcome.

Frequency: 2 issues per year; Circulation: 150

Publisher: Dept. of Philosophy, Carleton University

Subscription rates: No subscription fee

CARREFOUR

Dept. of Philosophy
University of Ottawa
Ottawa, ON K1N 6N5

Tel. 613-564-2294
Fax 613-564-7668

ISSN 0706-1250

Date of founding: 1979

Purpose: To provide an interdisciplinary forum for the discussion of problems that beset modernity. The journal remains, however, predominantly philosophical in orientation.

Sponsor: Société de philosophie de l'Outaouais; Department of Philosophy, University of Ottawa

Manuscript info: Most articles are devoted to philosophy. Manuscripts in any area of philosophy are welcome.

Manuscripts are refereed blind. About 50% of manuscripts are accepted; 75% require significant revision. About 90% of articles are invited. Instructions for manuscript preparation are included in the journal. Manuscripts should be sent to the Société de philosophie de l'Outaouais, 65 Université privé, Dept. de philosophie, Université d'Ottawa, Ottawa, Ontario, Canada K1N 6N5.

Book reviews: Reviews are not included.

Frequency: 2 issues per year; Circulation: 250

Publisher: Éditions Legas, CP 162 Stn. A, Ottawa, Ontario K1N 8T9

Subscription rates: Canada: Institutions $45, Individuals $20, Students $10; Outside Canada: Institutions $50, Individuals $25

DE PHILOSOPHIA

Editor: Justin Legault

Dept. of Philosophy
University of Ottawa
Ottawa, ON K1N 6N5

Tel. 613-564-2294
Fax 613-564-5952

ISSN 0228-412X

Date of founding: 1980

Purpose: To provide a forum for University of Ottawa students to have work of philosophical merit critiqued and published. Submissions from students anywhere are very welcome.

Sponsor: Student Association of the Department of Philosophy, University of Ottawa

Manuscript info: About 5-8 articles per year are devoted to philosophy. Manuscripts in any area of philosophy are welcome; graduate student manuscripts are preferred. Articles must be in French or English. Manuscripts are refereed blind; comments are not given to authors unless the manuscript is accepted for publication. About 75% of manuscripts are accepted; 25% require significant revision. Evaluation time averages 6 weeks. About 20% of articles are invited. Manuscripts should be sent to the editor.

Book reviews: Included. Unsolicited book reviews are welcome.

Frequency: Annual; Circulation: 200

Publisher: Philosophy Students' Association, Department of Philosophy, University of Ottawa

---

DIALOGUE

Editor: Steven Davis

Anglophone Ed.
Dialogue
EAA 2024
Simon Fraser University
Burnaby, BC V5A 1S6

Tel. 604-291-4979
Fax 604-291-4443
E-mail dialogue@sfu.ca

ISSN 0012-2173

Date of founding: 1962

Purpose: To publish scholarly articles, interventions, critical notices, and book reviews in philosophy in French and English.

Sponsor: Canadian Philosophical Association

Manuscript info: About 25 philosophy articles are published yearly. Papers in any area of philosophy are welcome. Backlog is 6-18 months. Manuscripts are refereed blind; referees' comments, which are signed only if the referee wishes, are given to authors. About 10% of manuscripts are accepted; average evaluation time is 3-4 months. English language manuscripts should be sent to the Anglophone editor, French language manuscripts to the Francophone editor: Claude Panaccio, Dept. de Philosophie, Universite du Québec a Trois-Rivieres, Québec G9A 5H7.

Book reviews: About 95% of book reviews are invited; unsolicited book reviews are welcome.

Frequency: Quarterly; Circulation: 1,500

Publisher: Wilfrid Laurier University Press for the Canadian Philosophical Association

Subscription rates: Membership: Ordinary and Associate $75; Joint $85; Retired $45; Student $17; Foreign individual subscriptions $45; Separate issues $15; Institutional subscriptions: Canadian $70; Foreign $75

EIDOS: THE CANADIAN GRADUATE JOURNAL OF PHILOSOPHY

Editor: Jason West

Dept. of Philosophy
University of Waterloo
Waterloo, ON N2L 3G1

Tel. 519-885-1211 Ext. 3809
Fax 519-746-3097
E-mail
eidos@artspas.watstar.uwaterloo.ca

ISSN 0707-2287

Date of founding: 1977

Purpose: To provide a bilingual channel for the publication of high-quality articles by graduate students in Canada and abroad.

Manuscript info: About 12-15 philosophy articles per year. Each issue of the journal is devoted to a specific theme and contains 2 special sections: Philosophy in Canada and Developing Themes. These sections are solicited. Otherwise, all manuscripts are refereed blind, and the referees' unsigned comments are given to the authors. About 30% of manuscripts are accepted; 90% require significant revision. Average evaluation time is 6 months. About 40% of articles are invited.

Book reviews: The number of invited book reviews varies; unsolicited reviews are welcome.

154

Frequency: Biannual;
Circulation: 180

Publisher: University of Waterloo Philosophy Graduate Student Association, Dept. of Philosophy, University of Waterloo

Subscription rates: $18; Institutions $35; Students $9 (Canadian funds)

ETHICA

Editor: Groupe de recherche Ethos

Univ. du Québec à Rimouski
300, allée des Ursulines
Rimouski, PQ G5L 3A1

Tel. 418-724-1784
Fax 418-724-1851

ISSN 0840-9935

Date of founding: 1989

Purpose: *Ethica* is an interdisciplinary journal that aims to facilitate exchanges between specialists of different scientific disciplines about the important ethics issues of our contemporary society.

Manuscript info: Twelve articles per year are devoted to philosophy. Manuscripts in ethics are preferred. There is no backlog. Manuscripts are refereed blind; unsigned comments are given to authors. About 90% of manuscripts are accepted; 5% require significant revision. Evaluation time averages 2 months. About 50% of articles are invited. Instructions for manuscript preparation are included in the journal. Manuscripts should be sent to the journal. Published mainly in French, only one-third of articles are in English.

Book reviews: Included; 90% are invited. Unsolicited book reviews are welcome.

Frequency: 2 issues per year

Publisher: Groupe de recherche Ethos

Subscription rates: $21.50;
Institutions $30; Students $16

GNOSIS: A JOURNAL OF PHILOSOPHIC INTEREST

Editor: Kenneth Todd

Dept. of Philosophy PR-202
Concordia University
1455 de Maisonneuve Blvd. West
Montréal, PQ H3G 1M8

Tel. 514-848-2500
Fax 514-848-3494

ISSN 0316-618X

Date of founding: 1973

Purpose: To publish work on philosophical topics by students, as well as professional philosophers and scholars.

Sponsor: Concordia University

Manuscript info: About 8-10 philosophy articles are published per year. Manuscripts are welcome in any area of philosophy. Backlog of accepted articles is 10 months. Refereeing is blind. About 50% of manuscripts are accepted; 5% require significant revision. Instructions for manuscripts are included in the journal. Manuscripts should be sent to the editor.

Book reviews: Unsolicited book reviews are welcome.

Frequency: Annual; Circulation: 150

Publisher: Concordia University

Subscription rates: $3; Institutions $5; Students $2. Prices subject to change without notice.

HORIZONS PHILOSOPHIQUES

Editor: Renée Asselin, Secretary

Collége Edouard-Montpetit
945 chemin de Chambly
Longueuil, PQ J4H 3M6

Tel. 514-679-2630 Ext. 487
Fax 514-677-2945

ISSN 1181-9227

Date of founding: 1979

Manuscript info: About 18 philosophy articles are published yearly. Manuscripts in any area of philosophy are welcome. Manuscripts are not refereed. About 80% of manuscripts are accepted; all require significant revision. Average evaluation time is 6-9 months. (We evaluate manuscripts twice a year, in June and in December.) Instructions for manuscript preparation are included in the journal. Manuscripts should be sent to Renée Asselin at the address listed.

Book reviews: Unsolicited book reviews are welcome.

Frequency: 2 issues per year; Circulation: 300

Publisher: Renée Asselin

Subscription rates: $16; Institutions $24; Students $14; add $4 postage.

HUMANIST IN CANADA

P.O. Box 3769
Station C
Ottawa, ON K1Y 4J8

Tel. 613-722-4652

ISSN 0018-7402

Date of founding: 1967

Purpose: To feature all aspects of modern humanism as a living philosophy, its history, development, critiques, influence, and role as basis of an international movement.

Manuscript info: About 12 philosophy articles are published per year. Manuscripts, of no more than 3,000 words, aimed at the intelligent layman are preferred. The backlog of accepted articles is 3 months. About 40-50% of manuscripts are accepted. The average time required to evaluate a manuscript is 2-4 months. About 10-20% of articles are invited. Instructions for manuscript preparation are available from the editor. Manuscripts should be sent to the editor.

Book reviews: About 10-20% of book reviews are invited; unsolicited book reviews are welcome.

Frequency: Quarterly; Circulation: 2,200

Publisher: Canadian Humanist Publications, Inc.

Subscription rates: $15 Canadian per year; $19 Canadian outside Canada, US $16 in US

INFORMAL LOGIC: REASONING AND ARGUMENTATION IN THEORY AND PRACTICE

Editors: A. Blair & R. Johnson

Department of Philosophy
University of Windsor
Windsor, ON N9B 3P4

Tel. 519-253-4232 Ext. 2332
Fax 519-973-7050
E-mail infolog@uwindsor.ca

ISSN 0824-2577

Date of founding: 1978

Purpose: To foster theory and good practice in informal logic and critical thinking from the perspectives of philosophy, rhetoric, speech communication, cognitive psychology, etc.

Sponsor: University of Windsor

Manuscript info: Approximately 12 articles are published per year. Manuscripts in informal logic, critical thinking, and all related fields of inquiry are welcome. Backlog of 9-12 months; manuscripts are blind refereed; unsigned comments are given to authors. One-third of manuscripts are accepted; 50% require significant revision. The average evaluation time is 4 months. About 15% of articles are

invited. Instructions for manuscript preparation are included in the journal; send all manuscripts to the editors at address listed. Managing editor: Mark Letteri.

Book reviews: Most book reviews are invited; unsolicited book reviews are welcome. Book review editor: Jonathan E. Adler.

Frequency: 3 issues per year; Circulation: 300

Publisher: J. Anthony Blair & Ralph H. Johnson

Subscription rates: Vol. 17 (1995): $30 CDN and US; Institutions $50 CDN and US. Outside Canada and US: $33, Institutions $55 US. Students $15 CDN and US. Rates include all applicable taxes and postal charges (surface mail).

JOURNAL OF AGRICULTURAL AND ENVIRONMENTAL ETHICS

Editors: Hugh Lehman & Frank Hurnik

Room 039 MacKinnon Building
University of Guelph
Guelph, ON N1G 2W1

Tel. 519-824-4120 Ext. 6925
Fax 519-837-9953
E-mail rvanderk@uoguelph.ca

ISSN 0893-4282

Date of founding: 1988

Purpose: To create a forum for discussion of moral issues arising from actual or projected social policies in regard to a range of questions relating to environmental concerns such as agricultural production, utilization of resources, animal welfare, etc.

Manuscript info: Preference is given to manuscripts in ethics related to agriculture and the environment. Manuscripts are refereed, blind if requested; unsigned comments are given to authors. About 30-40% of manuscripts are accepted; 50% require significant revision. Average evaluation time is 3 months. About 5-10% of articles are invited. Manuscript preparation instructions are included in the journal. Manuscripts should be sent to the editors.

Book reviews: Book reviews are included. Unsolicited book reviews are welcome.

Frequency: 2 issues per year; Circulation: 230

Publisher: Journal of Agricultural and Environmental Ethics, University of Guelph

Subscription rates: Within Canada: Individuals $35, Institutions $45, Students $18. Outside Canada: Individuals $38, Institutions $48, Students $21

JOURNAL OF BUSINESS ETHICS

Editor: Alex Michalos

Management & Administration
Univ. of Northern Brit. Columbia
3333 University Way
Prince George, BC V2N 4Z9

Tel. 604-960-6697
Fax 604-960-5544
E-mail michalos@unbc.edu

ISSN 0167-4544

Date of founding: 1981

Purpose: To provide a forum for discussion of ethical issues in business.

Manuscript info: About 30% of articles per year are devoted to philosophy. Manuscripts must be tied to business ethics at some level. Backlog is 18 months; manuscripts are refereed; the refereeing is blind. Authors are given unsigned comments. About 30% acceptance rate; about 40% require significant revision; the average evaluation time is 16 weeks. Instructions for manuscript preparation are included in the journal. Manuscripts should be sent to the editor.

Book reviews: About 90% are invited; unsolicited book reviews are welcome.

Frequency: 12 issues per year; Circulation: 1,100

Publisher: Kluwer Academic Publishers

Subscription rates: Private $139; Institutions $301, including postage; Society for Business Ethics $67

JOURNAL OF INDIAN PHILOSOPHY*

Editor: Phyllis Granoff

Dept. of Religious Studies
McMaster University
Hamilton, ON L8S 4K1

ISSN 0022-1791

Date of founding: 1970

Purpose: To facilitate study and research in Indian and comparative philosophy, with special emphasis upon history of logic, epistemology and philosophy of language.

Manuscript info: All articles are devoted to philosophy. Manuscripts in the areas of Indian philosophy and Indian comparative philosophy are preferred. Manuscripts based on direct acquaintance or original texts are given preference. Backlog is 12 months. Manuscripts are refereed blind; unsigned comments are given to authors. About 50% of manuscripts are accepted; 20% require significant revision. Evaluation time averages 3 months. Instructions for manuscript preparation are included in the journal.

Frequency: Quarterly; Circulation: 400

Publisher: Kluwer Academic Publishers, P.O. Box 17, 3300 AA Dordrecht, The Netherlands

Subscription rates: 105 Dfl, Institutions 256 Dfl; Postage included; required currency is Dfl or US.

LAVAL THÉOLOGIQUE ET PHILOSOPHIQUE

Editor: Les Facultés de Phil. & Theol.

Pavillon Félix-Antoine-Savard
Université Laval
Ste-Foy, PQ G1K 7P4

Tel. 418-656-7823
Fax 418-656-7267

ISSN 0023-9054

Date of founding: 1945

Purpose: The diffusion of knowledge in philosophy and theology.

Manuscript info: About 15 philosophy articles are published per year. Any area of philosophy is welcome; preference is given to erudite studies that genuinely advance knowledge. Backlog is 12 months. Manuscripts are refereed. The refereeing is blind. About 30% acceptance rate; 15% of accepted manuscripts require significant revisions. The average evaluation time is 6 months. About 20% of

articles are invited. Instructions are available from the editor.

Book reviews: About 90% of the book reviews are invited; unsolicited book reviews are welcome.

Frequency: 3 issues per year; Circulation: 800

Publisher: Les Facultés de Philosophie et de Théologie de l'Université Laval

Subscription rates: New rate: $25; Institutions $32

LEKTON*

Editor: Denis Fisette

Dept. de Philosophie
Univ. du Québec a Montréal,
BP 8888 Succ "A"
Montréal, PQ H3C 3P8

Tel. 514-987-3252
Fax 514-987-4644

ISSN 1180-2308

Date of founding: 1989

Purpose: Thématique. Consacré à un auteur ou à une problematique contemporaine. Interdisciplinaire mais à dominante philosophique et théorique. Echanges et débats entre chercheurs interuniversitaires.

Sponsor: Département de philosophie/Comité des Publications de l'UQAM

Manuscript info: About 12 philosophy articles per year. Manuscripts in any area of philosophy are welcome. Manuscripts are refereed blind; signed comments are given to authors. About 70% of manuscripts are accepted; 10% require significant revision. Average evaluation time is 3 weeks. About 10% of articles are invited.

Book reviews: Book reviews are not included.

Frequency: 2 issues per year; Circulation: 200

Publisher: Presses de l'Université du Québec

Subscription rates: $17; Institutions $25; Students $12; add $2 postage (Canadian funds)

MARITAIN STUDIES - ÉTUDES MARITAINIENNES

Editor: William Sweet

Dept. of Philosophy
St. Francis Xavier University
P.O. Box 5000
Antigonish, NS B2G 2W5

Tel. 902-867-2341
Fax 902-867-2448
E-mail wsweet@stfx.ca

ISSN 0826-9920

Date of founding: 1984

Purpose: To publish studies of major authors and themes in philosophy, particularly those found in the work of Jacques Maritain. Articles may be written in French or English.

Sponsor: Canadian Jacques Maritain Association - l'association canadienne Jacques-Maritain

Manuscript info: Manuscripts in any area of philosophy are welcome. Backlog of accepted articles is 6-12 months. Manuscripts are refereed blind; referees' unsigned comments are given to authors. Evaluation time

averages 3 months. About 75% of articles are invited.

Book reviews: Reviews are included; 50% are invited. Unsolicited book reviews are welcome.

Frequency: Annual; Circulation: 150

Publisher: Canadian Jacques Maritain Association

Subscription rates: Individuals $20; Students $10; Institutions $40; required currency is Canadian or equivalent.

MEDIAEVAL STUDIES

Editor: Jonathan Black

Pontifical Inst. of Med. Studies
59 Queen's Park Crescent East
Toronto, ON M5S 2C4

Tel. 416-926-1300 Ext. 3287
Fax 416-926-7258

ISSN 0076-5872

Date of founding: 1939

Purpose: To publish research on the Middle Ages; to publish medieval texts; to provide an organ for publication of such research lest these endeavors be wasted through unavailability.

Manuscript info: About 3 philosophy articles are published per year. Manuscripts given preference are those in medieval philosophy, or ancient and Renaissance philosophy that deal with hitherto unedited material (analysis and/or edition) and those based on a strong doctrinal argument. Manuscripts should be sent to the managing editor. Submit 3 doublespaced copies.

Frequency: Annual;
Circulation: 1,000

Publisher: Pontifical Institute of Mediaeval Studies

Subscription rates: $55 annually

PAIDEUSIS

Editor: William Hare

Department of Education
Dalhousie University
Halifax, NS B3H 3J5

E-mail whare@ac.dal.ca

ISSN 0838-4517

Date of founding: 1986

Purpose: To facilitate communication and interaction among philosophers of education in Canada.

Sponsor: Canadian Philosophy of Education Society

Manuscript info: About 6-8 articles per year are devoted to philosophy. Preference is given to manuscripts in philosophy of education. There is no backlog of accepted articles. Manuscripts are refereed blind. Referees' comments are given to authors (signature is optional). About 75% of manuscripts are accepted. Evaluation time averages 1 month. About 40% of articles are invited. Instructions for manuscript preparation are included in the journal. Manuscripts should be sent to the editor. Managing editor: Don Cochrane, Sub Post Office 6, Saskatoon, SK S7N OX1, Canada.

Book reviews: Reviews are included; 25% are invited. Unsolicited book reviews are welcome.

Frequency: 2 issues per year; Circulation: 120

Subscription rates: $8 Individuals; $12 Institutions; Canadian or American currency

PHILOSOPHIA MATHEMATICA

Editor: Robert Thomas

Dept. of Applied Mathematics
University of Manitoba
Winnipeg, MB R3T 2N2

Tel. 204-474-8126
Fax 204-275-0019
E-mail thomas@cc.umanitoba.ca

ISSN 0031-8019

Date of founding: 1964

Purpose: To disseminate new work in philosophy of pure and applied mathematics, including computing.

Sponsor: Canadian Society for History and Philosophy of Mathematics

Manuscript info: Papers of all lengths are accepted, in English or French. Manuscripts are refereed; signed reports are preferred. Instructions for manuscript preparation are in the journal. Articles are invited for special issues on selected topics. Manuscripts should be sent to the editor.

Book reviews: Only solicited reviews are welcome.

Frequency: 3 issues per year; Circulation: 200

Publisher: Distributed by University of Toronto Press

Subscription rates: Institutions $60; Individuals $29

PHILOSOPHIQUES

Editor: Josiane Ayoub

Dept. de Philosophie
Univ. du Québec à Montréal
CP 8888, Succ. Centre-Ville
Montréal, PQ H3C 3P8

Tel. 514-987-3252
Fax 514-987-6721
E-mail r14410@er.uqam.ca

ISSN 0316-2923

Date of founding: 1974

Purpose: To publish good papers in philosophy, with openness to all domains and schools of philosophy.

Sponsor: Société de Philosophie du Québec

Manuscript info: Twenty philosophy articles are published per year. Manuscripts are welcome in any area of philosophy; international quality is preferred. Language is French; translations are accepted. Backlog is 12 months. Manuscripts are refereed blind. Referees' comments, which are unsigned except when the referee asks that his or her name be given to author, are given to authors. About 50% of manuscripts are accepted; 50% of accepted manuscripts require significant revision. The average evaluation time is 3 months.

Book reviews: About 90% of the book reviews are invited; unsolicited book reviews are welcome. Preference is given to reviews of books written in French.

Frequency: Semi-annual;
Circulation: 800

Publisher: Editions Bellarmin

Subscription rates: By issue: $25, Students $25, Institutions $75; by subscription (2 issues): $50, Students $25, Institutions $75

PHILOSOPHY OF THE SOCIAL SCIENCES

Editor: I. C. Jarvie

Dept. of Philosophy
York University
4700 Keele St.
North York, ON M3J 1P3

Tel. 416-736-5113
Fax 416-736-5114
E-mail icj@nexus.yorku.ca

ISSN 0048-3931

Date of founding: 1971

Purpose: To publish scholarly papers in the philosophy of the social sciences.

Manuscript info: About 20 philosophy articles are published per year. The backlog of accepted articles is 12 months. Manuscripts are refereed. The refereeing is not blind; unsigned comments are given to authors. About 12% of manuscripts are accepted; 80% of accepted manuscripts require significant revision. The average evaluation time is 1-3 months. No articles are invited. Instructions for manuscript preparation can be obtained from the editorial office. Manuscripts should be sent to the editor.

Book reviews: All book reviews are invited; unsolicited book reviews are rarely accepted.

Frequency: Quarterly;
Circulation: 1,400

Publisher: Sage Publications, Inc.

Subscription rates: $51;
Institutions $126

PHOENIX

Editor: C. I. Rubincam

Trinity College
Toronto, ON M5S 1H8

Tel. 416-978-3037
Fax 416-978-4949
E-mail phoenix@epas.utoronto.ca

ISSN 0031-8299

Purpose: *Phoenix* encourages submissions in English and in French in every area of classical studies, including, most notably, Greek and Latin literature, Greek and Roman history and society, ancient philosophy, and classical art and archaeology.

Manuscript info: About 2-3 philosophy articles are published per year. Manuscripts in classical philosophy are preferred. Backlog is 9 months. Manuscripts are refereed blind; unsigned comments are given to authors. About 33% of manuscripts are accepted; 25% require significant revision. Evaluation time averages 4 months. No articles are invited. Instructions for manuscript preparation are in *Phoenix* 27 (1973), pp 1-3. Manuscripts should be sent to the editor.

Book reviews: Unsolicited book reviews are not welcome.

Frequency: Quarterly;
Circulation: 1,150

Publisher: University of Toronto Press

Subscription rates: $50;
Institutions $55

PROCEEDINGS OF THE FAR WESTERN PHILOSOPHY OF EDUCATION SOCIETY*

Editor: Evelina Orteza y Miranda

Dept. of Ed. Policy and Admin. St. University of Calgary
Calgary, AB T2N 1N4

Tel. 403-220-5675
Fax 403-282-3005

Date of founding: 1955

Purpose: To promote the study of philosophy of education and to provide information regarding its different interests and its development.

Sponsor: The Far Western Philosophy of Education Society

Manuscript info: The *Proceedings* consists of refereed papers presented at the annual meeting of the Society.

Frequency: Annual; Circulation: 150

Publisher: The Far Western Philosophy of Education Society

Subscription rates: Institutions $28;
Back issues $10

RUSSELL: THE JOURNAL OF THE BERTRAND RUSSELL ARCHIVES

Editor: Kenneth Blackwell

McMaster University Library
Hamilton, ON L8S 4L6

Tel. 905-525-9140 Ext. 24738
Fax 905-546-0625

ISSN 0036-0163

Date of founding: 1971

Purpose: To publish new studies on Russell's life and thought; to keep scholars up-to-date on new books; to publicize research opportunities in the *Russell Archives*, and to convey news of the Bertrand Russell Editorial Project.

Manuscript info: About 6 philosophy articles are published per year. Manuscripts on Russell's work in philosophy and significant developments since are preferred. Those shedding new light on Russell's life and thought are given preference. Manuscripts are refereed; unsigned comments are given to authors if useful in explaining rejection. About 50% of manuscripts are accepted; 70% of accepted manuscripts require significant revision. Some instructions for manuscript preparation are in the journal. Send manuscripts to the editor.

Book reviews: About 90% of the book reviews are invited; unsolicited book reviews are considered.

Frequency: Quarterly; Circulation: 500

Publisher: McMaster University Library Press

Subscription rates: $16; Institutions $28; add $4 postage (all Canadian funds)

ULTIMATE REALITY AND MEANING: INTERDISCIPLINARY STUDIES IN THE PHILOSOPHY OF UNDERSTANDING

Editors: Tibor Horvath & John Perry

Regis College
15 St. Mary Street
Toronto, ON M4Y 2R5

Tel. 416-922-2476
Fax 416-922-2898
E-mail perrj@max.cc.uregina.ca

ISSN 0709-549

Date of founding: 1978

Purpose: To collect studies about different ideas on ultimate reality and meaning, or horizons, or supreme values conceived by human mind from the early history of humankind until today and initiate systematic and structural reflection on it.

Sponsor: International Society for the Study of Human Ideas on Ultimate Reality and Meaning

Manuscript info: About 40% of articles per year are devoted to philosophy. Potential contributors should see "Notes for Contributors" published in each issue of the journal. Backlog is 1 to 2 years. Manuscripts are refereed; refereeing is not blind; 70% are accepted with invitation. About 50% require significant revision. Average evaluation time is 6 to 10 months. About 80% of articles are invited. Manuscripts should be sent to the general editor, Tibor Horvath, at address listed.

Frequency: Quarterly; Circulation: 500

Publisher: University of Toronto Press, Journal Dept.

Subscription rates: Individuals: Canada $25 plus GST; other countries $25 plus $5 postage; Institutions: Canada $43 plus GST; other countries $43 plus $5 postage; Cumulative Index Vols. 1-10 1978-1987 $20

ANALYSIS*

Editor: Peter Smith

Dept. of Philosophy
University of Sheffield
Sheffield, England S10 2TN

Fax 0742-798760
E-mail analysis@sheffield.ac.uk
http://www.shef.ac.uk/uni/academic/
N-Q/phil/analysis/homepage.html

ISSN 0003-2638

Date of founding: 1933

Purpose: Publishes short, analytic
articles only. Replies and rejoinders
are welcome.

Sponsor: The Analysis Trust

Manuscript info: About 48 articles
per year are published on topics in
contemporary analytical philosophy.
Some papers are refereed, blind when
possible. About 12% of manuscripts
are accepted. About 12% of articles
are invited replies. Average evaluation
time is 4 weeks. About 40% of articles
require revision before publication.
All authors of accepted papers are
asked to provide final versions on
disk, conforming to the journal's style.
Submit 2 typescripts to the editor.

Information about the journal and its
experimental electronic supplement,
Analyst, is available at
http://www.shelf.ac.uk/uni/academic/
N-Q/phil/analysis/homepage.html

Book reviews: Not included.

Frequency: Quarterly;
Circulation: 1,200

Publisher: Blackwell Publishers,
108 Cowley Road,
Oxford OX4 1JF, UK; also,
350 Main St.,
Malden, MA 02148 USA

Subscription rates: Individuals:
UK/Europe £12.50, N. America $25,
elsewhere £16.50; Institutions:
UK/Europe £21.50, N. America $42,
elsewhere £27.50

APPRAISAL

Editor: R. T. Allen

20 Ulverscroft Rd.
Loughborough, England LE11 3PU

Tel. 01509-215438
Fax 01509-215438
E-mail
101625.3010@compuserve.com

ISSN 1358-3336

Date of founding: 1996

Purpose: To develop and promote
constructive ways of thinking within
philosophy and other intellectual
disciplines.

Manuscript info: All contributions
should be in English, with end-notes
and frequent subheadings. Maximum
length of articles is about 10,000
words. Shorter items, such as discussions, working papers, notes, etc., are
especially welcome. Contributions
should be submitted on disk (consult
the editor for specifics) or in
scannable printed form.

Book reviews: Included.

Frequency: 2 issues yearly

Publisher: R. T. Allen

Subscription rates:
Individuals/Institutions: UK £5/8, rest of Europe £7/12, rest of world £9/16

ARISTOTELIAN SOCIETY: SUPPLEMENTARY VOLUME

Editor: Jonathan Wolff

University of London
Senate House, Malet Street
London, England WC1E 7HU

Tel. 0171-255-1724

ISSN 0309-7013

Date of founding: 1870

Purpose: To study philosophy in general, its development, its methods, and its problems.

Sponsor: The Aristotelian Society and the Mind Association

Manuscript info: Papers presented at the annual joint conference of the Aristotelian Society and the Mind Association in July.

Book reviews: Not included.

Frequency: Annual

Publisher: The Aristotelian Society

Subscription rates: Members £8, $16; Institutions £34.50, $64; Students £4, $8

BRITISH JOURNAL OF AESTHETICS

Editor: Peter Lamarque

Department of Philosophy
University of Hull
Hull, England HU6 7RX

Tel. 01482-465995
Fax 01482-466122,
E-mail p.v.lamarque@phil.hull.ac.uk

ISSN 0007-0904

Date of founding: 1960

Purpose: Discussion and research on the theory and philosophy of the arts and the principles of appreciation and criticism.

Sponsor: British Society of Aesthetics

Manuscript info: About 25 articles per year are devoted to philosophy. Manuscripts must be in the area of aesthetics/philosophy of art. Manuscripts are refereed blind; unsigned comments are given to authors. Average evaluation time is 3 months. Instructions for manuscript preparation are included in the journal.

Book reviews: Included; all are invited. Unsolicited book reviews are not welcome.

Frequency: Quarterly; Circulation: 1,500

Publisher: Oxford University Press

Subscription rates: British Society of Aesthetics members £20, students £10; Institutions £68 in UK and Europe, $124 in all other countries. Required currency is US dollars or pounds sterling to publisher; Sterling only to the Society.

BRITISH JOURNAL FOR THE PHILOSOPHY OF SCIENCE

Editor: David Papineau

Department of Philosophy
King's College London, Strand
London, England WC2R 2LS

Tel. 0171-873-2351
Fax 0171-873-2351
E-mail bjps@kcl.ac.uk

ISSN 0007-0882

Date of founding: 1950

Purpose: The journal is the official organ of the British Society for the Philosophy of Science, whose purpose is to study the philosophy of science, including the various special sciences and the social sciences.

Sponsor: The British Society for the Philosophy of Science

Manuscript info: About 30 articles per year are accepted. Backlog of accepted articles is 9 months. Manuscripts are refereed, and the refereeing is not necessarily blind. About 10% of manuscripts are accepted; 20% of accepted manuscripts require significant revision. Maximum time to evaluate a manuscript is 6 weeks. Instructions for manuscript preparation are included in the journal.

Book reviews: Included. About 90% of book reviews are invited. Unsolicited book reviews are welcome. Books for review should be sent to the editorial address.

Frequency: Quarterly; Circulation: 1,500

Publisher: Oxford University Press/British Society for the Philosophy of Science

Subscription rates: Members and students $35 (£17.50); Institutions $78 (£42); single copies $15; postage is included; Required currency is pounds sterling or US dollars.

BULLETIN OF THE HEGEL SOCIETY OF GREAT BRITAIN

Editor: Robert Stern

Department of Philosophy
University of Sheffield
Sheffield, England S10 2TN

Tel. 0114-2727944
Fax 0114-2798760
E-mail r.stern@sheffield.ac.uk

ISSN 0263-5232

Date of founding: 1979

Purpose: To publish papers, conference proceedings, and book reviews relating to the philosophy of G. W. F. Hegel.

Sponsor: Hegel Society of Great Britain

Manuscript info: Every issue is devoted entirely to philosophy. Manuscripts must be in an area related to the philosophy of G. W. F. Hegel. All articles are invited. Instructions for manuscript preparation are available from the editor.

Book reviews: Included; all are invited. Unsolicited book reviews are welcome.

Frequency: Biannual; Circulation: 300

Publisher: University of Sheffield

Subscription rates: Individuals $17 (£18.50); Institutions $24 (£12); postage is included; required currency is pounds sterling or US dollars.

BULLETIN OF THE INSTITUTE OF CLASSICAL STUDIES

Editor: R. R. K. Sorabji

Institute of Classical Studies
31-34 Gordon Square
London, England WC1H 0PY

Tel. 071-380-7498
Fax 071-383-4807

Date of founding: 1954

Purpose: Covers general classical studies, in Greek and Latin, including philosophy.

Sponsor: Institute of Classical Studies

Manuscript info: About 2 articles per year are devoted to philosophy, but a special supplementary volume, *Aristotle and After* (1996), is wholly devoted to philosophy, with papers by M. Frede, A. A. Long, H. von Staden, B. Inwood, S. Bobzien, H. Gottschalk, A. Falcon, R. Gaskin, T. Butler, M. Trapp, M. Roueché, and M. Rashed.

Book reviews: Not included.

Frequency: Annual;
Circulation: 800

Publisher: Institute of Classical Studies

Subscription rates: Bulletin 38: £25 plus postage

COGITO

Editor: A. J. Pyle

Dept. of Philosophy
University of Bristol
9 Woodland Rd.
Bristol, England BS8 1TB

Tel. 0272-303030 Ext. 3491
Fax 0272-732657

ISSN 0950-8864

Date of founding: 1987

Purpose: To bring philosophy to a wider readership by the publication of short, clear, nontechnical articles suitable for students and nonspecialists.

Sponsor: The Cogito Society

Manuscript info: About 30 articles per year are devoted to philosophy. Manuscripts in any area of philosophy are welcome. Manuscripts that are short, clear, and accessible to the general reader are preferred. Backlog of accepted articles is about 6 months. Manuscripts are refereed blind; comments are not given to authors. About 50% of manuscripts are accepted; 50% require significant revision. Evaluation time averages 1 month. About 25% of articles are invited. Instructions for manuscript preparation are included in the journal. Manuscripts should be sent to the editor.

Book reviews: Included; 25% are invited. Unsolicited book reviews are welcome.

Frequency: 2-3 issues yearly;
Circulation: 700

Publisher: Carfax Publishing Company, P.O. Box 25, Abingdon, Oxfordshire OX14 3VE

Subscription rates: Individuals £19; Institutions £84

167

COMMUNIQUÉ

Editor: Michal J. Eastcott

Sundial House Publications
Nevill Court, Tunbridge Wells
Kent, England TN4 8NJ

Tel. 01892-527631

ISSN 0264-5211

ECONOMICS AND PHILOSOPHY

Editors: John Broome
& Philippe Morgin

P.O. Box 1803
Bath, England BA2 7YF

Tel. 44(0)1225-835885
E-mail
economics-andphilosophy@bristol.ac.uk

ISSN 0266-2671

Date of founding: 1985

Purpose: To foster collaboration between economists and philosophers. The journal aims to promote the mutual enrichment of the disciplines of economics and philosophy.

Manuscript info: Ten philosophy articles per year. Backlog is 6 months. Manuscripts are refereed blind; unsigned comments are given to authors. About 10% of articles are accepted; 90% require significant revision. Average evaluation time is 3 months. Manuscript instructions are included in the journal. Manuscripts should be sent to the editors.

Book reviews: All book reviews are invited; unsolicited reviews are not accepted.

Frequency: 2 issues yearly; Circulation: 1,000

Publisher: Cambridge University Press

Subscription rates: US, Canada, and Mexico: Individuals $39, Institutions $78; Elsewhere: Individuals £25, Institutions £49

EFRYDIAU ATHRONYDDOL

Editors: Walford L. Gealy
& John Daniel

Dept. of Continuing Education
University of Wales, Aberystwyth
10-11 Laura Place, Aberystwyth
Ceredigion, Wales SY23 2AU

Tel. 01970-622680
Fax 01970-622686

ISSN 0142-3371

Date of founding: 1938

Purpose: To encourage Welsh-medium philosophy, to encourage research into Welsh thought, and to publish philosophy articles and reviews in the Welsh language.

Sponsor: Guild of Graduates, University of Wales; Mrs. H. D. Lewis in memory of the late Prof. H. D. Lewis

Manuscript info: The journal publishes papers read at the annual Welsh-medium Philosophy Conference sponsored by the Philosophical Section of the Guild of Graduates, University of Wales. Other individuals may also submit papers, unconnected with the conference. Five articles per year are devoted to philosophy. Manuscripts in any area of philosophy are welcome. There is no backlog. Manuscripts are not refereed. About 95% of articles are accepted; 70% require significant revision. Instructions for manuscript preparation are available from the editors. Manuscripts should be sent to the editors. Address given is for Walford L. Gealy. Address for joint editor John Daniel is Department of Philosophy, University of Wales Lampeter, Ceredigion, Wales.

Book reviews: Included; 90% are invited. Unsolicited book reviews are not welcome.

Frequency: Annual; Circulation: 95

Publisher: University of Wales Press, 6 Gwennyth St. Cathays, Cardiff, Wales CF2 4YD

Subscription rates: £3; postage charges 70p; required currency is pounds sterling.

ENVIRONMENTAL VALUES

Editor: Alan Holland

Department of Philosophy
Furness College, Lancaster University
Lancaster, England LA1 4YG

Fax 01524 592503
E-mail a.holland@lancaster.ac.uk

ISSN 0963-2719

Date of founding: 1992

Purpose: To be concerned with the basis and justification of environmental policy. It aims to bring together contributions from philosophy, law, economics, and other disciplines, which relate to present and future environment of humans and other species.

Manuscript info: About 15 articles per year are devoted to philosophy. Manuscripts related to environmental issues are preferred. Backlog of accepted articles is 6 months.

Manuscripts are refereed blind; comments are given to authors. About 30% of manuscripts are accepted; 50% require significant revision. Evaluation time averages 4-6 months. About 5% of articles are invited. Instructions for manuscript preparation are included in the journal. Manuscripts should be sent to the editor.

Book reviews: Included; 95% are invited. Unsolicited book reviews are not welcome.

Frequency: Quarterly; Circulation: 400

Publisher: White Horse Press, 10 High Street, Knapwell, Cambridge CB3 8NR

Subscription rates: Individuals $60, Institutions $120, Students $40; required currency is US dollars or pounds sterling.

EUROPEAN JOURNAL OF PHILOSOPHY

Editor: Mark Sacks

Department of Philosophy
University of Essex
England CO4 3SQ

Tel. 01206-872717
Fax 01206-873377
E-mail ejp@essex.ac.uk

ISSN 0966-8373

Date of founding: 1993

Purpose: To provide a platform to which philosophers, both inside and outside Europe, can turn to rediscover the diversity and variety of the European tradition.

Manuscript info: All articles (about 16 per year) are devoted to philosophy.

Manuscripts in any area of philosophy are welcome. Manuscripts are refereed blind. Referees' comments are sometimes given to authors. Referees may choose to waive anonymity. About 15% of manuscripts are accepted. Evaluation time averages 8 weeks. About 10% of articles are invited. Instructions for manuscript preparation are included in the journal. Manuscripts should be sent to the editor.

Book reviews: Included; all are invited. Unsolicited book reviews are not welcome.

Frequency: 3 issues yearly

Publisher: Blackwell Publishers, 108 Cowley Road, Oxford OX4 1JF

Subscription rates: UK/Europe: Individuals £32.50, Institutions £99; US: Individuals $38.50, Institutions $149

EXPLORATIONS IN KNOWLEDGE*

Editor: David Lamb

Dept. of Philosophy
University of Manchester
Manchester, England M13 9PL

Tel. 0703-264687

ISSN 0261-1376

Date of founding: 1984

Purpose: To publish papers on the philosophy of science; to throw light on the relationship between the scientific process and the advancement of knowledge and related moral problems.

Manuscript info: Ten articles per year are devoted to philosophy. Manuscripts in any area of philoso-

phy are welcome, but philosophy of science is preferred. Backlog of accepted articles is 12 months. Manuscripts are refereed blind. About 60% of manuscripts are accepted; 40% of accepted manuscripts require significant revision. Average time to evaluate a manuscript is 3 to 4 weeks. About 10% of articles are invited. Instructions for manuscript preparation are included in journal. Manuscripts should be sent to the editor.

Book reviews: Included. About 20% of book reviews are invited. Unsolicited book reviews are welcome.

Frequency: Biannual; Circulation: 200

Publisher: Sombourne Press, 294 Leigh Rd., Chandlers Ford, Eastleigh, Hants SO5 3AU

Subscription rates: £7, Institutions £10, single copies £4; postage is included; sterling currency is required.

EXPOSITORY TIMES

Editor: Cyril S. Rodd

61 Warblington Road
Emsworth, Hampshire
England PO10 7HG

Tel. 01243-372066

ISSN 0014-5246

Date of founding: 1889

Purpose: Interdenominational monthly journal for lecturers in theology and religious studies, ministers, clergy, and laymen. It contains sermon aids, extensive book reviews, and articles on theology and religious studies.

Manuscript info: About 2 to 3 articles per year are devoted to philosophy. Manuscripts in philosophy of religion are preferred. Backlog of accepted articles is 24 months. Manuscripts are not refereed. About 50% of articles are accepted; 10% of accepted articles require significant revision. Average time required to evaluate a manuscript is 2 weeks. About 30% of articles are invited. Manuscripts should be sent to the editor.

Book reviews: Included. All book reviews are invited. Unsolicited book reviews are not accepted.

Frequency: Monthly; Circulation: 7,000

Publisher: T. and T. Clark Ltd., 59 George Street, Edinburgh EH2 2LQ

Subscription rates: £19.95 UK, $39.95 US, $54.95 Canada, $54.95 Australia, £22.50 elsewhere; Students and new subscriptions £14.95 UK, $29.95 US, $39.95 Canada, $39.95 Australia, £17.50 elsewhere; Single copy £1.95; prices include postage.

FRANCIS BACON RESEARCH TRUST NEWSLETTER

Editor: Peter Dawkins

Francis Bacon Research Trust
Roses Farmhouse, Epwell Rd.
Upper Tysoe
Warwick, England CV35 0TN

Tel. 01295-688-185
Fax 01295-680-770
E-mail 100616.540@compuserve.com

Date of founding: 1980

Purpose: To search for truth by learning to love one another and all life—the means itself being equated with the goal.

Manuscript info: Several articles per year are devoted to philosophy. All are based on Francis Bacon's work.

Frequency: 2 issues yearly; Circulation: 140

Publisher: Francis Bacon Research Trust

Subscription rates: £20 plus postage

THE FREETHINKER

Editor: Peter Brearey

G. W. Foote & Company Ltd.
Bradlaugh House, 47 Theobalds Rd.
London, England WC1X 8SP

Tel. 0171-404-3126
Fax 01924-368338

ISSN 0016-0687

Date of founding: 1881

Purpose: Religions and theology (critical): freethought, humanism, atheism, agnosticism, secularism, rationalism; history, current affairs, literature, and arts from a secular humanist viewpoint.

Frequency: Monthly

Publisher: G. W. Foote & Co.

Subscription rates: 10£ UK (£7 unwaged); overseas: surface mail, including Republic of Ireland: £13, airmail: £2

HEYTHROP JOURNAL

Editor: T. J. Deidun

Heythrop Journal
Kensington Square
London, England W8 5HQ

Tel. 071-795-6600
Fax 071-795-4200
E-mail heythrop@ic.ac.uk

ISSN 0018-1196

Date of founding: 1960

Purpose: To foster dialogue among all schools in both philosophy and theology by means of academic articles, whether by members of the staff of Heythrop College or by others.

Sponsor: Heythrop College, University of London

Manuscript info: About 4-8 articles per year are devoted to philosophy. Manuscripts in any area of philosophy are welcome. Backlog of accepted articles is 8 to 12 months. Manuscripts are refereed blind. About 30% of articles are accepted; 80% of accepted articles require significant revision. Average time to evaluate a manuscript is 2 to 3 months. About 10% of articles are invited. Instructions for manuscript preparation are included in the journal. Style sheet is obtainable from the editor. Manuscripts should be sent to the editor.

Book reviews: Included. All book reviews are invited. Unsolicited book reviews are not welcome.

Frequency: Quarterly;
Circulation: 1,000

Publisher: Blackwell Publishers, 108 Cowley Road, Oxford OX4 1JF, UK

Subscription rates: Individuals £24 UK/Europe, $48 N. America, £30 elsewhere; Institutions £55 UK/Europe, $97 N. America, £60 elsewhere; Canadian customers please add 7% for GST.

HISTORY AND PHILOSOPHY OF LOGIC

Editor: Peter Simons

Department of Philosophy
University of Leeds
Leeds, England LS2 9JT

Tel. +44 113 233 3298
Fax +44 113 233 3265
E-mail p.m.simons@leeds.ac.uk

ISSN 0144-5340

Date of founding: 1980

Manuscript info: Manuscripts should be about logic. Historic types of manuscripts are preferred. Backlog is 9-12 months. Manuscripts are refereed (not blind); unsigned comments are given to authors. About 60% of articles are accepted; 62% of these require significant revision. Average time to evaluate a manuscript is 3 months. No articles are invited. Manuscripts should be sent to the editor or a board member.

Book reviews: Included. All book reviews are invited. Unsolicited book reviews are not welcome.

Frequency: Quarterly;
Circulation: 250

Publisher: Taylor & Francis Ltd., 1 Gunpowder Square, London EC4A 3DE

Subscription rates: Institutions $255, Individuals $130; any type of currency is acceptable.

HISTORY OF POLITICAL THOUGHT

Editor: Janet Coleman (co-editor)

Dept. of Government
London School of Econ./Poli. Sci.
Houghton Street
London, England WC2A 2AE

Tel. 0171-955 7196
Fax 0171-831-1707

ISSN 0143-781X

Date of founding: 1980

Purpose: To study political thought (philosophy and theory) in its historic context.

Sponsor: Conference for the Study of Political Thought

Manuscript info: All articles are devoted to political thought in its historical context. Manuscripts in the history of political ideas and political philosophy are preferred. Backlog is 6 months. Manuscripts are refereed blind; unsigned comments are given to authors. About 40% of manuscripts are accepted; 50% require significant revision. Evaluation time averages 4 months. Manuscripts should be sent to Janet Coleman for pre-1600 material; post-1600 material should be sent to co-editor Iain Hampsher-Monk, Dept. of Politics, Exeter University, Amory Building, Exeter EX4 4RJ.

Book reviews: Included. All book reviews are invited. Unsolicited book reviews are not welcome.

Frequency: Quarterly;
Circulation: 1,000

Publisher: J. K. B. Sutherland, Imprint Academic, P.O. Box No. 1, Thorverton, Exeter EX5 5YX; in US: Imprint Academic, c/o Royal

Mail Int., Yellowstone International, 87 Burlews Court, Hackensack, NJ 07601 USA

Subscription rates: £26.50 in UK, 29£ ($53.50) outside UK; Institutions £52 in UK, £62.50 ($115) outside UK; postage included; required currency is pounds or US dollars; credit cards are accepted.

IRISH PHILOSOPHICAL JOURNAL*

Editor: Bernard Cullen

Department of Scholastic Phil.
Queen's University
Belfast, Northern Ireland BT7 1NN

Tel. 232-24513 Ext. 3440

ISSN 0266-9080

Date of founding: 1984

Purpose: To provide a platform for philosophers working in Ireland, in all areas of philosophy and the history of philosophy. All other philosophers are welcome to submit manuscripts.

Manuscript info: About 12 articles per year are devoted to philosophy. Manuscripts in any area of philosophy are welcome. Backlog of accepted articles is 3 to 6 months. Manuscripts are refereed blind. The referees' unsigned comments are given to authors. About 50% of manuscripts are accepted; about 20% of accepted manuscripts require significant revision. Average time required to evaluate a manuscript is about 3 months. About 50% of articles are invited. Manuscripts should be sent to the editor.

Book reviews: Included. All book reviews are invited. Unsolicited book reviews are not welcome.

Frequency: Biannual;
Circulation: 500

Publisher: Bernard Cullen,
Department of Scholastic Philosophy,
Queen's University,
Belfast BT7 1NN, Northern Ireland

Subscription rates: £2.50,
Institutions £10, single copies £2;
postage included; sterling currency is
required.

JOURNAL OF APPLIED PHILOSOPHY

Editors: Stephen Clark &
Brenda Almond

Department of Philosophy
University of Liverpool
Liverpool, England L69 3BX

Tel. 0151-794-2788
Fax 0151-794-2789
E-mail srlclark@liverpool.ac.uk

ISSN 0264-3758

Date of founding: 1984

Purpose: To provide a focus for
philosophical research with a direct
bearing on areas of practical concern
that can be illuminated by the critical,
analytic approach of philosophy, and
by consideration of questions of value.

Sponsor: Society for Applied
Philosophy, Department of
Philosophy, University of Hull

Manuscript info: About 26 articles
per year are devoted to philosophy.
Clearly written and accessible manuscripts in applied philosophy and
ethics are preferred. Manuscripts are
refereed (not blind); unsigned comments are given to authors. About
15% of manuscripts are accepted;
40% require significant revision.

Average time to evaluate a manuscript is 2 months. Manuscripts
should be sent to co-editor, Stephen
Clark, Philosophy Dept., University
of Liverpool, POB 147, Liverpool
L69 3BX.

Book reviews: Included. Book
reviews are invited; unsolicited book
reviews are not welcome.

Frequency: 3 issues yearly;
Circulation: 800

Publisher: Blackwell Publishers,
108 Cowley Road,
Oxford OX4 1JF, UK:
or 350 Mail St., Malden, MA 02148

Subscription rates: £37 per volume, p.a., $78; Institutions £92 per
volume, p.a., $201; required currency
is pounds or US dollars.

JOURNAL OF THE BRITISH SOCIETY FOR PHENOMENOLOGY

Editor: Wolfe Mays

Institute of Advanced Studies
Manchester Metropolitan University
All Saints
Manchester, England MI5 6BH

Tel. 0161-247-1973
Fax 0161-247-6390
E-mail w.mays@mmu.ac.uk

ISSN 0007-1773

Date of founding: 1970

Purpose: To publish papers in phenomenology, general philosophy, and
problems relating to the philosophy
of human sciences.

Sponsor: British Society for
Phenomenology

Manuscript info: About 20 articles per year are devoted to philosophy. Manuscripts in phenomenology and existential philosophy are preferred, but good manuscripts on general philosophical topics are also published. Backlog of accepted articles is 24 months. Manuscripts are refereed, and the refereeing is not blind. The referees' unsigned comments are given to authors. About 30% of manuscripts are accepted; 3% of accepted manuscripts require significant revision. Average time to evaluate a manuscript is 6 weeks.

Book reviews: Included. All book reviews are invited. Unsolicited book reviews are not welcome.

Frequency: 2-3 issues yearly; Circulation: 450

Publisher: Haigh and Hochland Ltd.; Precinct Centre, Oxford Road, Manchester MI3 8QA

Subscription rates: £30, outside Britain $54; Institutions £33, outside Britain $60; Single copies £10, outside Britain $18

JOURNAL OF HELLENIC STUDIES

Editor: Richard Hunter

Pembroke College
Cambridge, England CB2 1RF

Tel. 01223-338100
Fax 01223-338163
E-mail rlh10@cus.cam.ac.uk

ISSN 0075-4269

Date of founding: 1881

Purpose: To act as the organ for the Society for the Promotion of Hellenic Studies, founded in 1879 to advance the study of Greek language, literature, history, and art.

Sponsor: Society for the Promotion of Hellenic Studies, 31-34 Gordon Square, London WC1H 0PP

Manuscript info: One or more articles and some book reviews per year are devoted to ancient philosophy. Manuscripts in any area of ancient philosophy are welcome. Backlog of accepted articles is 12 months. Manuscripts are refereed; unsigned comments are given to authors. About 25% of manuscripts are accepted. Average time to evaluate a manuscript is 3 months. Instructions for manuscript preparation are available from the sponsor. Manuscripts should be sent to the editor.

Book reviews: Included. All book reviews are invited. Unsolicited book reviews are not welcome.

Frequency: Annual; Circulation: 3,000

Publisher: Society for the Promotion of Hellenic Studies

Subscription rates: £27 or $60; Institutions £41 or $90; Students £15; required currency is sterling or US dollars.

JOURNAL OF MEDICAL ETHICS

Editor: Raanan Gillon

Humanities Prog.
Mech. Eng. Bldg.
Imperial Col. of Sci. Tech., Med.
Exhibition Rd.
London, England SW7 2AZ

Tel. 0181-866-2950
Fax 0181-723-5899

ISSN 0306-6800

Date of founding: 1975

Purpose: To promote the study of contemporary medico-moral problems.

Sponsor: The Institute of Medical Ethics and the British Medical Association

Manuscript info: About 9 articles per year are devoted to philosophy. Manuscripts in medical or health care ethics are preferred. Backlog of accepted articles is 6 to 12 months. Manuscripts are refereed (not blind); unsigned comments are often given to authors. About 30% of manuscripts are accepted; 50% require significant revision. Average evaluation time is 3 to 6 months. About 5% of the articles are invited.

Book reviews: Included. About 90% of book reviews are invited. Unsolicited book reviews are not welcome.

Frequency: Bimonthly; Circulation: 1,500

Publisher: British Medical Association, BMA House, Tavistock House East, Tavistock Square, London WC1H 9JR

JOURNAL OF MORAL EDUCATION

Editor: Monica Taylor

c/o NFER, The Mere
Upton Park, Slough
Berkshire, England SL1 2DQ,

Tel. 01753-574123
Fax 01753-691632

ISSN 0305-7240

Date of founding: 1971

Purpose: To provide a unique interdisciplinary forum for consideration of all aspects of moral education and development across the lifespan. Analyses, reports and evaluations address a range of value issues. Particular topics are addressed in special issues.

Sponsor: The Norham Foundation

Manuscript info: Approximately 8 articles per year are devoted to philosophy. Manuscripts in ethics and moral education are preferred. Backlog is 6-12 months. Manuscripts are refereed blind. The referees' unsigned comments are given to authors. About 33-50% of manuscripts are eventually accepted; 80% of accepted manuscripts require significant revision. Average time to evaluate a manuscript is 4 months. About 25% of articles are invited. Instructions for manuscript preparation are included in the journal.

Book reviews: Included. All book reviews are invited. Unsolicited book reviews are not welcome.

Frequency: 4 issues yearly; Circulation: 800

Publisher: Carfax Publishing Company, P.O. Box 25, Abingdon, Oxfordshire OX14 3UE, United Kingdom; and P.O. Box 2025, Dunnellon, FL 34430-2025 USA

Subscription rates: Individuals £25 ($50 US & Canada); Institutions £80 ($160 US & Canada); postage included.

JOURNAL OF THE PHILOSOPHY OF EDUCATION SOCIETY OF GREAT BRITAIN

Editor: Richard Smith

School of Education
University of Durham
Durham, England DH1 1TA

Tel. 091-374-3508
Fax 091-374-3506
E-mail r.d.smith@durham.ac.uk

ISSN 0309-8249

Date of founding: 1978

Purpose: To publish articles on all aspects of the philosophy of education from contributors throughout the English-speaking world.

Sponsor: The Philosophy of Education Society of Great Britain

Manuscript info: About 20 articles per year are devoted to philosophy. Manuscripts should be related to the philosophy of education. Backlog is 9 months. Manuscripts are refereed blind; unsigned comments are given to authors. About 30% of manuscripts are accepted; 40% require significant revision. Average evaluation time is 3 months. About 20% of articles are invited. Instructions for manuscript preparation are included in the journal. Manuscripts should be sent to the editor.

Book reviews: Included; 80% are invited. Unsolicited book reviews are welcome.

Frequency: 3 issues yearly; Circulation: 1,200

Publisher: Blackwell Publishers

Subscription rates: Individuals: UK/Europe £60, rest of world £72, N. America $116; Institutions: UK/Europe £175, rest of world £196, N. America $316. The journal is free to members of the Education Society of Great Britain. Contact the editor for details of membership.

LOCKE NEWSLETTER

Editor: Roland Hall

Summerfields, The Glade
Escrick, York, England YO4 6JH

Tel. 01904-728408
E-mail rh1@york.ac.uk

ISSN 0307-2606

Date of founding: 1970

Purpose: To publish articles, notes, and queries about all aspects of John Locke's work or life, or on related authors; to review books on Locke; to give information about recent work on Locke; to debate issues arising directly from Locke's philosophy.

Manuscript info: About 6 articles per year are devoted to philosophy.

Book reviews: Included.

Frequency: Annual; Circulation: 500

Publisher: Roland Hall, Department of Philosophy, Lancaster University

Subscription rates: £12, or $22, postage is free; concessionary rate for individuals: £8, or $15.

MIND

Editor: Mark Sainsbury

King's College, London
Strand, London
England WC2R 2LS

Tel. 0171-873-2757
Fax 0171-836-1799
E-mail mindjournal@kcl.ac.uk

ISSN 0026-4423

Date of founding: 1876

Purpose: To serve as a professional journal of philosophy.

Sponsor: Mind Association, Department of Philosophy, University of Manchester

Manuscript info: 20 main articles, 10 discussions, and 60 reviews are published each year, all on philosophy. Good manuscripts in any area of philosophy are welcome. Manuscripts are refereed blind. About 8% of manuscripts are accepted. Average time to evaluate a manuscript is 2 months. Manuscripts should be sent to the Editorial Secretary, *Mind*, Department of Philosophy, King's College London, Strand, London WC2R 2LS.

Book reviews: Included. About 90-100% of book reviews are invited. Unsolicited book reviews are welcome.

Frequency: Quarterly; Circulation: 3,200

Publisher: Oxford University Press, Walton St., Oxford OX2 6DP

Subscription rates: £21 UK and EEC, $40 elsewhere; Institutions £35 UK and EEC, $62 elsewhere; required currency is pounds or dollars.

MIND AND LANGUAGE

Editor: Sarah Patterson

Philosophy Department
Birkbeck College
Malet Street
London, England WC1E 7HX

Tel. 0171-631-6536
Fax 0171-631-6564
E-mail
mind-lang@philosophy.bbk.ac.uk

ISSN 0268-1064

Date of founding: 1986

Purpose: To unite the work of linguists, philosophers, psychologists, and workers in artificial intelligence who are currently engaged in the study of a single, though complex subject, centered around phenomena of mind and language.

Manuscript info: Manuscripts should contain original material that anyone engaged in research on the phenomena of mind and language would find relevant and important. The presentation of this material should make the article accessible to readers from disciplines other than that of the author. Backlog of accepted articles is 6 months. Manuscripts are refereed, and authors may request that their names be withheld from the referees.

Book reviews: Included. All book reviews are invited. Unsolicited book reviews are welcome.

Frequency: Quarterly; Circulation: 521

Publisher: Blackwell Publishers, 108 Cowley Road, Oxford OX4 1JF

Subscription rates: £44, $81; Institutions £122, $228; postage is included; required currency is US dollars or sterling. Discounted rates for members of APA and SPP.

NEW HUMANIST

Editor: Jim Herrick

Bradlaugh House
47 Theobald's Road
London, England WC1X 8SP

Tel. 0171-430-1371
Fax 0171-430-1271

ISSN 0306-512X

Date of founding: 1972

Purpose: To disseminate humanist ideas and ideals in the areas of philosophy, history, literature, science, and current affairs.

Sponsor: Rationalist Press Association

Manuscript info: Six articles per year are devoted to philosophy. Manuscripts in any area of philosophy are welcome; preference is given to those relating to humanist themes. Backlog of accepted articles is 6 months. Manuscripts are not refereed. About 10% of articles are invited. Instructions for manuscript preparation are available by request. Manuscripts should be sent to the editor.

Book reviews: Included; 100% are invited. Unsolicited book reviews are not welcome.

Frequency: Quarterly; Circulation: 2,000

Publisher: Rationalist Press Association, Bradlaugh House, 47 Theobald's Road, London WC1X 8SP

Subscription rates: £12

NEW LEFT REVIEW

Editor: Robin Blackburn

6 Meard St.
London, England W1V 3HR

Tel. 0171-734-8830
Fax 0171-734-0059
E-mail
100306.3473@compuserve.com

ISSN 0028-6060

Date of founding: 1960

Purpose: Political, sociological, and cultural review.

Manuscript info: The number of articles per year devoted to philosophy is variable. Manuscripts in any area of philosophy are welcome. Backlog of accepted articles is 6 months. Manuscripts should be sent to the editor.

Book reviews: Included.

Frequency: 6 issues yearly; Circulation: 10,000

Publisher: New Left Review

Subscription rates: Individuals £22.50 UK, $54 Canada, £26 ($47 US) overseas, £34 ($61 US or $67 Canada) airmail; Institutions £48 UK, £51.50 ($93 US) overseas, £59.50 ($107 US) airmail; required currency is pounds, US or Canadian dollars.

ONE EARTH*

Editor: Betsy Van Der Lee

Findhorn Foundation
The Park, Forres
Moray, Scotland IV36 0TZ

Tel. 0309-691641
Fax 0309-691639

179

Date of founding: 1980

Manuscript info: Ten articles per year are devoted to philosophy. Manuscripts in any area of philosophy are welcome. Manuscripts are not refereed. About 50% of manuscripts are accepted. About 90% of articles are invited. Manuscripts should be sent to the editor.

Book reviews: Included. Unsolicited book reviews are welcome.

Frequency: Quarterly; Circulation: 4,400

Publisher: One Earth Magazine, Findhorn Foundation, Forres, IV36 0TZ

Subscription rates: $20; Single copies $5; required currency is US dollars or British pounds.

PEGASUS NEWSLETTER*

Editor: Editorial Board

Runnings Park, Croft Bank
West Malvern
Worcestershire, England WR14 4BP

Tel. 0684-565253

Date of founding: 1989

Purpose: To represent all activities at Runnings Park; to serve as a bridge, an interface between the spiritual/ psychic and the business world.

Sponsor: Runnings Park

Manuscript info: All articles are devoted to philosophy. Manuscripts in any area of philosophy are welcome. Manuscripts are not refereed. About 50% of manuscripts are accepted; 25% require significant revision. Evaluation time averages 1 month.

Manuscripts should be sent to the journal.

Book reviews: Included; all are invited. Unsolicited book reviews are welcome.

Frequency: Quarterly; Circulation: 350

Publisher: Runnings Park

Subscription rates: £36; required currency is sterling.

PHILOSOPHICAL INVESTIGATIONS

Editor: D. Z. Phillips

Department of Philosophy
University of Wales, Swansea
Singleton Park, Swansea
West Glam, Wales SA2 8PP

Tel. 01792-295189
Fax 01792-295893
E-mail t.tessin@swansea.ac.uk

ISSN 0190-0536

Date of founding: 1978

Purpose: To publish philosophical papers in every branch of philosophy; to provide selected critical notices and book reviews.

Manuscript info: Twenty articles per year are devoted to philosophy. Manuscripts in any area of philosophy are welcome. Backlog of accepted articles is 12 months. Manuscripts are refereed, and the refereeing is not blind. The referees' signed comments are sometimes given to authors. About 40% of manuscripts are accepted; 5% of accepted manuscripts require significant revision. Average time to evaluate a manuscript is 1 month. About 1% of articles are invited.

Book reviews: Included. About 99% of book reviews are invited. Unsolicited book reviews are not welcome.

Frequency: Quarterly; Circulation: 400

Publisher: Blackwell Publishers, 108 Cowley Road, Oxford OX4 1JF, UK

Subscription rates: £17.75, Institutions £42.50, Single copies £5

PHILOSOPHICAL QUARTERLY

Editor: Roger Squires

Dept. of Moral Philosophy
University of Saint Andrews
St. Andrews, Scotland KY16 9AL

Tel. 01334-476161
Fax 01334-462485
E-mail pq@st-andrews.ac.uk

ISSN 0031-8094

Date of founding: 1951

Purpose: To serve as a general philosophical journal.

Sponsor: Scots Philosophical Club and University of Saint Andrews

Manuscript info: About 25 to 30 articles and 25 to 30 discussions and critical notices per year are devoted to philosophy. Manuscripts in any area of philosophy are welcome. Backlog of accepted articles is 8 months. Manuscripts are refereed, and the refereeing is not blind unless requested by the contributors. The referees' comments are not normally signed, but are given to authors at the discretion of the editors. About 5-10% of manuscripts are accepted; 50% of manuscripts require significant revision.

Book reviews: Included. All book reviews are invited. Unsolicited book reviews are not welcome.

Frequency: Quarterly; Circulation: 1,300

Publisher: Blackwell Publishers, 108 Cowley Road, Oxford OX4 1JF, UK

Subscription rates: £21, Europe £21.50, North America $44, rest of world £27.50; Institutions £62, Europe £62, North America $134, rest of world £83; Student rate $23

PHILOSOPHY

Editor: Anthony O'Hear

Royal Institute of Philosophy
14 Gordon Square
London, England WC1H 0AG

Tel. 0171-387-4130
Fax 0171-383-4061
E-mail I.Purkiss@mailbox.uscc.ac.uk

ISSN 0031-8191

Date of founding: 1926

Purpose: To publish original articles and book reviews concerned with the study of philosophy in all its branches: logic, metaphysics, epistemology, ethics, aesthetics, social and political philosophy, and the philosophies of religion, science, and education.

Sponsor: The Royal Institute of Philosophy

Manuscript info: About 25 articles plus 16 discussions per year are devoted to philosophy.

Book reviews: Included.

Frequency: Quarterly; Circulation: 2,850

Publisher: Cambridge University Press

Subscription rates: £25 ($45) for members of the Royal Institute of Philosophy; £116 ($204) for institutional subscribers

PHILOSOPHY NOW: A MAGAZINE OF PHILOSOPHY

Editor: Richard Lewis

226 Bramford Rd., Ipswich
Suffolk, England IP1 4AS

Tel. +44-473-240185
Fax +44-171-873-2270
E-mail r.lewis@kcl.ac.uk

ISSN 0961-5970

Date of founding: 1991

Purpose: To make philosophy accessible to people with little or no formal training in the subject, and to provide some relatively light and amusing reading matter for people who are already involved in philosophy.

Manuscript info: Approximately 40 articles per year are devoted to philosophy. Manuscripts in any area of philosophy are welcome. Preference is given to clearly written, jargon-free manuscripts that will be intelligible to newcomers to philosophy. About 70% of manuscripts are refereed. The refereeing is blind; unsigned comments are given to authors. About 30% of manuscripts are accepted; 20% require significant revision. Evaluation time averages 6 months. About 10% of articles are invited. Instructions for manuscript preparation are included in the journal. Manuscripts should be sent to the editor.

Book reviews: Included; 30% are invited. Unsolicited book reviews are welcome.

Frequency: 4 issues yearly;
Circulation: 4,200

Publisher: *Philosophy Now*

Subscription rates: Rates for US subscribers: Individuals $25, Institutions $34; required currency is pounds or US dollars.

PHILOSOPHY, PSYCHIATRY, AND PSYCHOLOGY

Editor: K. W. M. Fulford

Department of Philosophy
University of Warwick
Coventry, England CV4 7AL

Tel 44-1203 524961
Fax 44-1203 523019
E-mail pysak@snow.warwick.ac.uk

ISSN 1071-6076

Date of founding: 1994

Purpose: The journal advances philosophical inquiry in psychiatry and abnormal psychology while making clinical material and theory more accessible to philosophers.

Sponsor: Assoc. for Advance of Phil. & Psych.; Royal Coll. Psychiatrists Phil. Group; Royal Inst. of Phil.

Manuscript info: All articles are devoted to philosophy. Preference is given to manuscripts that address the interdisciplinary areas of philosophy, psychiatry, and clinical psychology. Backlog is 3 months. Manuscripts are refereed blind; unsigned comments are given to authors. About 15% of manuscripts are accepted; 90% require significant revision.

Evaluation time averages 90 days. About 10% of articles are invited. Instructions for manuscript preparation are included in the journal. Manuscripts should be sent to the editor at address listed, or to co-editor John Sadler, Dept. of Psychiatry, University of Texas Southwest Medical Center, 5323 Harry Hines Blvd., Dallas, TX 75235-9070 USA.

Book reviews: Not included, but review articles are commissioned to coincide with important publications.

Frequency: Quarterly; Circulation: 500

Publisher: Johns Hopkins University Press, 2715 N. Charles St., Baltimore, MD 21218 USA

Subscription rates: $65; Institutions $99; for postage outside the United States, add $4.50 for Canada and Mexico, $9 elsewhere. For student and other special rates, apply to the editor.

PHRONESIS

Editor: R. W. Sharples

Department of Greek and Latin University College London Gower Street, London, England WC1E 6BT

Tel. 0171-380-7492 Fax 0171-209-2324

ISSN 0031-8868

Date of founding: 1955

Purpose: To publish articles covering all aspects of ancient Greek and Roman philosophy.

Manuscript info: Approximately 15 articles per year are devoted to

ancient philosophy. Backlog of accepted articles is at the maximum 12 months. Manuscripts are refereed at the editor's discretion. The referees' unsigned comments are given to authors. About 17% of manuscripts are accepted; 20% of accepted manuscripts require significant revision. No articles are invited.

Book reviews: Included. All book reviews are invited. Unsolicited book reviews are not welcome.

Frequency: 3 issues yearly; Circulation: 1,100

Publisher: Van Gorcum & Comp. BV, P.O. Box 43, 9400 AA Assen, The Netherlands

Subscription rates: In Holland, Dfl 110, Students Dfl 75; abroad, including postage, Dfl 135, Students Dfl 100; Single copies Dfl 45 plus postage and handling.

POLIS

Editor: Peter P. Nicholson

Department of Politics University of York Heslington York, England YO1 5DD

Tel. 01904-43-3549 Fax 01904-43-3563

ISSN 0412-257X

Date of founding: 1978

Purpose: To promote exchange of ideas concerning ancient Greek political thought between students of the subject in the disciplines of classics, ancient history, philosophy, and politics.

Sponsor: Society for the Study of Greek Political Thought

Manuscript info: Six articles per year are devoted to philosophy. Manuscripts in political thought and philosophy are preferred. Manuscripts are refereed blind; unsigned comments are given to authors. About 50% of manuscripts are accepted; 10% of accepted manuscripts require significant revision. Average time to evaluate a manuscript is 2 months. About 50% of articles are invited. Instructions for manuscript preparation are available from the editor. Manuscripts should be sent to the editor.

Book reviews: Included. All book reviews are invited. Unsolicited book reviews are not welcome.

Frequency: Biannual; Circulation: 200

Publisher: The Editor

Subscription rates: £8, Foreign £9; postage included; required currency is pounds sterling, or US dollars may be sent to the American Chapter, Director, Kent F. Moors, Dept. of Political Science, Duquesne University, Pittsburgh, PA 15282-0001.

PRIMA PHILOSOPHIA

Editor: Sabine Sara Gehlhaar

Flat 5, 21 Essex Road
Dartford/Kent, England DA1 2AU

Tel. 0044-1322-401-755
Fax 0044-1322-401-755

ISSN 0933-5749

Date of founding: 1986

Purpose: To advance philosophical research on all fields known (general character, no special fixation besides importance in philosophical question context).

Manuscript info: About 25-30 articles per year are devoted to philosophy. Manuscripts in any area of philosophy are welcome. Backlog of accepted articles is 3 months. Manuscripts are not refereed. About 90% percent of manuscripts are accepted; 5% require significant revision. About 10% of articles are invited. Instructions for manuscript preparation are included in the journal. Manuscripts should be sent to the editor.

Book reviews: Included; 70% are invited. Unsolicited book reviews are welcome.

Frequency: Quarterly; Circulation: 250

Publisher: Traude Junghans, Brahmsstr 8b, D-27474 Cuxhaven, Germany

Subscription rates: 84 DM Individuals, 68 DM Students; required currency is Deutsche marks, pounds, or US dollars.

PROCEEDINGS OF THE ARISTOTELIAN SOCIETY

Editor: Jonathan Wolff

The Aristotelian Society
University of London
Senate House, Malet Street
London, England WC1E 7HU

Tel. 0171-255-1724

ISSN 0066-7374

Date of founding: 1870

Purpose: To advance public education in philosophy; to publish proceedings to this end.

Sponsor: The Aristotelian Society

Manuscript info: Fifteen articles per year are devoted to philosophy. Manuscripts in any area of philosophy are welcome, but mainstream, analytical ones are preferred. A small percentage of manuscripts are refereed, and the refereeing is not blind. About 90% of articles are invited. The length of manuscripts should be 6,000 words. Manuscripts should be sent to the editor.

Book reviews: Not included.

Frequency: 3 issues yearly

Publisher: The Aristotelian Society; Dist: Journal Subscriptions Dept., Marston Book Services, P.O. Box 87, Oxford OX2 0DT

Subscription rates: £8, $16; Institutions £33.50, $62; Students £4, $8; postage included; required currency is sterling or US dollars.

PROCEEDINGS OF THE LEEDS PHILOSOPHICAL AND LITERARY SOCIETY, LITERARY & HISTORICAL SECTION

Editor: I. S. Moxon

School of History
University of Leeds
Leeds, England LS2 9JT

Tel. 0113-233-3544
Fax 0113-234-2759

ISSN 0024-0281

Date of founding: 1925

Purpose: The *Proceedings*, which are monograph publications subsequently bound into numbered volumes by institutional subscribers, exist to publish academic work of high quality, which may not be commercially viable, in any field of the humanities.

Manuscript info: Manuscripts in any area of philosophy are welcome. Backlog is 24 months. Manuscripts are refereed (not blind); unsigned comments are given to authors. About 66% of manuscripts are accepted; 66% require significant revision. Evaluation time averages 6 months. Manuscripts should be sent to the editor.

Book reviews: Not included.

Frequency: 1-3 issues yearly; Circulation: 500

Publisher: Leeds Philosophical and Literary Society Ltd., City Museum, Calverley Street, Leeds LS1 3AA

Subscription rates: Monographs vary in size and are individually priced.

RADICAL PHILOSOPHY

Editor: Editorial Collective

Secretary: Jean Grimshaw
North View, Dundry Lane, Dundry
Bristol, England BS18 8JG

Tel. 071-226-2724
Fax 071-704-6027

ISSN 0300-211X

Date of founding: 1971

Purpose: To provide an alternative to analytic philosophy; to counter the ignorance of modern continental thought evident in analytic philosophy; to argue for the philosophical significance of socialism.

Manuscript info: All articles are devoted to philosophy or philosophical aspects of social and cultural thought. Manuscripts in any area of philosophy are welcome. Clearly written manuscripts are preferred. Manuscripts are refereed, and the refereeing is not blind. The sometimes signed comments are given to authors in summarized form. About 20% of manuscripts are accepted; 25% of accepted manuscripts require significant revision. Average time to evaluate a manuscript is 3 months. About 15% of articles are invited. Manuscripts should be sent to the editor.

Book reviews: Included. About 90% of book reviews are invited.

Frequency: 6 issues yearly; Circulation: 2,500

Publisher: Radical Philosophy Ltd., 33 Cowl Road, Wolverhampton WV6 0JN, England

Subscription rates: Overseas rates: Individuals £22/$36 (surface mail), £30/$48 (airmail); Institutions £40/$60 (surface mail), £58/$85 (airmail); UK rates: Individuals £16, Institutions £36

RATIO

Editor: John Cottingham

Department of Philosophy
University of Reading
Reading, England RG6 2AA

Tel. 01734-318325
Fax 01734-318295
E-mail j.g.cottingham@reading.ac.uk

ISSN 0034-0066

Date of founding: 1957

Purpose: To publish readily accessible articles in all branches of philosophy; to provide accessibility to the nonspecialist.

Manuscript info: About 12-15 articles per year are devoted to philosophy. Manuscripts in any area of philosophy are welcome. Manuscripts of 6,000 or fewer words are preferred. Manuscripts are refereed blind. About 10% of manuscripts are accepted; 10% of accepted manuscripts require significant revision. Average time to evaluate a manuscript is 4 weeks. No articles are invited, except for special issues. Since 1995, 1 issue each year is devoted to invited papers on a special topic. Manuscripts should be sent to the editor.

Book reviews: Included. All book reviews are invited. Unsolicited book reviews are not welcome.

Frequency: 3 issues yearly; Circulation: 520

Publisher: Blackwell Publishers, 108 Cowley Road, Oxford OX4 1JF

Subscription rates: £31, overseas £41; Institutions £49.50, overseas £65.

RELIGIOUS STUDIES

Editors: P. A. Byrne & J. S. K. Ward

King's College, The Strand
London, England WC2R 2LS

Tel. 071-836-5454 Ext. 3794
Fax 071-873-2255
E-mail p.byrne@kcl.ac.uk

ISSN 0034-4125

Date of founding: 1965

Purpose: Primarily concerned with central problems in the philosophy of religion as these arise out of classical and contemporary discussions and from varied religious traditions.

Manuscript info: Publishes 32 articles per year. Papers should relate to topics described under "Purpose"; papers from other branches of the study of religions accepted if of general scholarly interest. Backlog is 10-12 months. Manuscripts are refereed blind; unsigned comments are given to authors as appropriate. About 25% of manuscripts are accepted; 2% require significant revision. Average time to evaluate a manuscript is 3 months. Instructions for manuscript preparation are included in the journal.

Book reviews: Included. All book reviews are invited. Unsolicited book reviews are not welcome.

Frequency: Quarterly; Circulation: 1,250

Publisher: Cambridge University Press, The Pitt Building, Trumpington Street, Cambridge, England CB2 1RP

Subscription rates: $75, Institutions $153, Single copies $40; postage is included for subscribers; required currency is pounds or US dollars.

SCOTTISH JOURNAL OF RELIGIOUS STUDIES

Editor: Malory Nye

Dept. of Religious Studies
University of Stirling
Stirling, Scotland FK9 4LA

Tel. 01786-473171 Ext. 6240
Fax +44 1786 451335
E-mail mn2@stir.ac.uk

ISSN 0143-8301

Date of founding: 1980

Purpose: To promote a critical investigation of all aspects of the study of religion.

Sponsor: University of Stirling

Manuscript info: About 8-10 articles per year are devoted to philosophy. Manuscripts in philosophy of religion and Asian philosophy are preferred. Backlog of accepted articles is 6 months. Manuscripts are refereed blind. About 60% of manuscripts are accepted; 20% of accepted manuscripts require significant revision. Average time to evaluate a manuscript is 3 months. About 20% of articles are invited. Instructions for manuscript preparation are included in the journal. Manuscripts should be sent to the editor.

Book reviews: Included. About 10% of book reviews are invited. Unsolicited book reviews are welcome.

Frequency: Biannual; Circulation: 200

Publisher: Department of Religious Studies, University of Stirling

Subscription rates: Individuals £7 ($14 overseas); Institutions £15 ($30 overseas); Single copies to individuals £4 ($8 overseas); Single copies to institutions £8 ($16 overseas).

SELF-KNOWLEDGE

Editor: Shanti Sadan

29 Chepstow Villas
London, England W11 3DR

Tel. +44 0171 727 7846
Fax +44 0171 792 9817

Date of founding: 1950

Purpose: To study spiritual thought and practice with special reference to Advaita Vedanta and Adhyatma Yoga (the Yoga of Self-Knowledge and Mysticism).

Sponsor: Shanti Sadan

Manuscript info: About 20 articles per year are devoted to philosophy.

Frequency: Quarterly; Circulation: 200

Publisher: Shanti Sadan

Subscription rates: £9, Single copies £2.25

SOCIAL EPISTEMOLOGY

Editor: Joan Leach

Science Communication Group
Imperial College of Science
Technology and Medicine
London, England SW7 2AZ

Tel. 44-171-594-8753
Fax 44-171-594-8763
E-mail j.leach@ic.ac.uk

ISSN 0269-1728

Date of founding: 1987

Purpose: The journal is committed to both examining and exhibiting the social structure of knowledge; thus, its policy is to publish "collaborations" that are the collective product of several contributors.

Sponsor: Taylor & Francis, Ltd.

Manuscript info: About half of all articles are devoted to philosophy. Manuscripts in any area of philosophy are welcome, although preference is given to those of interest to non-philosophers. Backlog is 6-12 months. Manuscripts are refereed; signed comments are given to authors. About 10% of manuscripts are accepted; 70% require significant revision. Average evaluation time is 1-6 months. About 75% of articles are

invited. Instructions for manuscript preparation are in the journal. Manuscripts should be sent to the editor.

Book reviews: Offers for synthetic essay-reviews are welcome. A preference is given to reviews to which the author of the book responds.

Frequency: Quarterly; Circulation: 400

Publisher: Taylor & Francis Ltd., 1 Gunpowder Square, London EC4A 3DE

Subscription rates: $60/£35; Institutions $120/£69

STUDIES IN HISTORY AND PHILOSOPHY OF SCIENCE

Editor: Nicholas Jardine

Dept. of History & Phil. of Sci.
University of Cambridge
Free School Lane
Cambridge, England CB2 3RH

Tel. 0-223-334546
Fax 0-223-334554

ISSN 0039-3681

Date of founding: 1970

Purpose: To encourage studies of the sciences that integrate philosophical, historical, and sociological considerations.

Manuscript info: About 15-20 articles per year are devoted to philosophy. Manuscripts in philosophy of science are preferred. Manuscripts that combine philosophical with historical and/or sociological considerations are given preference. Backlog of accepted articles is 1 year. Manuscripts are refereed blind; referees' unsigned comments are given to authors at the editor's discretion. About 30% of manuscripts are accepted; 70% of accepted manuscripts require revision.

Book reviews: Included. About 80% of book reviews are invited. Unsolicited book reviews are welcome.

Frequency: Quarterly;
Circulation: 1,000

Publisher: Elsevier Science Ltd., The Boulevard, Langford Lane, Kidlington, Oxford OX5 1GB

Subscription rates: Institutions: North, Central, and South America $271 US, rest of world £170. Customers in North America send subscription enquires to Elsevier Science Inc., 660 White Plains Rd., Tarrytown, NY 10591-5153 US; rest to Elsevier at UK address listed previously.

UTILITAS: JOURNAL OF UTILITARIAN STUDIES

Editor: Roger Crisp

St. Anne's College
Oxford, England OX2 6HS

Tel. 01865-274819
Fax 01865-274899
E-mail roger.crisp@st-annes.ox.ac.uk

ISSN 0953-8208

Date of founding: 1989

Purpose: To serve as a cross-disciplinary, international forum for the study of all aspects of thought in which utilitarianism has made a contribution.

Sponsor: International Society for Utilitarian Studies, Bentham Project

Manuscript info: About 75% (12 articles per year) are devoted to philosophy. Preference is given to manuscripts in the areas of moral and political philosophy. Backlog of accepted articles is about 6 months. Manuscripts are refereed blind; comments are given to authors. About 20% of manuscripts are accepted; 30% require significant revision. Evaluation time averages 3-4 months. About 50% of articles are invited. Manuscripts should be sent to the editor. There are no special stylistic requirements for a first submission.

Book reviews: Included; 90% are invited. Unsolicited book reviews are welcome.

Frequency: 3 issues yearly;
Circulation: 400

Publisher: Edinburgh University Press, 22 George Square, Edinburgh EH8 9LF

Subscription rates: Individuals: UK and EC £27.50, overseas £29.75/$49.75; Institutions: UK and EC £55, overseas £59.50/$99.50; payment by cheque or Visa/Mastercard

JOURNALS: SELECTED INTERNATIONAL

ARCHIV FÜR GESCHICHTE DER PHILOSOPHIE

Editors: D. Frede & W. Bartuschat

Philosophisches Seminar
Universität Hamburg
Von-Melle-Park 6, D-20146 Hamburg
Germany

Tel. 40/4123 Ext. 3338
Fax 4940 4123 4785

home page http://www.degruyter.de/journals/agp.html

ISSN 0003-9101

Date of founding: 1889

Purpose: History of philosophy

Manuscript info: Manuscripts are accepted only in the area of history of philosophy. Backlog of accepted articles is up to 24 months. Manuscripts are refereed blind; unsigned comments are given to authors. About 20% of articles are accepted; 50% require significant revision. Average evaluation time is 2 months. Send manuscripts from US and Canada to Steven Nadler, Dept. of Philosophy, University of Wisconsin, 600 North Park St., Madison, WI 53706 US; send all others to Redaktion Hamburg.

Book reviews: Included. Book reviews are invited. Unsolicited book reviews are not welcome.

Frequency: 3 issues yearly;
Circulation: 700

Publisher: Walter de Gruyter & Co., Postfach 303421, D-10728 Berlin

Subscription rates: 198 DM

AUSTRALASIAN JOURNAL OF PHILOSOPHY

Editor: Robert Young

La Trobe University
Bundoora VIC 3083
Australia

Tel. 03-9479-2424
Fax 03-9479-3639
E-mail phiajp@lure.latrobe.edu.au
http://www.arts.su.edu.au/Arts/departs/philos/APS/AJP/AJP.htm

ISSN 0004-8402;

Date of founding: 1923

Purpose: To promote the study of philosophy.

Sponsor: Australasian Association of Philosophy

Manuscript info: About 30 articles per year are devoted to philosophy; manuscripts in any area of philosophy are welcome. Backlog is 12 months. Manuscripts are refereed blind; unsigned comments are given to authors. About 8-9% of manuscripts are accepted; 75% require significant revision. Average evaluation time is 3-4 months. No articles are invited. Instructions for manuscript preparation are included in the journal. Manuscripts should be sent to the editor.

Book reviews: All book reviews are invited; unsolicited book reviews are not welcome.

Frequency: Quarterly;
Circulation: 1,300

190

Publisher: Australasian Association of Philosophy

Subscription rates: A$40; Institutions A$70; Students A$20; currency US$, A$, NZ$

CRÍTICA: REVISTA HISPANOAMERICANA DE FILOSOFÍA

Editor: Carolina Celorio Vizcaíno

Inst. de Invest Fil.
UNAM, Circuito Mario de la Cueva
Coyoacàn, 04510
Mexico DF 70-447

Tel. 622-74-29
Fax 622-74-27

ISSN 0011-1503

Date of founding: 1967

Purpose: To publish articles and discussions specializing in philosophical themes of contemporary interest.

Sponsor: Instituto de Investigaciones Filosoficas, UNAM

Manuscript info: About 15 to 20 articles are published each year. Manuscripts in any area of philosophy are welcome, but manuscripts discussing major contemporary problems are preferred. No backlog of accepted articles. Manuscripts are refereed blind. The referees' unsigned comments are given to authors. About 40% of manuscripts are accepted; 50% of accepted manuscripts require significant revision. Average time to evaluate a manuscript is 1 month.

Book reviews: Included. All book reviews are invited.

Frequency: 3 issues yearly; Circulation: 800

Publisher: Carolina Celorio, Secretario de Redacción, Instituto de Investigaciones Filosóficas, Universidad Nacional Autónoma de México

Subscription rates: Individuals $30 (N$60 Mexican pesos), Institutions $36 (N$90 Mexican pesos); Single copies: Individuals $10 (N$20 Mexican pesos); Institutions $12 (N$30 Mexican pesos); required currency is Mexican pesos or US dollars.

DIALECTICA: INTERNATIONAL REVIEW OF PHILOSOPHY OF KNOWLEDGE

Editor: Henri Lauener

P.O. Box 5907
CH-3001 Bern
Switzerland

Tel. 031/6313590

ISSN 0012-2017

Date of founding: 1947

Purpose: Philosophie de la connaissance et spécialement méthodologie et philosophie des sciences.

Manuscript info: About 30 articles per year are devoted to philosophy. Those in the areas of philosophy of sciences, methodology, and epistemology are preferred. Backlog is 6 months. Manuscripts are refereed blind; comments are not given to authors. About 30% of manuscripts are accepted; 10% require significant revision. Average evaluation time is 3 months. Instructions for manuscript preparation are included in the journal's last number of the year.

Book reviews: Included. Unsolicited book reviews are welcome.

Frequency: Quarterly; Circulation: 700

Publisher: Dialectica

Subscription rates: SFr 70 for individuals and students; SFr 120 for institutions; postage charges SFr 8; required currency is SFr.

ERKENNTNIS: AN INTERNATIONAL JOURNAL OF ANALYTIC PHILOSOPHY

Editor: W. Spohn & C. Hempel

W. Essler, Fachgruppe Philosophie
Universität Konstanz
Postfach 5560 D21, D-78434
Konstanz
Germany

Tel. 0049-7531-88-2503
Fax 0049-7531-88-4121
E-mail
wolfgang.spohn@uni-konstanz.de

ISSN 0165-0106

Date of founding: 1930

Purpose: To serve as an international journal of analytic philosophy.

Manuscript info: About 40 articles per year are devoted to philosophy. Manuscripts about analytic and systematic philosophy are preferred. Average time elapsing from first submission to publication is 18 months. Manuscripts are refereed blind; unsigned comments are given to authors. About 25% of manuscripts are accepted; 60% of accepted manuscripts require significant revision. Average evaluation time is 5 months. About 10% of articles are invited. Manuscripts should be sent to

Editorial Office, *Erkenntnis*, Kluwer Academic Publishers.

Book reviews: Included.

Frequency: 6 issues (2 vol.) yearly; Circulation: 600

Publisher: Kluwer Academic Publishers, P.O. Box 17, NL-3300 AA Dordrecht, The Netherlands

Subscription rates: $52, Institutions $173.50 per volume; postage included; required currency is dollars or Dfl.

GRAZER PHILOSOPHISCHE STUDIEN

Editor: Rudolf Haller

Philosophisches Institut
Universität Graz
Heinrichsstrasse 26, A-8010 Graz
Austria

Tel. 0316-380-2297/2298
Fax (316)356144
E-mail rudolf.haller@kfunigraz.ac.at

ISSN 0165-9227

Date of founding: 1975

Purpose: To bring into closer contact the different traditions of analytical philosophy and to emphasize the contribution of Austrian philosophers to this movement.

Manuscript info: Sixteen to 20 articles per year are devoted to philosophy. Manuscripts in any area of philosophy are welcome; short papers on current philosophical themes are preferred. Backlog is 6 months. Manuscripts are refereed (not blind); unsigned comments are given to authors. About 60% of manuscripts are accepted; 30% require significant revision. Average time required to evaluate a manuscript is 6 months. Manuscripts should be sent to the editor.

Book reviews: Included. All book reviews are invited. Unsolicited book reviews are not welcome.

Frequency: Biannual;
Circulation: 350

Publisher: Editions Rodopi, Keizersgracht 302-304, 1016 EX Amsterdam, Netherlands

Subscription rates: Vary, with institutional rates twice the individual rates; postage varies; required currency is US dollars or Dutch guilders.

INQUIRY: AN INTERDISCIPLINARY JOURNAL OF PHILOSOPHY

Editor: Alastair Hannay

University of Oslo
P.O. Box 1024 Blindern
N-0315 Oslo
Norway

Tel. 47-22856962
Fax 47-22856963

ISSN 0020-174X

Date of founding: 1958

Purpose: To publish articles, discussions of articles, and review of discussions with a view to promoting integrative perspectives in philosophy and integrative research in the sciences.

Manuscript info: About 30 articles per year are devoted to philosophy. Manuscripts in any area of philosophy are welcome. Backlog of accepted articles is 6 months. Manuscripts are refereed. 8% of manuscripts are accepted; 5% require significant revision. Average evaluation time is 6 weeks. About 15% of articles are invited. Instructions for manuscript preparation are given in the journal. Manuscripts should be sent to the editor.

Book reviews: Review articles only. All book reviews are invited. Unsolicited book reviews are not welcome.

Frequency: Quarterly;
Circulation: 1,000

Publisher: Universitetsforlaget A/S, (Scandinavian University Press), P.O. Box 2959, Toyen, N-0608 Oslo; US Address: Scandinavian University Press North America, 875-84 Massachusetts Ave., Cambridge, MA 01239; Fax 617-354-0875; Toll-free 800-498-2877

Subscription rates: $65, Institutions $129; postage included; required currency is Nkr or dollars. Visa/American Express/ Mastercard/Eurocard accepted.

INTERNATIONAL JOURNAL OF PHILOSOPHICAL STUDIES

Editor: Dermot Moran

Editorial Office, Department of Philosophy
University College Dublin
Belfield, Dublin 4
Ireland

Tel. 353-1-706-8123
Fax 353-1-269-3469
E-mail dermot.moran@ucd.ie

ISSN 0967-2559

Date of founding: 1951

Purpose: To publish articles of the highest academic quality on all areas of philosophy, including scholarly articles on the history of philosophy. The journal seeks to promote dialogue between analytic and continental styles of philosophy.

Sponsor: National University of Ireland

Manuscript info: There are 12-16 philosophy articles per year. Some issues are dedicated to a single topic. Manuscripts are independently refereed; unsigned comments are normally given to authors. Evaluation time averages 3 months. Manuscripts should be sent in triplicate to the editor. Editorial Board: Karl-Otto Apel, Johann Wolfgang Goethe-Univ., Frankfurt, Germany; Jonathan Barnes, Univ. de Genéve, Switzerland; Werner Beierwaltes, Ludwig-Maximilians-Univ., München, Germany; Seyla Benhabib, Harvard Univ., Cambridge, USA; Desmond Clarke, Univ. College, Cork, Ireland; John Cleary, St. Patrick's College, Maynooth, Ireland; John Dillon, Trinity College, Dublin, Ireland; David Evans, Queen's Univ. of Belfast, Northern Ireland; Karsten Harries, Yale Univ., New Haven, USA; Klaus Jacobi, Albert-Ludwigs Univ., Freiburg, Germany; Richard Kearney, Univ. College Dublin, Ireland; Thomas McCarthy, Northwestern Univ., Evanston, USA; James McEvoy, Univ. Catholique de Louvain, Belgium; Alasdair MacIntyre, Univ. of Notre Dame, USA; Ernan McMullin, Univ. of Notre Dame, USA; Kevin Mulligan, Univ. de Genéve, Switzerland; Onora O'Neill, Newnham College, Cambridge, England; Philip Pettit, Australian National University, Canberra, Australia; Otto Pöggeler, Ruhr-Univ. Bochum, Germany; Paul Ricoeur, Univ. of Paris, France/Univ. of Chicago, USA; Richard Rorty,

Univ. of Virginia, Charlottesville, USA; Richard Sorabji, King's College, London, England; Charles Taylor, McGill Univ., Montréal, Canada; Timothy Williamson, Univ. College, Oxford, England; Marcus Wörner, Univ. College, Galway, Ireland

Book reviews: Book reviews and longer Critical Notices normally are invited. Book review editor: Maria Baghramian; e-mail baghram@macollamh.ucd.ie

Frequency: 3 issues/year (from 1997); Circulation: 700

Publisher: Routledge, 11 New Fetter Lane, London EC4P 4EE, England

Subscription rates: Individual: £30 UK/EC, $45 US, £32 elsewhere; Institutions: £64 UK/EC, $96 US, £68 elsewhere

---

KANT-STUDIEN

Editor: Gerhard Funke

Kant-Studien-Redaktion
Universität Mainz
Colonel-Kleinmann-Weg 2
D-55128 Mainz
Germany

Tel. 06131 39 2793
Fax 06131 395141
E-mail kant@goofy.zdv.uni-mainz.de

home page http://www.degruyter.de/journals/kant.html

ISSN 0022-8877

Date of founding: 1896

Sponsor: Kant-Gesellschaft

Manuscript info: About 25 articles per year are devoted to philosophy.

Book reviews: Included.

Frequency: Quarterly; Circulation: 900

Publisher: Walter de Gruyter & Co.

Subscription rates: 175 DM

MANUSCRITO-REVISTA INTERNATIONAL DE FILOSOFIA

Editors: Marcelo Dascal & Michael Wrigley

CLE-Unicamp, CP 6133
13081-970 Campinas SP
Brazil

Tel. 0055-192-393269
Fax 0055-192-393269
E-mail clehc@bruc.bitnet

ISSN 0100-6045

Date of founding: 1977

Purpose: To promote discussion and research in all areas of philosophy. *Manuscrito* publishes articles in English, French, Spanish, and Portuguese.

Manuscript info: Twelve articles per year are devoted to philosophy. Manuscripts in any area of philosophy are welcome. Manuscripts are refereed blind; unsigned comments are given to the authors. About 60% of manuscripts are accepted; 70% require significant revision. Average evaluation time is 4 months. About 20%t of articles are invited. Send 2 copies of manuscript, and abstract in English, to Editor Marcelo Dascal, Dept. of Phil., Tel-Aviv Univ., 69978 Tel-Aviv, Israel, and Associate Editor M. Wrigley at listed address.

Book reviews: Included. All book reviews are invited. Unsolicited book reviews are welcome.

Frequency: Biannual; Circulation: 700

Publisher: Centro de Logica, Epistemologia e Historia das Ciencias, Univ. Estadual de Campinas, CP 6133, 13081 Campinas, Sao Paulo

Subscription rates: $55; Single copies $30; postage included; required currency is US dollars.

PHILOSOPHIA*

Filosofisk Institut
Aarhus Universitet
DK-8000 Aarhus C
Denmark

Tel. 0045-89422215

ISSN 0108-1632

Date of founding: 1965

Sponsor: Filosofisk Forening 1 Aarhus, Filosofisk Institut, Aarhus Universitet, DK-8000 Aarhus C

Manuscript info: About 20 articles per year are devoted to philosophy. Manuscripts in any area of philosophy are welcome. Manuscripts are not refereed. About 50% of manuscripts are accepted; 50% of accepted manuscripts require significant revision. About 60% of articles are invited. Manuscripts should be sent to Aarhus Universitet.

Book reviews: Included. About 75% of book reviews are invited. Unsolicited book reviews are welcome.

Frequency: Biannual; Circulation: 500

Publisher: Philosophia, Filosofisk Institut, Aarhus Universitet, DK-8000 Aarhus C

Subscription rates: 200 DKr, Institutions 275 DKr

PHILOSOPHICAL PAPERS

Editor: Michael Pendlebury

Department of Philosophy
Univ. of the Witwatersrand
P.O. WITS
Johannesburg 2050
South Africa

Tel. 011-716-2757
Fax 011-403-1174
E-mail 103philp@muse.arts.wits.ac.za

ISSN 0556-8641

Date of founding: 1972

Purpose: To publish submitted and invited articles, notes, and critical studies in all branches of philosophy within the broad analytical tradition.

Sponsor: Departments of Philosophy, Rhodes University, and University of the Witwatersrand

Manuscript info: Manuscripts in any area of philosophy are welcome. Manuscripts are usually refereed. The referee's unsigned comments are given to authors on request if the paper is rejected. About 20% of manuscripts are accepted; 30% require significant revision. Average time to evaluate a manuscript is 6 weeks. Instructions for manuscript preparation are included in the journal.

Book reviews: Only occasional critical studies.

Frequency: 3 issues yearly; Circulation: 500

Publisher: Department of Philosophy, Rhodes University, P.O. Box 94, Grahamstown 6140, South Africa

Subscription rates: Individuals $20, Institutions $60, Students $12; postage included; any negotiable currency is acceptable.

PHILOSOPHY AND LITERATURE

Editor: Denis Dutton

School of Fine Arts
University of Canterbury
Christchurch,
New Zealand

Tel. 64-3-366-7001
Fax 64-3-364-2858
E-mail d.dutton@fina.canterbury.ac.nz

ISSN 0190-0013

Date of founding: 1976

Purpose: To provide a forum for scholars who wish to explore the relationship between philosophy and literary arts.

Sponsor: Whitman College

Manuscript info: Manuscripts are refereed, and the refereeing is blind when manuscripts are submitted with a detachable title-author page. Unsigned comments are given to authors when possible. Fewer than 10% of manuscripts are accepted; fewer than 20% require significant revision. Average evaluation time is 3 months. Instructions for manuscript preparation are included in the journal. Manuscripts should be sent to the editor, or to the co-editor, Patrick Henry, Whitman College, Walla Walla, WA 99362 USA.

Book reviews: Included. All book reviews are invited.

Frequency: Biannual

Publisher: Johns Hopkins University Press, Box 19966, Baltimore, MD 21211 USA;
E-mail jlorder@jhunix.hcf.jhu.edu

Subscription rates: $23 US, Institutions $48 US, Students $18 US; postage $5.50 US for airmail outside the continental USA.

SOPHIA: JOURNAL OF PHILOSOPHICAL THEOLOGY AND CROSS-CULTURAL PHILOSOPHY OF RELIGION

Editor: Purushottama Bilimoria

c/o Patrick Hutchings-Assoc. Ed.
Dept. of Phil., Melbourne Univ.
P.O. Box 4230, Parkville VIC 3052
Australia

Tel. 61-0-3-93445142 Ext. 4778
Fax 61-03-92445454
E-mail
zsophia@ariel.its.unimelb.edu.au

ISSN 0038-1527

Date of founding: 1962

Purpose: To provide a forum for discussion of issues in philosophical theology and cross-cultural philosophy of religions that are of contemporary interest and critical to cultural understanding.

Manuscript info: About 15 to 20 articles per year are devoted to philosophy, theology, and religions.
Manuscripts in any of these areas are welcome. Most manuscripts are refereed blind; comments are given to authors. About 60% of manuscripts are accepted; 30% require significant revi-

sion. Average evaluation time is 4 months. About 5% of articles are invited. Instructions for manuscript preparation are included in the journal.

Book reviews: Included; about 80% are invited. Unsolicited book reviews are welcome.

Frequency: 2-3 issues yearly;
Circulation: 650

Publisher: Society for Philosophy of Religion and Philosophical Theology, Inc.

Subscription rates: Individuals: Aust-NZ $15, US $18, UK £8, other countries $12.50 US; Institutions: Aust-NZ $20, US $25, UK £10, other countries $15 US

SORITES: ELECTRONIC QUARTERLY OF ANALYTIC PHILOSOPHY

Editor: Lorenzo Peña

CSIC Institute of Philosophy
Spanish Inst. Advanced Studies
Pinar 25
E-28006 Madrid
Spain

Fax +341 564 52 52
E-mail sorites@olmo.csic.es

ftp://olmo.csic.es/pub/sorites

ISSN 1135-1349

Date of founding: 1995

Purpose: *Sorites* is an electronic journal of analytical philosophy dedicated to the promotion of analytical standards of rigour and clarity in all fields of pure and applied philosophy.

Manuscript info: Papers in all fields of pure and applied philosophy are welcome. The journal can be accessed through Gopher or anonymous FTP at the Internet site olmo.csic.es, directory/pub/sorites. Editorial e-mail boxes are sorites@olmo.csic.es and sorites@pinar2.csic.es Manuscripts are refereed by members of the board of advisors or other specialists. Preferred format for manuscript submissions is WordPerfect 5.1; contact the editors for alternative formats.

Book reviews: Included.

Frequency: Quarterly

Publisher: Colectivo Sorites

Subscription rates: Free access via the Internet

Publishers

The following listing of publishers contains all information contained in the *Directory of American Philosophers, 1996-97*, published by the Philosophy Documentation Center. This includes Canadian publishers. Also included are publishers from the United Kingdom, as listed in the *International Directory of Philosophers, 1997-98*.

Although every effort has been made to ensure the accuracy of this information, in some cases no response has been received to our inquiries for updated information. In such cases, we have attempted to provide up-to-date information from other sources. These entries are marked with an asterisk to let the reader know that we were not able to confirm the information first-hand.

PUBLISHERS: UNITED STATES

ABARIS BOOKS, LTD.

70 New Canaan Ave.
Norwalk, CT 06850

Tel. 203-849-1655
Fax 203-849-9181

Date of founding: 1973

Ser Publ: Janus: authoritative translations of classics in philosophy and science consisting of major works from the late medieval period and Renaissance up to the end of the nineteenth century.

ABINGDON PRESS*

201 Eighth Ave., South, P.O. Box 801
Nashville, TN 37202-0801

Tel. 615-749-6404
Fax 615-749-6512

Date of founding: 1789

ABLEX PUBLISHING CORPORATION*

355 Chestnut St.
Norwood, NJ 07648

Tel. 201-767-8450
Fax 201-767-6717

Date of founding: 1977

ACADEMIC RESOURCES CORP.

P.O. Box 344
Delmar, NY 12054

Tel. 518-439-5978

Date of founding: 1936

Ser Publ: History of Psychology, ed. by Robert Watson; Early Modern Philosophy, ed. by Stanley Tweyman; Monographs in Islamic Religion and Theology, ed. by Parviz Morewedge; Studies in Islamic Philosophy and Science, ed. by the Society for the Study of Islamic Philosophy and Science.

ACORN PRESS, THE

P.O. Box 3279
Durham, NC 27715-3279

Tel. 919-471-3842
Fax 919-477-2622

Date of founding: 1980

Other info: Titles published to date are essentially in Indic philosophy, but scholarly manuscripts outside of this area are also welcome. We are the distributors of Chetana, Bombay, one of the leading publishers of philosophical works in India.

ADDISON-WESLEY PUBLISHING COMPANY, INC.*

Reading, MA 01867

Tel. 617-944-3700
Fax 617-944-9338

AGORA PUBLICATIONS

17 Dean St.
Millis, MA 02054

Tel. 508-376-4313
Fax 508-376-4313
E-mail
anderson@vaxvmsx.babson.edu

Date of founding: 1994

Ser Publ: The Theater of the Mind (Plato's dialogues), and The World of the Mind, both edited by Lieselotte Anderson and Ron Waite. The purpose of each series is to give teachers, students, and the general reader of classic texts an encounter with cherished and lasting ideas in a live listening experience. Each work is sold as a set of audio cassettes and accompanying paperback text, unabridged and in contemporary English.

ALBA HOUSE*

2187 Victory Blvd.
Staten Island, NY 10314-6603

Tel. 718-761-0047
Fax 718-761-0057

Other info: Alba House publishes works in the field of Christian philosophy.

AMERICAN ACADEMY OF RELIGION

1703 Clifton Rd., Suite G-5
Atlanta, GA 30329-4019

Tel. 404-727-7920
Fax 404-727-7959

Jour Publ: *Journal of the American Academy of Religion*

Ser Publ: Academy Series, ed. by Barbara A. Holdrege, publishes recent dissertations in religion; Reflection and Theory in the Study of Religion Series publishes books that make primary contributions to understanding theoretical and methodological issues in arising scholarly work in religious studies; Texts and Translations Series, ed. by Terry Godlove, aims to make available to the religious studies community important printed materials that are now inaccessible; Cultural Criticism Series, ed. by Cleo McNelly Kearns, publishes work that addresses the relation between religion and cultural studies, feminism, postcolonial and multicultural criticism, science and technology, environmentalism, peace studies, gay and lesbian studies, electronic media and the arts; The Religions Series, ed. by Paul B. Courtright, publishes books in textual and historical studies that highlight the many religions studied by AAR members.

AMERICAN ATHEIST PRESS

P.O. Box 140195
Austin, TX 78714-0195

Tel. 512-458-1244
E-mail info@atheist.org

Date of founding: 1959

Jour Publ: *American Atheist Newsletter; American Atheist Magazine*

Other info: Publishes paperback books.

ANALYTIC PRESS, THE

365 Broadway
Hillsdale, NJ 07642

Tel. 201-358-9477
Fax 201-358-0621
E-mail
orders@leahq.mhs.compuserve.com

Date of founding: 1982

Jour Publ: *Psychoanalytic Inquiry:* a topical journal for mental health professionals; *Psychoanalytic Dialogues:* a journal of relational perspectives

Ser Publ: The Psychonalytic Inquiry Book Series, ed. by Joseph D. Lichtenberg; The Psychoanalytic Study of Society, Volumes 10-19, ed. by L. Bryce Boyer and Ruth M. Boyer; The Relational Perspectives Book Series, ed. by Stephen A. Mitchell

Other info: Telephone number for orders: 800-926-6579 or 201-666-4110; fax number for orders: 201-666-2394

ANDREWS UNIVERSITY PRESS

Information Services Bldg., Suite 213
Berrien Springs, MI 49104-1700

Tel. 616-471-3392
Fax 616-471-6224
E-mail aupress@andrews.edu

Date of founding: 1965

Other info: Publishes 2 widely used texts in the philosophy of education.

ANTHONY PUBLISHING COMPANY*

206 Gleasondale Road
Stow, MA 01775

Tel. 508-897-7191
Fax 508-897-0894

Date of founding: 1979

Ser Publ: Four volumes on the *I Ching*, ed. by Carol K. Anthony, purpose: to make the ancient psychology and metaphysics of the *I Ching* available to western readers in a highly usable way.

ARETÉ PRESS*

P.O. Box 1060
Claremont, CA 91711-1060

Tel. 909-624-7770
Fax 909-398-1840

Date of founding: 1978

ARIEL PRESS

289 S. Main St., Suite 205
Alpharetta, GA 30201

Tel. 770-664-4886
Fax 770-664-4974

Date of founding: 1975

Ser Publ: Life of Spirit, ed. by Carl Japikse and Robert Leichtman; purpose: to explore the nature and purpose of spirit and how we can contact and use it; Art of Living, ed. by Carl Japikse and Robert Leichtman; purpose: personal growth and how we can enrich our lives.

ASIAN HUMANITIES PRESS

P.O. Box 3523
Fremont, CA 94539

Tel. 510-659-8272
Fax 510-659-0501

Date of founding: 1976

Ser Publ: Nanzan Studies in Asian Religions, ed. by Paul L. Swanson: scholarly texts and studies, as well as translations of religious, philosophical, and cultural material dealing with Asia; Religions of the World, ed. by Noble Ross Reat: trade and undergraduate-level course adoption-oriented books dealing with all the major religions of the world, from a historical, philosophical, and doctrinal viewpoint.

Other info: Publishes trade books in Oriental and Asian philosophy and religions (original works as well as translations) that have potential for undergraduate course adoption. Publishing proposals should be initiated with a query letter and project outline.

AVEBURY

Old Post Rd.
Brookfield, VT 05036-9704

Tel. 802-276-3162
Fax 802-276-3837
E-mail aveburypub@aol.com

Ser Publ: Avebury Series in Philosophy, ed. by David Lamb; Avebury Series in Philosophy of Science, ed. by David Lamb

BAKER BOOK HOUSE

P.O. Box 6287
Grand Rapids, MI 49516-6287

Tel. 616-676-9185
Fax 616-676-9573,
E-mail bakerbooks@aol.com

Date of founding: 1949

BARRON'S EDUCATIONAL SERIES, INC.

250 Wireless Blvd.
Hauppauge, NY 11788

Tel. 516-434-3311
Fax 516-434-3723

Date of founding: 1941

Ser Publ: Existentialism

BASIC BOOKS, INC.
A DIVISION OF HARPERCOLLINS

10 East 53rd Street
New York, NY 10022

Tel. 212-207-7057
Fax 212-207-7203

Date of founding: 1952

Other info: Basic Books publishes an entire range of philosophy in some form or other with few omissions.

BEACON PRESS

25 Beacon Street
Boston, MA 02108

Tel. 617-742-2110

Date of founding: 1854

Other info: Beacon Press publishes trade books that have potential for course adoption in feminist philosophy, political philosophy, ethics, philosophy of mind, and theology. Proposals should include author's CV and a short description of the work.

BEAR & COMPANY*

P.O. Drawer 2860
Santa Fe, NM 87504-2860

Tel. 505-983-5968
Fax 505-989-8386

Date of founding: 1980

Ser Publ: Meditation with the Medieval Mystics, ed. by Matthew Fox et al.: a series designed to make the teachings and beliefs of medieval thinkers accessible to modern readers.

BEHRMAN HOUSE*

235 Watchung Ave.
West Orange, NJ 07052

Tel. 201-669-0447
Fax 201-669-9769

Date of founding: 1921

BERG PUBLISHERS, LTD.*

13950 Park Center Rd.
Herndon, VA 22071-3222

Tel. 401-273-0061
Fax 401-273-6120

Date of founding: 1983

Jour Publ: *Diogenes*

Ser Publ: The Peirce Seminar Papers: An Annual of Semiotic Papers, ed. by Michael Shapiro: an annual of essays applying Charles Peirce's sign theory to problems of an interdisciplinary nature.

BERGHAHN BOOKS, INC.

165 Taber Ave.
Providence, RI 02906

Tel. 401-861-9330
Fax 401-521-0046
E-mail berghahnbk@aol.com

Date of founding: 1994

Jour Publ: *Diogenes; European Judaism; Sartre Studies International*

BLACKWELL PUBLISHERS

350 Main St.
Malden, MA 02148

Tel. 617-388-8200
Fax 617-388-8210
E-mail solde@world.std.com
http://www.blackwellpublishers.co.uk/

Date of founding: 1984

Jour Publ: *Noûs; Philosophical Books; Philosophical Investigations; The Philosophical Quarterly; Pacific Philosophical Quarterly; Metaphilosophy; Journal of Political Philosophy; European Journal of Philosophy*

Ser Publ: Philosophical Theory, ed. by John McDowell, Philip Pettit and Crispin Wright: advances philosophical theory by focusing on specific issues within the broad area of contemporary philosophy; Great Debates in Philosophy, ed. by Ernest Sosa: presents important current issues in philosophy in the form of a debate; Aristotelian Society Monographs, ed. by the Society's monographs committee, reflect current research in a variety of areas.

Other info: Blackwell Publishers publishes books and journals in all areas of philosophy, both analytic and continental, and specializes in paperback books for students and professional philosophers; anthologies and reference works.

BOLCHAZY-CARDUCCI PUBLISHERS, INC.

1000 Brown St., Unit 101
Wauconda, IL 60084

Tel. 708-526-4344
Fax 708-526-2867,
E-mail bolchazy@delphi.com

Date of founding: 1979

Jour Publ: *The Classical Bulletin* (ISSN 00009-8337)

Other info: Publisher of books–scholarly and textbooks–on the ancient world.

BRANDEN PUBLISHING COMPANY

17 Station St., Box 843
Brookline Village, MA 02147-0843

Tel. 617-734-2045
Fax 617-734-2046

Date of founding: 1965

BRAZILLER, GEORGE, INC.

60 Madison Avenue
New York, NY 10010

Tel. 212-889-0909

Date of founding: 1955

Ser Publ: International Library of Systems Theory and Philosophy, ed. by Ervin Laszlo: a collection that offers critical and creative examination of philosophical perspectives of systems theory and a forum for international work.

BROWN AND BENCHMARK PUBLISHERS

Sluice Dock
Guilford, CT 06437

Tel. 800-243-6532
Fax 203-453-6000,
E-mail lauriet@wcbc.com

Date of founding: 1971

BUCKNELL UNIVERSITY PRESS

Lewisburg, PA 17837

Tel. 717-524-3674
Fax 717-524-3760,
E-mail medgertn@bucknell.edu

Date of founding: 1969

Jour Publ: *Bucknell Review*

CAMBRIDGE UNIVERSITY PRESS*

40 West 20th St.
New York, NY 10011-4211

Tel. 212-924-3900
Fax 212-691-3239
http:www.cup.cam.ac.uk/

Jour Publ: *Philosophy; Religious Studies; The Behavioral and Brain Sciences; Social Philosophy and Policy*

Ser Publ: Modern European Philosophy, ed. by Raymond Geuss; Texts in German Philosophy, ed. by Raymond Geuss; Cambridge Studies in Philosophy, ed. by Ernest Sosa; Cambridge Studies in Philosophy and Law, ed. by Jules Coleman; Cambridge Studies in Philosophy and Public Policy, ed. by Douglas MacLean; Cambridge Studies in Philosophy and the Arts, ed. by Salim Kemal and Ivan Gaskell; Cambridge Studies in Probability, Induction and Decision Theory, ed. by Brian Skyrms; Studies in Rationality and Social Change, ed. by Jon Elster and Mike MacPherson; Studies in Marxism and Social Theory, ed. by Jon Elster, John Roemer, and G. A. Cohen; Cambridge Companions; Cambridge Philosophical Texts in Context, ed. by Dan Gerber and John Cottingham; Cambridge Studies in the Philosophy of Biology, ed. by Michael Ruse.

Other info: Publishes textbooks, monographs and reference books in all major subdisciplines within analytic philosophy, continental philosophy, history of philosophy, political philosophy, decision theory, philosophy and law, philosophy of science, and aesthetics.

CATHOLIC UNIVERSITY OF AMERICA PRESS

620 Michigan Avenue, N.E.
Washington, DC 20064

Tel. 202-319-5052
Fax 202-319-5802
E-mail mcgonagle@cua.edu

Date of founding: 1939

Ser Publ: Studies in Philosophy and the History of Philosophy, ed. by Jude P. Dougherty: a series of occasional volumes of collected papers.

Other info: Also publishes works of original scholarship in monograph form and works intended for supplemental reading assignments in courses. Customer service: P.O. Box 4852, Hampden Station, Baltimore, MD 21211 Tel. 410-516-6953, Fax 410-516-6998.

CHANDLER & SHARP PUBLISHERS, INC.

11A Commercial Boulevard
Novato, CA 94949-6117

Tel. 415-883-2353
Fax 415-883-4280

Date of founding: 1972

Ser Publ: Chandler & Sharp Publications in Political Thought and Theory

CHRISTIAN CLASSICS/A DIVISION OF THOMAS MORE

200 E. Bethany
Allen, TX 75002

Tel. 800-822-6701
Fax 800-688-8356

Date of founding: 1966

CHRISTOPHER PUBLISHING HOUSE

24 Rockland St.
Commerce Green
Hanover, MA 02339

Tel. 617-826-7474
Fax 617-826-5556

Date of founding: 1910

Other info: Publishes in all fields of philosophy; special interest in philosophy of religion.

CLARK UNIVERSITY PRESS

950 Main Street
Worcester, MA 01610

Tel. 508-793-7414
E-mail plongo@vax.clarku.edu

Jour Publ: *Idealistic Studies*

COLLEGIATE PRESS

6458 Lake Shore Drive
San Diego, CA 92119

Tel. 619-697-4182
Fax 619-698-0761

Date of founding: 1986

COLUMBIA UNIVERSITY PRESS

562 West 113th Street
New York, NY 10025

Tel. 212-666-1000 Ext. 7145
Fax 212-316-3100

Date of founding: 1893

Ser Publ: Agora Paperback Editions: translations and commentary on classic works in philosophy; Ancient Commentators on Aristotle, ed. by Richard Sorabji: translations of ancient Greek commentaries on Aristotle; Cornell Studies in the Philosophy of Religion, ed. by William P. Alston

CONTINUUM PUBLISHING COMPANY

370 Lexington Ave.
New York, NY 10017

Tel. 212-953-5858

Date of founding: 1980

Other info: Occasionally publishes and/or translates scholarly or general books in the field of philosophy. Potential authors or translators should query publisher before submitting manuscripts.

CORNELL UNIVERSITY PRESS

Sage House
512 East State St., P.O. Box 250
Ithaca, NY 14851

Tel. 607-277-2338
Fax 607-277-2374

Date of founding: 1869

Ser Publ: Agora Paperback Editions: translations and commentary on classic works in philosophy; Ancient Commentators on Aristotle, ed. by Richard Sorabji: translations of ancient Greek commentaries on Aristotle; Cornell Studies in the Philosophy of Religion, ed. by William P. Alston

Other info: Publishes in all fields of philosophy with special interest in moral theory, practical ethics, social/political philosophy, feminist philosophy, history of philosophy, philosophy of mathematics and religion, theory of knowledge, and classical philosophy.

COUNCIL OF SOCIETIES FOR THE STUDY OF RELIGION

Valparaiso University
Valparaiso, IN 46383-6493

Tel. 219-464-5515
Fax 219-464-6714
E-mail cssr@exodus.valpo.edu

Date of founding: 1970

Jour Publ: *Religious Studies Review; Council of Societies for the Study of Religion Bulletin*

Ser Publ: Council of Societies for the Study of Religion Directory of Departments and Programs of Religious Studies in North America; Council of Societies for the Study of

Religion Directory of Faculty of Departments and Programs of Religious Studies in North America.

CROSSROAD PUBLISHING COMPANY

370 Lexington Ave.
New York, NY 10017

Tel. 212-532-3650
Fax 212-532-4922

Date of founding: 1981

Other info: Publishes books on religion, spirituality, and counseling.

DARTMOUTH PUBLISHING COMPANY

Ashgate Publishing Company
Old Post Road
Brookfield, VT 05036-9704

Tel. 802-276-3162
Fax 802-276-3837
E-mail ashgatepub@aol.com

Ser Publ: International Research Library of Philosophy, John Skorupski, General Editor: the series collects a wide range of important and influential essays in philosophy published in the last 20 years. The Library constitutes a representative sampling of the best contemporary work in philosophy, divided into 4 series: Metaphysics and Epistemology; Philosophy of Logic, Mathematics and Science; Language and Mind. Applied Legal Philosophy Series, Tom D. Campbell, General Editor: encourages publication of books that adopt a theoretical approach to the study of particular areas of law, or deal with general theories of law in a way that is directed at issues of practical, moral, and political concern in specific legal contexts. The approach is analytical and theoretical.

Other info: 10 volumes currently available. 3-5 new volumes per year. 15% discount for standing orders.

WALTER DE GRUYTER, INC.

200 Saw Mill River Rd.
Hawthorne, NY 10532-1592

Tel. 914-747-0110
Fax 914-747-1326
http://www.degruyter.de/

Date of founding: 1919

Jour Publ: *Archiv für Geschichte der Philosophie; Kant-Studien.*

Ser Publ: Monographien und Texte zur Nietzsche-Forschung, ed. by Ernst Behler and Mazzino Montinari; Peripatoi, ed. by Paul Moraux; Phänomenologisch-psychologische Forschungen, ed. by Carl F. Graumann and Johannes Linschoten; Quellen und Studien zur Geschichte der Philosophie, ed. by Paul Wilpert; Quellen und Studien zur Philosophie, ed. by Günther Patzig and Erhard Scheibe.

DHARMA PUBLISHING

Editorial Offices
2425 Hillside Ave.
Berkeley, CA 94704

Tel. 510-548-5407
Fax 510-845-7540
E-mail 74547.1132@compuserve.com

Date of founding: 1972

Jour Publ: *Reports from the Field,* c/o Steve Randall, 19 Justin Dr., San Francisco, CA 94112

Ser Publ: Time, Space and Knowledge Series, ed. by Jack Petranker et al.: a series that explores the nature of time and space in order to move beyond conventional modes of thinking. Four titles in the series reunite science, philosophy, and direct experience through analysis and exercises, unveiling a profoundly liberating way of investigating human nature and the world; Crystal Mirror, ed. by Elizabeth Cook et al.: provides a comprehensive history of the Buddhist Dharma in India, Tibet, and other Asian countries. The series explores the life of the Buddha, the unfolding of the Dharma, and the growth of the Sangha over 2,000 years. Includes lineage lists, maps, biographies, overview of Buddhist texts, and bibliographies.

Other info: Business address: 2910 San Pablo Ave., Berkeley, CA 94702; Tel. 510-548-5407, Fax 510-548-2230

DIALOGUE PUBLISHING CO.

P.O. Box 11071
Honolulu, HI 96828

Tel. 808-943-6759
Fax 808-943-6759

Date of founding: 1982

Jour Publ: *Journal of Chinese Philosophy; International Journal of I Ching Studies* (in planning)

Ser Publ: Contemporary Studies in Chinese Philosophy, ed. by Chung-Ying Cheng: to present significant results of studies in Chinese philosophy.

DORRANCE PUBLISHING COMPANY, INC.*

643 Smithfield St.
Pittsburgh, PA 15222-2505

Tel. 412-288-4543
Fax 412-288-1786

Date of founding: 1920

Other info: For book orders:
Tel. 800-788-7654.

DOUBLEDAY & COMPANY, INC.*

Editorial Offices
1540 Broadway
New York, NY 10036

Tel. 212-782-6500

DOVER PUBLICATIONS, INC.

31 East 2nd Street
Mineola, NY 11501

Tel. 516-294-7000
Fax 516-742-6953

Date of founding: 1941

Ser Publ: Western Philosophy: a series that makes available to philosophers, students, and readers in general some of the classics of Western philosophical thought in a convenient format and at a low cost; History of Religions, Oriental Thought, Ancient Egypt: a series whose purpose is similar to that of the Western philosophy series, but with a comparative, intellectual orientation. Books include numerous classics in Eastern philosophies.

Other info: Dover's books in Western philosophy are almost exclusively paperback reprints, often revised editions, of important works in general philosophy, the philosophy of science, linguistic philosophy, metaphysics, political philosophy, and logic.

DUFOUR EDITIONS, INC.*

P.O. Box 7
Chester Springs, PA 19425-0007

Tel. 215-458-5005
Fax 215-458-7013

Date of founding: 1948

DUKE UNIVERSITY PRESS

Box 90660
Durham, NC 27708-0660

Tel. 919-687-3600
Fax 919-688-4574

Date of founding: 1921

Jour Publ: *Poetics Today; Journal of Medieval and Early Modern Studies*

Ser Publ: Post-Contemporary Interventions; The Roman Jakobson Series in Linguistics and Poetics

DUQUESNE UNIVERSITY PRESS

600 Forbes Avenue
Pittsburgh, PA 15282-0101

Tel. 412-396-6610
Fax 412-396-5780

Date of founding: 1927

Other info: Areas of publishing concentration include ethics and moral philosophy. Additional fax number: 412-396-5984.

EASTERN PRESS

P.O. Box 881
Bloomington, IN 47402-0881

Date of founding: 1981

EERDMANS, WILLIAM B., PUBLISHING COMPANY

255 Jefferson Avenue, SE
Grand Rapids, MI 49503

Tel. 616-459-4591
Fax 616-459-6540

Date of founding: 1911

Other info: Wm. B. Eerdmans Publishing Company publishes material generally in the areas of philosophy of religion, philosophical theology, and ethics. The majority of publications would fall in the areas of theology and biblical studies.

ENVIRONMENTAL ETHICS BOOKS

University of North Texas
P.O. Box 13496
Denton, TX 76203-6396

Tel. 817-565-2727
Fax 817-565-4448
E-mail ee@unt.edu

Other info: Environmental Ethics Books is a reprint series for important books in the field of environmental ethics. Currently, it has 4 books available.

FAIRLEIGH DICKINSON UNIVERSITY PRESS

285 Madison Avenue
Madison, NJ 07940

Tel. 201-593-8564
Fax 201-593-8564,
E-mail fdupress@fdu.edu

Date of founding: 1968

FORDHAM UNIVERSITY PRESS

University Box L
Bronx, NY 10458-5172

Tel. 718-817-4782
Fax 718-817-4785

Date of founding: 1907

Ser Publ: American Philosophy, Continental Philosophy (Perspectives in), and Moral Philosophy and Moral Theology Series

FORTRESS PRESS

Box 1209, 426 S. 5th St.
Minneapolis, MN 55440

Tel. 612-330-3433
Fax 612-330-3455

Date of founding: 1893

Other info: Fortress Press publishes books in philosophical theology and religious studies.

FRANCISCAN PRESS*

Quincy University
1800 College Ave.
Quincy, IL 62301-2670

Tel. 217-228-5670
Fax 217-228-5672

Date of founding: 1991

Other info: The Press has taken over the list of the now-defunct Franciscan Herald Press of Chicago. Herald Press titles remaining in print, including primary and secondary works in medieval philosophy and theology, are available.

FREE PRESS

866 Third Avenue
New York, NY 10022

Tel. 212-702-2000
Fax 212-605-4872
E-mail peter_burger@prenhall.com

Date of founding: 1947

GARLAND PUBLISHING, INC.

1000A Sherman Avenue
Hamden, CT 06514

Tel. 203-281-4487
Fax 203-230-1186

Date of founding: 1969

Ser Publ: Essays on Early Modern Philosophers, ed. by Vere Chappell; Sources and Studies in the History and Philosophy of Classical Science, General Editors: Alan C. Bowen and Francesca Rochberg-Halton; Garland Series in Applied Ethics, General Editor: Alan Goldman; Political Theory and Poltical Philosophy, General Editor: Maurice Cranston; Harvard Dissertations in Philosophy, General Editor: Robert Nozick; The Philosophy of George Berkeley, General Editor: George Pitcher

GEORGETOWN UNIVERSITY PRESS

3619 O St. NW
Washington, DC 20007

Tel. 202-687-5912
Fax 202-687-6340
E-mail
samplesj@gusun.georgetown.edu

Date of founding: 1964

Ser Publ: Moral Traditions and Moral Arguments, ed. by James F. Keenan, SJ

GINN PRESS*

160 Gould St.
Needham Heights, MA 02194-2310

Tel. 617-455-7000
Fax 617-455-1294

GORDON AND BREACH PUBLISHERS

2 Gateway Center, 11th Floor
Newark, NJ 07102

Tel. 201-643-7500
Fax 201-643-7676

Jour Publ: *World Futures: The Journal of General Evolution*

Ser Publ: The World Futures General Evolution Series, ed. by E. Laszlo

Tel. 212-614-7850
Fax 212-614-7886
E-mail grove@escape.com

Date of founding: 1992

GREEN, WARREN H., INC.

8356 Olive Boulevard
St. Louis, MO 63132

Tel. 314-991-1335
Fax 314-997-1788

Date of founding: 1966

Other info: Toll-free number: 800-537-0655

GREENWOOD PUBLISHING GROUP, INC.

88 Post Road West, P.O. Box 5007
Westport, CT 06881

Tel. 203-226-3571
Fax 203-222-1502

Ser Publ: Contributions in Philosophy: this series publishes important new monographs on the history of philosophy, avenues of philosophical inquiry, and analysis of individual thinkers and works; Bibliographies and Indexes in Philosophy: this series is designed to provide bibliographical and index materials for scholars, librarians, and other researchers concerned with key issues in philosophy; Bio-Bibliographies in Philosophy: a series of reference volumes on individual philosophers, historical and contemporary, international in scope.

GROVE/ATLANTIC, INC.

841 Broadway, 4th Flr.
New York, NY 10003-4793

GUILFORD PUBLICATIONS

72 Spring St.
New York, NY 10012-9941

Tel. 800-365-7006
Fax 212-966-6708
E-mail staff@guilford.com

Date of founding: 1978

Ser Publ: Critical Perspectives, ed. by Douglas Kellner, will publish state-of-the-art texts in the fields of philosophy, social and political theory, and cultural criticism that offer innovative treatments of politics, culture, and everyday life; The Conduct of Science, ed. by Steve Fuller, presents work from a variety of disciplines on how science is practiced. Topics such as peer review, the nature of scientific discovery, fraud/deception/self-deception, and policy, as well as other themes in the sociology, politics, and philosophy of science, will be considered in historical and contemporary context. Interdisciplinary Studies in Social Theory Series, ed. by John Paul Jones III, Wolfgang Natter, and Theodore R. Schatzki, arose out of the activities of the Committee on Social Theory at the University of Kentucky, which each year sponsors a public lecture series focused on a key area of inquiry in contemporary social thought. Avowedly interdisciplinary, each volume will contain provocative essays from humanists and social scientists, demonstrating the breadth of disciplinary perspectives that bear on central theoretical issues and furthering cross-disciplinary exchange. The Democracy and Ecology Series, ed. by James

O'Connor, is published in collaboration with the journal *Capitalism, Nature, Socialism.* Asking hard questions about what went wrong with the worlds that global capitalism and state socialism created, the series will also forge new paths to the kind of world that might be rebuilt from the wreckage of ecologically and socially bankrupt ways of life.

HACKETT PUBLISHING COMPANY

P.O. Box 44937
Indianapolis, IN 46244-0937

Tel. 317-635-9250
Fax 317-635-9292

Date of founding: 1972

Other info: Hackett is an independently owned publisher dedicated to publishing works of lasting value in the humanities for both students and scholars. Branch editorial office: P.O. Box 7, Cambridge, MA 02139; 617-497-6303, Fax 617-661-8703.

HARCOURT BRACE COLLEGE PUBLISHERS

301 Commerce St., Suite 3700
Fort Worth, TX 76102

Tel. 817-334-7529
Fax 817-334-0947
E-mail dtatom@harbrace.com

Date of founding: 1919

Ser Publ: Philosophy, ed. by Robert C. Solomon; Religion, ed. by Robert Ferm

HARLAN DAVIDSON, INC.

773 Glenn Ave.
Wheeling, IL 60090-6019

Tel. 708-541-9720

Fax 708-541-9830

Date of founding: 1972

Ser Publ: Crofts Classics Series, ed. by Samuel Beer: classics in philosophy, political science, and literature in authoritative, inexpensive paperbound editions, for classroom adoption in colleges and universities

HARPER SAN FRANCISCO

Div. of Harper Collins Publ.
1160 Battery St.
San Francisco, CA 94111-1213

Tel. 415-477-4400
Fax 415-477-4444

Date of founding: 1817

HARPERCOLLINS

10 E. 53rd St.
New York, NY 10022-5299

Tel. 212-207-7000
Fax 212-207-7797
http://www.harpercollins.com/

Date of founding: 1817

HARVARD UNIVERSITY PRESS

79 Garden Street
Cambridge, MA 02138-9983

Tel. 617-495-2600
Fax 617-495-5898

Date of founding: 1913

HASKELL HOUSE PUBLISHERS, LTD.

Box 420, Blythebourne Station
Brooklyn, NY 11219

Tel. 718-435-4400
Fax 715-635-7050

Date of founding: 1960

Ser Publ: Studies in Philosophy, ed. by H. Smith: a series of monographs in philosophy and aesthetics.

HIMALAYAN PUBLISHERS

R.R. 1, Box 405
Honesdale, PA 18431

Tel. 717-253-3022
Fax 717-253-9078

Date of founding: 1977

Other info: Books published provide a unique synthesis of Eastern and Western disciplines. Subject matter 0includes holistic health, preventive medicine, yoga, meditation, diet and nutrition, philosophy, psychology, and commentaries on Indian texts.

HOPE PUBLISHING HOUSE*

P.O. Box 60008
Pasadena, CA 91116-6008

Tel. 818-792-6123
Fax 818-792-2121

Date of founding: 1983

HOUGHTON MIFFLIN COMPANY*

222 Berkeley St.
Boston, MA 02116

Tel. 617-351-5000
Fax 617-351-1117

Date of founding: 1832

HUMAN KINETICS PUBLISHERS, INC.

1607 N. Market St.
Champaign, IL 61820-2200

Tel. 217-351-5076
Fax 217-351-2674

Date of founding: 1974

Jour Publ: *Journal of the Philosophy of Sport*

Other info: HKP also publishes books in sport philosophy.

HUMANA PRESS

999 Riverview Dr. #208
Totowa, NJ 07512-1165

Tel. 201-256-1699
Fax 201-256-8341

Date of founding: 1977

Ser Publ: Biomedical Ethics Reviews, ed. by James M. Humber and Robert F. Almeder: yearly volumes that examine a variety of concepts, case histories, and literature in contemporary biomedical ethics; Contemporary Issues in Biomedicine, Ethics, and Society, ed. by John W. Davis, Barry Hoffmaster, and Sarah J. Shorten: provides in-depth treatment of single issues in medical and social ethics today.

HUMANITIES PRESS INTERNATIONAL, INC.

165 First Ave.
Atlantic Highlands, NJ 07716

Tel. 908-872-1441
Fax 908-872-0717

Date of founding: 1951

Jour Publ: *Journal of Phenomenological Psychology; Research in Phenomenology; New Vico Studies; Review of Existential Psychology and Psychiatry*

213

Ser Publ: Contemporary Studies in Philosophy and the Human Sciences, ed. by Hugh J. Silverman and Graeme Nicholson: explores recent developments in philosophy, stressing fundamental issues and current styles of philosophical thought; Philosophy and Literary Theory, ed. by Hugh J. Silverman: a series highlighting interdisciplinary studies that take a philosophical or theoretical position with respect to literature, literary study, and the practice of criticism; Key Concepts in Critical Theory, ed. by Roger S. Gottlieb: a new series consisting of volumes edited by recognized scholars on such concepts as justice, democracy, and alienation, presents traditional and contemporary analyses of these concepts and explores the variety of theoretical contexts and political programs in which the selected concept has functioned; intended for students of political philosophy.
Society/Religion//Religion/Society, edited by Roger Gottlieb: explores the connections and dissonances between post-secular society and the worlds of spirituality as they occur in such environments as the spiritual implications of the new physics, abortion rights, deep ecology, feminist spirituality, etc. The series examines the reentry of spiritual ideas into social life–at the same time as religion and spirituality itself are being transformed by social crisis, political movements, and the new intellectual perspectives.

Other info: Humanities Press publishes titles in the areas of philosophy, ethics, social sciences, political theory, philosophy of religion, comparative religion, Buber studies, history, aesthetics, and art theory, among others.

INDIANA UNIVERSITY PRESS

601 N. Morton St.
Bloomington, IN 47404-3797

Tel. 812-855-6804
Fax 812-855-7931,
E-mail iupress@indiana.edu

Date of founding: 1950

Jour Publ: *Discourse: Journal for Theoretical Studies in Media and Culture*, ed. by Roswitha Mueller and Kathleen Woodward; *Hypatia: A Journal of Feminist Philosophy*, ed. by Linda Lopez McAlister; *Differences: A Journal of Feminist Cultural Studies,* ed. by Naomi Schor and Elizabeth Weed

Ser Publ: Medical Ethics, ed. by David H. Smith and Robert M. Veatch, seeks to publish works that address ethical issues related to medical advances, research, and experimentation; Studies in Continental Thought, ed. by John Sallis, embraces work in all areas of continental philosophy–from 19th century German idealism to current philosophical developments; Indiana Series in the Philosophy of Religion, ed. by Merold Westphal, fosters critical reflection on religion from a variety of perspectives; Indiana Series in the Philosophy of Technology, ed. by Don Ihde, encourages analysis of the impact of a wide range of technologies upon human life and society.

Other info: Internet addresses: http://www.indiana.edu/~iupress
Toll-free telephone: 1-800-842-6796

INNER TRADITIONS INTERNATIONAL, LTD.*

One Park St.
Rochester, VT 05767

Tel. 802-767-3174
Fax 802-767-3726

Date of founding: 1975

Other info: Books are published about both Eastern and Western philosophy. Authors include R. A. & Isha Schwaller de Lubicz, Alain Daniélou, Nicholas Roerich, Sir Richard Burton, Harish Johari, and the ancient Sufi masters.

INTERNATIONAL PUBLISHERS CO., INC.

239 West 23rd Street, 5th Floor
New York, NY 10011-2302

Tel. 212-366-9816
Fax 212-366-9820

Date of founding: 1924

Ser Publ: Collected Works of Karl Marx and Frederick Engels in 50 volumes

Other info: Other titles on Marxist dialectics, historical materialism, and works influenced by Marxist philosophy. Free catalog on request.

INTERVARSITY PRESS

P.O. Box 1400
Downers Grove, IL 60515

Tel. 708-887-2500
Fax 708-887-2520
E-mail staff@ivpress.com

Date of founding: 1947

Ser Publ: Contours of Christian Philosophy, ed. by C. Stephen Evans: a series of introductory-level textbooks in ethics, metaphysics, philosophical theology and philosophy of religion. The books explore the implications that Christian convictions might have for the philosophical issues discussed as well as the implications of the various topics for Christian theology. Contours of Christian Theology, ed. by Gerald Bray: a new series of concise introductory texts focusing on the main themes of Christian theology, exploring contemporary issues with insights from evangelical and other traditions.

Other info: InterVarsity Press has strengthened its academic line with the release of *Philosophers Who Believe*, featuring autobiographical essays by Mortimer Adler, Alvin Plantinga, and others.

J A I PRESS, INC.

55 Old Post Rd. #2, P.O. Box 1678
Greenwich, CT 06836-1678

Tel. 203-661-7602
Fax 203-661-0792

Date of founding: 1972

Jour Publ: *Journal of Social and Evolutionary Systems*

Ser Publ: Research in Philosophy and Technology, ed. by Carl Mitcham; Knowledge & Society, ed. by Shirley Gurenstein

JOHNS HOPKINS UNIVERSITY PRESS

2715 N. Charles St.
Baltimore, MD 21218-4319

Tel. 301-338-6900
Fax 301-338-6998
http://www.press.jhu.edu/real_home.html

Date of founding: 1878

Jour Publ: *Diacritics; Philosophy and Literature; American Journal of Philology;*

Human Rights Quarterly; Kennedy Institute of Ethics Journal; New Literary History

JONES AND BARTLETT PUBLISHERS, INC.

40 Tall Pine Dr.
Sudbury, MA 01776

Tel. 508-443-5000
Fax 508-443-8000
E-mail custserv@jbpub.com

Date of founding: 1983

Ser Publ: Series in Moral Philosophy, ed. by Robert Ginsberg, offers textbooks addressed to complex issues and problems of being human in the troubled world of the twentieth-century, including environment, feminism, human rights, love and sex, war and peace, meaning and responsibility; Series in Philosophy of Culture, ed. by Robert Ginsberg, introduces students to global awareness through study of the philosophical heritage of Africa, Asia, Latin America, and Native America; Series in Applied Ethics, ed. by Sterling Harwood, publishes books exploring business ethics, biomedical ethics, philosophy of law, ethics of the professions; Series in Logic and Scientific Methodology, ed. by Gary Jason, publishes books exploring any area in the teaching of logic and science: induction, deduction, symbolic logic, computer logic, critical thinking, and scientific reasoning. Jones and Barlett is actively seeking student-centered books in all fields of philosophy, including nursing ethics, philosophy of science, aesthetics, philosophy of religion, media ethics, philosophy of technology, philosophy of woman, human values, philosophy and film, philosophy and history, and philosophy for the future.

Video programs, computer disks, and other visual and electronic aids may be distributed in conjunction with texts. Philosophy Editorial Office is located at 30 Granada Court, Portola Valley, CA 94028-7737; phone 415-851-0182; fax 415-851-5015. Inquiries and submissions are welcome.

Other info: Philosophy Div.: Arthur C. Bartlett, Sr. V.P. & Publisher; Nancy E. Bartlett, Philosophy Editor; Robert Ginsberg, General Editor; E-mail: jnbartlett@aol.com. Toll-free telephone: 800-832-0034.

KLUWER ACADEMIC PUBLISHERS

101 Philip Dr.
Norwell, MA 02061-1677

Tel. 617-871-6600
Fax 617-871-6528
E-mail kluwer@world.std.com
http://kapis.www.wkap.nl/

Date of founding: 1853

Jour Publ: *Argumentation; Biology and Philosophy; Erkenntnis; Husserl Studies; International Journal for Philosophy of Religion; Journal of Business Ethics; Journal for General Philosophy of Science; Journal of Indian Philosophy; Journal of Medicine and Philosophy; Journal of Value Inquiry; Journal of Philosophical Logic; Law and Philosophy; Man and World; Minds and Machines; Philosophical Studies; Studia Logica; Studies in Philosophy and Education; Synthese; Theoretical Medicine;* and others

Ser Publ: Kluwer publishes more than 30 series in philosophy.

Other info: Distributor for US and Canada: Kluwer Academic Publishers at US address listed. Distributor outside US and Canada: Kluwer Academic Publishers Group Distr. Ctr.,

P.O. Box 322, 3300 AH Dordrecht,
The Netherlands, 078-39-2392;
E-mail: kluwer@wkap.nl

KRAUS REPRINT*

358 Saw Mill River Rd.
Millwood, NY 10546-1035

Tel. 914-762-2200
Fax 914-762-1195

Date of founding: 1946

Other info: Kraus publishes reprints
of books and journals in a wide variety of fields, including many titles in
philosophy and religion.

KRIEGER PUBLISHING COMPANY

P.O. Box 9542
Melbourne, FL 32902-9542

Tel. 407-724-9542
Fax 407-951-3671

Date of founding: 1969

Other info: Books are published on philosophy, religion, and phenomenology.

PETER LANG PUBLISHING, INC.

275 Seventh Ave., 28th Floor
New York, NY 10001-6708

Tel. 212-647-7700
Fax 212-647-7707

Date of founding: 1982

Ser Publ: New Directions in
Philosophy, ed. by Anatole Anton;
Revisioning Philosophy, ed. by David
Appelbaum; Historia Critica
Philosophiae, ed. by Paul Richard
Blum; New Perspectives in
Philosophical Scholarship, ed. by
James Duerlinger; Asian Thought and
Culture, ed. by Charles Wei-Hsun

Fun; New Studies in Aesthetics, ed. by
Robert Ginsberg; Literature and the
Sciences of Man, ed. by Peter Heller;
Studies in Contemporary Continental
Philosophy, ed. by Galen A. Johnson;
Studies in Moral Philosophy, ed. by
John Kekes; John MacMurray Studies,
ed. by Frank Kirkpatrick; Studies in
European Thought, ed. by E. Allen
McCormick; Hermeneutic
Commentaries, ed. by Pietro Pucci;
Contemporary Existentialism, ed. by
Howard K. Slaatte; Soviet and East
European Studies in Aesthetics and
the Philosophy of Culture, ed. by
Willis H. Truitt; Emory Vico Studies,
ed. by Donald P. Verene; Conflict and
Consciousness, ed. by Charles P.
Webel; Applied Philosophy, ed. by
Farhang Zabeeh; Catholic Thought
from Lublin, ed. by A. Woznicki.

Other info: Customer service:
800-770-5264; 212-647-7706

LANGUAGE PRESS

7703 N. Alden St., Box 342
Whitewater, WI 53190

Tel. 414-473-8822

Ser Publ: Philosophical Psychology,
ed. by Warren Shibles: books on
death, emotion, rational love, ethics,
and lying; Philosophy for Children,
ed. by Warren Shibles: a series whose
purpose is to make philosophy available to young people from grade
three through high school; Metaphor
Series; Emotion Series.

Other info: Press is interested in
manuscripts that stress clarification of
concepts and humanism and promote
practical application of philosophy
and psychology toward solving
human problems.

LARSON PUBLICATIONS

4936 Route 414
Burdett, NY 14818-9795

Tel. 607-546-9342
Fax 607-546-9344

Date of founding: 1981

Ser Publ: The Notebooks of Paul
Brunton, ed. by Paul R. Cash and
Timothy J. Smith: East-West synthesis,
modern reformulation of traditional
wisdom teachings.

LEHIGH UNIVERSITY PRESS

30 Library Dr.
Bethlehem, PA 18015-3067

Tel. 610-758-3933
Fax 610-974-2823
E-mail inlup@lehigh.edu

Date of founding: 1986

Other info: Specializing in eigh-
teenth-century studies and the history
of science and technology.

LIBERTARIAN PRESS, INC.*

P.O. Box 309
Grove City, PA 16127-0309

Tel. 412-458-5861

Date of founding: 1952

LIBERTY FUND, INC.

8335 Allison Pointe Trail, Suite 300
Indianapolis, IN 46250-1687

Tel. 317-842-0880
Fax 317-577-9067

Date of founding: 1960

Other info: Liberty Fund is an educational foundation established to
encourage study of the ideal of a society of free and responsible individuals. It publishes books in history,
political thought, and economics as
well as philosophy.

LIBRA PUBLISHERS, INC.

3089C Clairemont Dr., Suite 383
San Diego, CA 92117

Tel. 619-571-1414

Date of founding: 1960

Jour Publ: *Adolescence; Family Therapy:
The Journal of the California Graduate
School of Family Psychology*

LONG BEACH PUBLICATIONS

P.O. Box 14807
Long Beach, CA 90803

Tel. 310-439-7347
Fax 310-439-7347 Ext. 58

Date of founding: 1982

Other info: Long Beach Publications
was established to publish works in
Asian thought and comparative philosophy and religion.

LOUISIANA STATE UNIVERSITY PRESS

P.O. Box 25053
Baton Rouge, LA 70894-5053

Tel. 504-388-6294
Fax 504-388-6461
E-mail uppress@lsuvm.sncc.lsu.edu

Date of founding: 1935

Other info: The focus of our philosophy program is political theory and
ideas. We are publishing the Collected

218

Works of Eric Voegelin (34 volumes projected), and we have published a number of works that explore aspects of Voegelin's thought.

LOYOLA UNIVERSITY PRESS

3441 N. Ashland Ave.
Chicago, IL 60657-1301

Tel. 312-281-1818
Fax 312-281-0885

Date of founding: 1912

M I T PRESS*

55 Hayward St.
Cambridge, MA 02142

Tel. 617-253-1584

Date of founding: 1961

Jour Publ: *Computational Linguistics; Thesis Eleven: Interpreting Modernity; Linguistic Inquiry*

Ser Publ: Studies in Contemporary German Social Thought, ed. by Thomas McCarthy, makes available to an English-speaking audience primary and secondary materials dealing with the major strands of social theory, as practiced in modern Germany; Learning, Development, and Conceptual Change, ed. by Lila Gleitman, Susan Carey, Elissa Newport, and Elizabeth Spelke: books in developmental and cognitive psychology exploring the formation of concepts and mental structures; Computational Models of Cognition and Perception, ed. by Jerome A. Feldman, Patrick J. Hayes, and David E. Rumelhart, explores such subject domains as knowledge representation, natural language understanding, problem solving, learning and generalization; Representation and Mind, ed. by

Ned Block and Hilary Putnam, consists of work in philosophy of mind and of psychology.

Other info: The MIT Press publishes other books outside series on continental philosophy, social theory, linguistic theory, and philosophy of science; Bradford Books, a separate imprint of the Press since 1981, publishes books on philosophy of mind and science.

MACMILLAN PUBLISHING COMPANY*

866 Third Ave.
New York, NY 10022

Tel. 212-702-2000

MAGI BOOKS, INC.

33 Buckingham Drive
Albany, NY 12208

Tel. 518-482-7781

Date of founding: 1964

MAISONNEUVE PRESS

P.O. Box 2980
Washington, DC 20013-2980

Tel. 301-277-7505
Fax 301-277-2467

Date of founding: 1988

Ser Publ: Post-Modern Positions, ed. by Robert Merrill: examines epistemological, aesthetic, and sociological shifts of post-modernism; Critical Studies in Community Development and Architecture, ed. by Dennis Crow: integrates new developments in poststructural philosophy and social theory to urban planning and architecture. Transformation: Marxist Boundary Work in Theory, Economics, Politics, and Culture; ed. by Mas'ud Zavarzadch, Teresa Ebert, and Donald Morton: deploys classical Marxist theory to the new terrains of capitalism without borders.

Other info: Maisonneuve Press was founded to promote work bridging the gap between serious scholarship and political/social transformation. To build a network and mailing list, we are interested in hearing from those who share this commitment.

MARQUETTE UNIVERSITY PRESS

Marquette University, Cudahy Hall
P.O. Box 1881
Milwaukee, WI 53201-1881

414-288-1564
Fax 414-288-3300

Date of founding: 1916

Jour Publ: *Philosophy and Theology:* Marquette University Quarterly; *Renascence:* Values in English Literature

Ser Publ: St. Thomas Aquinas Lecture Series, ed. by Roland Teske: to honor St. Thomas Aquinas; Mediaeval Philosophical Texts in Translation, ed. by Roland Teske: to perpetuate knowledge in humanistic studies and to help offset decline in knowledge of Latin; The Pere Marquette Theology Series: a series of annual public lectures to honor the explorer Pere Jacques Marquette; Marquette Studies in Philosophy, ed. by Andrew Tallon; Marquette studies in Theology, ed. by Andrew Tallon; Reformation Texts With Translation, ed. by Kenneth Hagen.

Other info: Press is primarily directed to publishing works and translations of scholars in philosophy and theology with emphasis on Jesuit learning and history. The press also has titles in history, foreign languages, and education.

MARXIST EDUCATIONAL PRESS

University of Minnesota
116 Church St. SE
Minneapolis, MN 55455-0112

Tel. 612-922-7993
E-mail marquit@physics.spa.umn.edu

Date of founding: 1977

Jour Publ: *Nature, Society, and Thought:* a Journal of Dialectical and Historical Materialism

Ser Publ: Studies in Marxism: monographs and collections of papers on application of dialectical and historical materialism to various fields; Marxist Dimensions, ed. by James Lawler: collections of papers on dialectical and historical materialism in a given field of inquiry.

Other info: Also publishes books under imprint MEP Publications.

MAYFIELD PUBLISHING COMPANY

1280 Villa Street
Mountain View, CA 94041

Tel. 415-960-3222
Fax 415-960-0328,
E-mail 74512.2233@compuserve.com

Date of founding: 1946

Other info: Mayfield is a publisher of college textbooks. Sponsoring Editor in Philosophy: James Bull.

MCGRAW-HILL COLLEGE DIVISION

1221 Avenue of the Americas
43rd Floor
New York, NY 10020-1095

Tel. 212-512-2987
Fax 212-512-6260

Ser Publ: The Heritage Series, ed. by Tom Regan: brief introductory texts and anthologies.

Other info: McGraw-Hill College Division publishes textbooks in philosophy.

MCPHERSON & COMPANY

P.O. Box 1126
Kingston, NY 12401-0126

Tel. 914-331-5807
Fax 914-331-5807

Date of founding: 1973

Other info: The main foci of McPherson & Company are literary fiction and art "criticism." Books issued in both areas have proved to be of interest to philosophers. Texts on art are usually published under our DOCUMENTEXT imprint. Catalog available on request.

MELLEN, EDWIN, PRESS, THE

415 Ridge St., P.O. Box 450
Lewiston, NY 14092-0450

Tel. 716-754-2266
Fax 716-754-4056

Date of founding: 1974

Ser Publ: Studies in the History of Philosophy, ed. by H. Richardson: monographs, translations, and specialized studies in the history of philoso-phy; Problems in Contemporary Philosophy, ed. by H. Richardson: monographs dealing with particular problems analyzed philosophically; Texts and Studies in Religion, ed. by H. Richardson: history of Western religious and philosophical tradition (including classical and mediaeval philosophy); Studies in Asian Thought and History, ed. by H. Richardson: Asian philosophy (including classical).

MERCER UNIVERSITY PRESS

6316 Peake Road
Macon, GA 31210

Tel. 912-752-2880
Fax 912-752-2264

Date of founding: 1979

Jour Publ: *The Personalist Forum*

Ser Publ: International Kierkegaard Commentary Series, ed. by Robert L. Perkins; North American Paul Tillich Society–Mercer University Press Series on Paul Tillich Studies, ed. by John J. Carey; Studies in American Biblical Hermeneutics, ed. by Charles Mabee: a series that hopes to promote interdisciplinary, interdenominational, and intercommunity conversation with the Bible as the formative text of the American experience.

MILK BOTTLE PRODUCTIONS, INC.

P.O. Box 10325
Arlington, VA 22210-1325

Tel. 703-525-1860
Fax 703-525-0617
E-mail ndopa@cap1.capaccess.org

Date of founding: 1992

Ser Publ: MBPI produces "No Dogs or Philosophers Allowed," the philosophy television program seen on PBS and other educational stations. It also produces other philosophical multimedia and does research into new ways to distribute Socratic discourse, including CD-ROM, video-on-demand, and online services.

Other info: WWW address: http://www.access.digex.net/ ~kknise ly/philosophy.tv.html

WILLIAM MORROW & COMPANY*

1350 Avenue of the Americas
New York, NY 10019

Tel. 212-261-6500
Fax 212-261-6595

Date of founding: 1926

NEW YORK UNIVERSITY PRESS

Washington Square
New York, NY 10003

Tel. 212-998-2575
Fax 212-995-3833

Date of founding: 1916

Ser Publ: Nomos, the yearbook of the American Society for Political and Legal Philosophy, ed. by John W. Chapman and Ian Shapiro, is a collection of essays that focus on the problem of uniting the several social sciences, law, and philosophy.

NICOLAS-HAYS, INC.

P.O. Box 612
York Beach, ME 03910-0612

Tel. 207-363-4393
Fax 207-363-5799

Date of founding: 1976

NORTHERN ILLINOIS UNIVERSITY PRESS

320A Williston
DeKalb, IL 60115-2854

Tel. 815-753-1826
Fax 815-753-1845

Date of founding: 1965

Other info: NIUP publishes in history of philosophy, ethics, and political theory.

NORTHWESTERN UNIVERSITY PRESS

625 Colfax St.
Evanston, IL 60208-4210

Tel. 708-491-5313
Fax 708-491-8150
E-mail nupress@nwu.edu

Ser Publ: Studies in Phenomenology and Existential Philosophy, John McCumber and David M. Levin, General Editors: translations of the important works of phenomenology and existential philosophy, as well as original works in these fields.

W. W. NORTON & COMPANY, INC.

500 Fifth Avenue
New York, NY 10110

Tel. 212-354-5500
Fax 212-869-0856

Date of founding: 1923

OHIO STATE UNIVERSITY PRESS

180 Pressey Hall, 1070 Carmack Rd.
Columbus, OH 43210-1002

Tel. 614-292-6930
Fax 614-292-2065

Date of founding: 1957

OHIO UNIVERSITY PRESS

Scott Quadrangle
Athens, OH 45701

Tel. 614-593-1155
Fax 614-593-4536

Date of founding: 1964

Ser Publ: Continental Thought Series, ed. by J. Claude Evans: monographs and original investigations whose purpose is to foster philosophy and theoretical human science in the twentieth-century continental tradition.

C. OLSON AND COMPANY

P.O. Box 100
Santa Cruz, CA 95063-0100

Tel. 408-458-9004

Date of founding: 1981

OPEN COURT PUBLISHING

332 S. Michigan Ave., Suite 2000
Chicago, IL 60604

Tel. 312-939-1500
Fax 312-939-8150

Date of founding: 1887

Ser Publ: Paul Carus Lectures Series, whose purpose is to further free and original philosophical enquiry. Biannually, a lecturer chosen by the APA delivers the Lectures, which are subsequently published by Open Court; Library of Living Philosophers, ed. by Lewis Edwin Hahn: a series of volumes, each containing a leading philosopher's intellectual autobiography, critical articles by 20-30 philosophers, and the philosopher's replies to each, with a full bibliography and other information.

Other info: Specializes in books on ethics, continental philosophy, philosophy of religion, philosophy of science, epistemology, and Indian and Chinese philosophy. The *Monist*, formerly published by Open Court, is now published by Hegeler Institute.

OX BOW PRESS

P.O. Box 4045
Woodbridge, CT 06525-0045

Tel. 203-387-5900
Fax 203-387-0035

Date of founding: 1977

OXFORD UNIVERSITY PRESS

198 Madison Avenue
New York, NY 10016

Tel. 212-726-6000
Fax 212-726-6449
http://www.oup.co.uk/

Jour Publ: *British Journal of Aesthetics; Mind; Common Knowledge; British Journal for the Philosophy of Science; Journal of Semantics*

Ser Publ: Philosophy of Mind Series, ed. by Owen Flanagan; Clarendon Aristotle Series, ed. by J. L. Ackrill and Lindsay Judson; Clarendon Edition of the Philosophical Works of Thomas Hobbes, ed. by Noel Malcolm; Clarendon Edition of the Works of John Locke, ed. by M. A. Stewart; Clarendon Library of Logic and Philosophy, ed. by L. Jonathan Cohen; Clarendon Plato Series, ed. by M. J. Woods; The Glasgow Edition of the Works and Correspondence of Adam Smith, Marxist Introductions, ed. by Steven Lukes; Oxford Logic Guides; Oxford Readings in Philosophy; The Collected Works of Jeremy Bentham, ed. by J. R.

Dinwiddy; Environmental Ethics and Science Policy, ed. by Kristin Shrader-Frechette; Logic and Computation in Philosophy, ed. by Clark Glymour, Teddy Seidenfeld, and Wilfried Sieg; Oxford Ethics Series, ed. by Derek Parfit; Vancouver Studies in Cognitive Science, ed. by Steven Davis.

Other info: The press publishes scholarly, college, and trade books in philosophy, including contemporary as well as classical works. Philosophy Eds (both at address listed): Robert Miller, 212-726-6219, E-mail rbm@oup-usa.org; Cynthia Read, 212-726-6030

P J D PUBLICATIONS, LTD.*

P.O. Box 966
Westbury, NY 11590-0966

Tel. 516-626-0650
Fax 516-626-5546

Date of founding: 1968

Ser Publ: What Are We Living For? A Practical Philosophy, ed. by C. D. Leake

PACHART PUBLISHING HOUSE

1130 San Lucas Circle
Tucson, AZ 85704

Fax 602-297-4797

Date of founding: 1970

Jour Publ: *Philosophy in Science*: contains articles on philosophical ramifications of astronomy and cosmology.

Ser Publ: Philosophy in Science Library, ed. by M. Heller and J. Zycinski: books on philosophical issues arising within the sciences, discussed at a level accessible to intelli-

gent laymen, as well as scholarly monographs.

Other info: Pachart Foundation, a non-profit association.

PALACE PUBLISHING

RD 1, Box 320
Moundsville, WV 26041

Tel. 304-845-1380
Fax 304-845-9819

Other info: Publishes in fields of religion and philosophy, including vedic, interfaith, new age, and metaphysics.

PATHFINDER PRESS, INC.

410 West Street
New York, NY 10014

Tel. 212-741-0690
Fax 212-727-0150

Date of founding: 1970

Jour Publ: Distributes *New International: A Magazine of Marxist Politics and Theory.*

Ser Publ: Although not formally a series, the works of George Novack, one of the foremost American Marxist scholars, are an integrated collection.

Other info: Also available from Pathfinder are theoretical writings of Marx, Engels, Lenin, and Trotsky.

PAULIST PRESS

997 MacArthur Boulevard
Mahwah, NJ 07430

Tel. 201-825-7300
Fax 201-825-8345

Date of founding: 1865

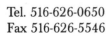

Ser Publ: History of Philosophy Series, ed. by Frederick Copleston.

PENDRAGON PRESS

41 Ferry Rd.
Stuyvesant, NY 12173-9720

Tel. 518-828-3008
Fax 518-828-2368
E-mail pendpress@aol.com

Date of founding: 1976

Ser Publ: Aesthetics in Music Series: this series contains several anthologies, spanning ancient times to the present, which serve more fully to explore music in an aesthetic sense.

PENGUIN USA

375 Hudson St.
New York, NY 10014-3657

Tel. 212-366-2000
Fax 212-366-2666
http://www.penguin.com/

PENNSYLVANIA STATE UNIVERSITY PRESS

820 N. University Drive
University Park, PA 16802

Tel. 814-865-1327
Fax 814-863-1408
E-mail sgt3@psu.edu

Date of founding: 1956

Jour Publ: *Philosophy and Rhetoric; Journal of Speculative Philosophy—New Series*

Ser Publ: Literature and Philosophy, ed. by A. J. Cascardi: a new series that will publish a wide range of subjects in philosophy and literature, including studies of the social and his-

torical issues that relate to the two fields. Drawing on the resources of the Anglo-American and continental traditions, the series is open to philosophically informed scholarship covering the entire range of contemporary critical thought. Re-Reading the Canon, Nancy Tuana, General Editor: a new series that will consist of edited collections of essays, original and previously published, offering feminist reinterpretations of the writings of major figures in the Western philosophical tradition.

PERIPATETIC PRESS, THE

Box 68
Grinnell, IA 50112

Tel. 515-236-5861

Date of founding: 1979

Ser Publ: Translations of Aristotle's works, by Hippocrates G. Apostle: 9 translations to date.

PHANES PRESS, INC.

P.O. Box 6114
Grand Rapids, MI 49516

Tel. 616-458-8869
Fax 616-458-8869
E-mail phanes@cris.com

Date of founding: 1984

Jour Publ: *Alexandria: The Journal of the Western Cosmological Traditions*

Other info: Phanes Press publishes books on the spiritual and philosophical traditions of the Western world with an emphasis on Neoplatonism. Also distributes 300 titles from other publishers.

PHILOSOPHY DOCUMENTATION CENTER

Bowling Green State University
Bowling Green, OH 43403-0189

Tel. 419-372-2419
Fax 419-372-6987
E-mail phildoc@opie.bgsu.edu
http://www.bgsu.edu/pdc/

Date of founding: 1966

Jour Publ: *Journal of Philosophical Research; Teaching Philosophy*

Ser Publ: *Directory of American Philosophers, International Directory of Philosophy and Philosophers; The Philosopher's Phone Book*

Other info: Publishes bibliographies and other reference works in philosophy, including *Philosophy in Cyberspace*; collects information about on-going philosophical activity in the US and abroad; provides typesetting, subscription fulfillment and marketing services; publishes instructional software for philosophers; offers discount prices on philosophy books from more than 100 publishers through its "Books in Philosophy" distribution business.

Other info: Toll-free telephone: 1-800-444-2419

PICKWICK PUBLICATIONS

Dikran Y. Hadidian, Editor

4137 Timberlane Dr.
Allison Park, PA 15101-2932

Tel. 412-487-2159
Fax 412-487-8862

Date of founding: 1982

Jour Publ: *Ex Auditu*: An International Journal of Theological Interpretation of Scripture

Ser Publ: Princeton Theological Monograph Series

PIERIAN PRESS, INC.

P.O. Box 1808
Ann Arbor, MI 48106-1808

Tel. 313-434-5530
Fax 313-434-6409

Date of founding: 1968

Other info: Publishes 1 book in philosophy, used for a textbook as well as a reference book.

PORTER SARGENT PUBLISHERS, INC.

11 Beacon Street, Suite 1400
Boston, MA 02108

Tel. 617-523-1670
Fax 617-523-1021

Date of founding: 1914

Ser Publ: Extending Horizons Books: presents topics in contemporary affairs, viewpoints rarely offered, methods and modes of social change, and framework of alternative structures. Directed primarily to the college course adoption market.

PRAEGER PUBLISHERS, INC.*

88 Post Road West
Westport, CT 06881

Tel. 203-226-3571

Date of founding: 1950

PRENTICE HALL, INC.*

1 Lake St.
Upper Saddle River, NJ 07458

Tel. 201-592-2000
http://www.prenhall.com/

Ser Publ: Foundations of Philosophy Series, ed. by Tom L. Beauchamp, Elizabeth Beardsley and Monroe Beardsley: a series that presents the integral field of philosophy in separate volumes, each written by an expert in his/her field; Occupational Ethics Series, ed. by John Atwell and Elizabeth Beardsley: a series designed to introduce and explore the ethical dilemmas encountered in various occupations.

PRESBYTERIAN AND REFORMED PUBLISHING CO.*

P.O. Box 817
Phillipsburg, NJ 08865-0817

Tel. 908-454-0505
Fax 908-859-2390

Date of founding: 1931

PRINCETON UNIVERSITY PRESS

41 William Street
Princeton, NJ 08534

Tel. 609-258-4900
Fax 609-258-6305

Date of founding: 1905

Jour Publ: *Philosophy and Public Affairs*

Ser Publ: Studies in Moral, Political, and Legal Philosophy, ed. by Marshall Cohen: historical and systemic studies in this broadly conceived area.

Other info: Publishes scholarly books in philosophy.

PROBE BOOKS

1900 Firman Dr. 100
Richardson, TX 75081

Tel. 214-480-0240
Fax 214-644-9664
E-mail 74152.214@compuserve.com

Date of founding: 1973

Other info: Probe Books publishes philosophy from a Judeo-Christian perspective.

PROMETHEUS BOOKS, INC.

59 John Glenn Drive
Amherst, NY 14228-2197

Tel. 716-691-0133
Fax 716-564-2711

Date of founding: 1969

Ser Publ: Frontiers of Philosophy, ed. by Peter H. Hare; Contemporary Issues, ed. by Robert M. Baird and Stuart E. Rosenbaum; Great Minds; Great Books in Philosophy; Prometheus Lecture Series (by invitation only); Russian Studies; Skeptic's Bookshelf; Women's Studies.

Other info: Publishes both philosophy books and general books. Approximately 70 new books published per year, including hard cover and paperback. Submissions welcome.

PURDUE UNIVERSITY PRESS

1532 South Campus Courts–E
West Lafayette, IN 47907-1532

Tel. 317-494-2038
Fax 317-496-2442

Date of founding: 1960

Ser Publ: Purdue Series in the History of Philosophy, ed. by Joseph Kockelmans et al.: provides text and commentary on one work of a major Western philosopher; intended for undergraduate and graduate students and for scholars needing commentary and information on current research.

REFERENCE AND RESEARCH SERVICES

511 Lincoln St.
Santa Cruz, CA 95060

Tel. 408-426-4479

Date of founding: 1982

Ser Publ: Social Theory: A Bibliographic Series, ed. by Joan Nordquist: bibliographies of the work of contemporary social theorists and critical literature about their work.

RELIGIOUS EDUCATION PRESS

5316 Meadow Brook Road
Birmingham, AL 35242

Tel. 205-991-1000
Fax 205-991-9669

Date of founding: 1974

Other info: Publishes books only, including philosophy of education, with special attention to moral education.

RIDGEVIEW PUBLISHING COMPANY

Box 686
Atascadero, CA 93423

Tel. 805-466-7252

Ser Publ: The Philosopher's Annual, ed. by P. Grim, C. J. Martin, and P. Athay: a yearly collection of recent articles of special merit and worthy of special attention; Philosophical Perspectives, ed. by James E. Tomberlin: a yearly publication containing essays by distinguished philosophers on a particular field of philosophy; Philosophical Issues, ed. by Enrique Villanueva: a yearly publication that contains papers by leading philosophers, originally presented at international conferences sponsored by Sociedad Filosofica Ibero Americana; North American Kant Society Studies in Philosophy: a yearly publication on Kant or on topics related to Kant and his legacy in modern philosophy.

RODOPI, EDITIONS, BV

233 Peachtree St. NE, Suite 404
Atlanta, GA 30303-1504

Tel. 404-523-1964
Fax 404-522-7116,
E-mail e.van.der.zee@rodopi.nl

Date of founding: 1966

Jour Publ: *Grazer Philosophische Studien; Perspektiven der Philosophie*

Ser Publ: Critical Studies, ed. by Myriam Diaz-Diocaretz; Currents of Encounter: Studies on the Contact between Christianity and other Religions, Beliefs, and Cultures; Elementa: Schriften zur Phpilosophie und ihrer Problemgeschichte, ed. by Rudolph Berlinger and Wiebke Schrader; Elementa-Texte, ed. by Rudolph Berlinger et al.; Fichte-Studien, ed. by Klaus Hammacher et al; Fichte-Studien/Supplementa, ed. by Klaus Hammacher et al.; InterActions; International

Bibliography of Austrian Philosophy, ed. by Fabian, Haller, and Heinrichs; International Series in the Psychology of Religion, ed. by J. A. van Belzen and J. M. van der Lans; Lier en Boog Studies (Subject: Philosophy of Art/Aesthetics); Philosophie & Repräsentation/Philosophy and Representation, ed. by Petra Gehring et al.; Postmodern Studies, ed. by Theo D'haen and Hans Bertens; Poznan Studies in the Philosophy of the Sciences and the Humanities, ed. by Leszek Nowak; Rodopi Philosohical Studies, ed. by Fransisco Miro Quesada and Ernest Sosa; Schriftenreihe zur Philosophie Karl R. Poppers und des Kritischen Rationalismus, ed. by Kurt Salamun; Studien zur Interkulturellen Philosophie/Studies in Intercultural Philosophy/Etudes de philosophie interculturelle, ed. by Heinz Kimmerle and Ram Adhar mall; Studien zur Österreichischen Philosohie, ed. by Rudolf Haller; Studien zur Österreichischen Philosophie Supplement, ed. by Fabian, Haller, and Heinrichs; Studies in the History of Ideas in the Low Countries, ed. by Hans W. Blom et al.; Value Inquiry Book Series, ed. by Robert Ginsberg: philosophical books in all areas of value inquiry, including social and political thought, ethics, applied philosophy, feminism, religious values, values in higher education, medical and health values, values in science and technology, formal axiology, history of ideas, semiotics, peace theory, law and society, and theory of culture.

FRED B. ROTHMAN & CO.

10368 West Centennial Rd.
Littleton, CO 80127

Tel. 303-979-5657

Fax 303-978-1457
E-mail orders@rothman.com

Date of founding: 1945

Ser Publ: Modern Legal Philosophy Series

ROUTLEDGE, INC.

29 West 35th St.
New York, NY 10001-2299

Tel. 212-244-3336
Fax 212-563-2269
E-mail info@routledge.com
http://www.routledge.com

Ser Publ: Continental Philosophy, ed. by Hugh J. Silverman: explores and develops topics, themes, and figures in contemporary continental philosophy, opening space for discussion and debate in the Anglo-American context; Thinking Gender, ed. by Linda Nicholson: publishes innovative work in feminism and gender theory, with an emphasis on studies that stem from the continental tradition in philosophy and social thought.

Other info: Formerly Methuen, Inc. Address of London office: Routledge, 11 New Fetter Lane, London EC4P 4EE, UK

ROWMAN & LITTLEFIELD PUBLISHERS, INC.

4720-A Boston Way
Lanham, MD 20706

Tel. 301-459-3366
Fax 301-459-2118

Date of founding: 1947

Ser Publ: Studies in Social and Political Philosophy, ed. by James P. Sterba: analyzes and critically evaluates the major political and social ideals, institutions, and practices of our time; New Feminist Perspectives, ed. by Rosemarie Tong: feminist philosophical evaluations of ethics, jurisprudence, political theory, public policy, epistemology, science, and aesthetics, as well as analyses of feminist thought; Issues in Academic Ethics, ed. by Steven M. Cahn: the first multivolume series devoted to the emerging field of ethics in higher education; Point/Counterpoint: Philosophers Debate Contemporary Issues, ed. by James P. Sterba and Rosemarie Tong: co-authored books arguing two sides of a controversial question; Studies in Epistemology and Cognitive Theory, ed. by Paul K. Moser: original, single-authored works that focus on the following: theory of knowledge, philosophical psychology, theories of rationality, theories of perception, and philosophy of language.

Other info: Rowman and Littlefield continues to seek manuscripts, projects, and ideas for new series. The editor-in-chief is Jonathan Sisk. The philosophy acquisitions editor is Jennifer K. Ruark.

RUDRA PRESS*

P.O. Box 13390
517 NE 20th Ave., Ste. 206
Portland, OR 97232

Tel. 617-576-3394
Fax 617-868-3524

Date of founding: 1980

Ser Publ: Dynamic Stillness, ed. by Linda Barnes: a series that introduces to the West the practice of Trika Yoga, a practice based in the Tantric tradition of Kashmir Shaivism; Kashmir Shaivism Translation Series: translates into English classic texts on Kashmir Shaivism.

RUNAWAY PUBLICATIONS

P.O. Box 1172
Ashland, OR 97520-0040

Tel. 503-482-2578

Date of founding: 1977

Ser Publ: The Patriot

Other info: Contact Person: James L. Berkman, M. A.

SAGE PUBLICATIONS, INC.*

2455 Teller Rd.
Newbury Park, CA 91320

Tel. 805-499-0721
Fax 805-499-0871

Date of founding: 1965

Jour Publ: *Philosophy of the Social Sciences; Political Theory; Rationality and Society*

Ser Publ: Theory, Culture and Society, ed. by Mike Featherstone: caters for the resurgence of interest in culture within contemporary social science and the humanities; Masters in Social Theory, ed. by Jonathan H. Turner: provides both scholarly analysis and summarizes the basic, core idea of the individual master; Key Issues in Social Theory, ed. by Jeffrey C. Alexander and Jonathan H. Turner: crystallizes key issues in contemporary theoretical debate; Media, Culture and Society, ed. by John Corner et al.; Inquiries in Social Construction, ed. by Kenneth J. Gergen and John Shotter: a series designed to facilitate, across discipline and national boundaries, an emergent dialogue within the social sciences, which many believe presages a major shift in the Western intellectual tradition.

Other info: Web site URL:
http://www.sagepub.com

SAINT MARTIN'S PRESS, INC. *

175 5th Ave.
New York, NY 10010-7848

Tel. 212-982-3900
Fax 212-777-6359

Ser Publ: Mind Matters Series,
ed. by Judith Hughes

SCARECROW PRESS, INC.*

52 Liberty Street
Metuchen, NJ 08840

Tel. 908-548-8600
Fax 908-548-5767

Date of founding: 1950

Other info: Reference titles in the
humanities and social sciences,
including philosophy. Toll-free
telephone number: 800-537-7107

SCHENKMAN BOOKS, INC.*

Main St., Box 119
Rochester, VT 05767

Tel. 802-767-3702
Fax 802-767-9528

Date of founding: 1961

SCHOLARS PRESS

P.O. Box 15399
Atlanta, GA 30333-0399

Tel. 404-727-2320
Fax 404-727-2348

Jour Publ: *International Studies in
Philosophy*

SHAMBHALA PUBLICATIONS, INC.

300 Massachusetts Ave.
Boston, MA 02115

Tel. 617-424-0030
Fax 617-236-1563

Date of founding: 1969

Ser Publ: Shambhala Dragon
Editions, ed. by Samuel Bercholz,
offers a treasury of readings in the
sacred knowledge of Asia. In presenting the works of authors both ancient
and modern, we seek to make these
teachings accessible to lovers of wisdom everywhere.

SHARPE, M. E., INC.

80 Business Park Dr.
Armonk, NY 10504

Tel. 914-273-1800
Fax 914-273-2106
E-mail mesinfo@usa.net

Date of founding: 1957

Jour Publ: *Russian Studies in
Philosophy; Chinese Studies in Philosophy*

Other info: All articles are published
translations from the Soviet Union
and China.

SHOE STRING PRESS, INC., ARCHON BOOKS

P.O. Box 657
North Haven, CT 06473-0657

Tel. 203-239-2702
Fax 203-239-2568

Date of founding: 1952

SIMON AND SCHUSTER*

1230 Avenue of the Americas
New York, NY 10020

Tel. 212-698-7000
http://www.superlibrary.com/

SMITH, PETER, PUBLISHER, INC.

5 Lexington Avenue
Magnolia, MA 01930-3915

Tel. 508-525-3562
Fax 508-525-3674

Date of founding: 1929

SNOW LION PUBLICATIONS, INC.

P.O. Box 6483
Ithaca, NY 14851

Tel. 607-273-8519
Fax 607-273-8508,
E-mail 75061.1026@compuserve.com

Date of founding: 1980

Ser Publ: Studies in Indo-Tibetan
Buddhism

Other info: Snow Lion specializes in
books on Tibetan Buddhist philosophy, culture, and politics. A scholarly
set of books from University of
Virginia covering the four philosophic schools and the four meditational
schools of Tibetan Buddhism is now
in process.

SOUTH END PRESS

116 St. Botolph
Boston, MA 02115

Tel. 617-266-0629
Fax 617-266-1595

Date of founding: 1979

Other info: We publish books in radical social philosophy and radical politics in general.

SOUTHERN ILLINOIS UNIVERSI-
TY PRESS

P.O. Box 3697
Carbondale, IL 62902-3697

Tel. 618-453-2281
Fax 618-453-1221

Date of founding: 1956

SOUTHERN METHODIST
UNIVERSITY PRESS

Box 415
Dallas, TX 75275-0415

Tel. 214-768-1432
Fax 214-768-1428

Date of founding: 1937

SPRING PUBLICATIONS, INC.

299 E. Quassett Rd.
Woodstock, CT 06281-3308

Tel. 203-974-3428
Fax 203-974-3195,
E-mail spring@neca.com

Date of founding: 1941

Jour Publ: *Spring: A Journal of
Archetype and Culture*

Ser Publ: Dunquin Series; Jungian
Classics Series; Spring Fever Seminar
Series

SPRINGER-VERLAG

175 Fifth Avenue
Attn: Journals Managing Editor
New York, NY 10010

Tel. 212-460-1500

Fax 212-473-6272
E-mail em-helpdesk@springer.de

Date of founding: 1842

Jour Publ: *Archive for History of Exact Sciences*

Other info: Toll-free telephone: 800-777-4643; WWW site: http://www.springer-ny.com

STATE UNIVERSITY OF NEW YORK PRESS

State University Plaza
Albany, NY 12246

Tel. 518-472-5000
Fax 518-472-5038
E-mail rwde@snycenvm.bitnet

Date of founding: 1966

Ser Publ: SUNY Series in Systematic Philosophy, ed. by Robert C. Neville; SUNY Series in Philosophy, ed. by Georg C. Lucas, Jr.; SUNY Series in Hegelian Studies, ed. by William Desmond; SUNY Series in Indology, ed. by Wilhelm Halbfass; SUNY Series in Chinese Philosophy, ed. by David Hall and Roger Ames; SUNY Series in Logic and Language, ed. by John T. Kearns; SUNY Series in the Philosophy of the Social Sciences, ed. by Lenore Langsdorf; SUNY Series in Jewish Philosophy, ed. by Kenneth Seeskin; SUNY Series in Contemporary Continental Philosophy, ed. by Dennis J. Schmidt

STILLPOINT PUBLISHING*

Div. of Stillpoint Internat'l
P.O. Box 640, Meetinghouse Road
Walpole, NH 03608

Tel. 603-756-9281
Fax 603-756-9282

Date of founding: 1983

SUSQUEHANNA UNIVERSITY PRESS*

Susquehanna University
Selinsgrove, PA 17870-1001

Tel. 717-372-4175
Fax 717-372-4310

Date of founding: 1981

SWEDENBORG FOUNDATION, INC.

P.O. Box 549
West Chester, PA 19381-0549

Tel. 610-430-3222
Fax 610-430-7982

Date of founding: 1849

Ser Publ: Swedenborg Studies Monographs: scholarly studies related to Swedenborg, his influence on others, or Swedenborgian thought.

Other info: The Foundation publishes the theological and philosophical works of Emanuel Swedenborg, and contemporary books related to the spiritual quest. For information, write David Eller, Executive Director, at the address listed.

TAYLOR & FRANCIS/FALMER PRESS

1900 Frost Road, Ste. 101
Bristol, PA 19007-1598

Tel. 215-785-5800
Fax 215-785-5515

Date of founding: 1798

Jour Publ: *Annals of Science; History and Philosophy of Logic; History and Philosophy of Life Sciences; Qualitative*

Studies in Education; Social Epistemology

TEACHERS COLLEGE PRESS*

1234 Amsterdam Avenue
New York, NY 10027

Tel. 212-678-3929
Fax 212-678-4149

Date of founding: 1904

Ser Publ: John Dewey Lecture Series; Advances in Contemporary Educational Thought.

TEMPLE UNIVERSITY PRESS*

Broad and Oxford Streets
Philadelphia, PA 19122

Tel. 215-204-8787
Fax 215-204-4719

Date of founding: 1969

Ser Publ: Ethics and Action, ed. by Tom Reagan: a series whose purpose is to make available distinguished works on the major moral issues of the day; The Arts and Their Philosophies, ed. by Joseph Margolis: original studies in aesthetics and the philosophy of art from a variety of philosophical orientations; Themes in the History of Philosophy, ed. by Edith Wyschogrod: a series that aims to publish outstanding works on past philosophical figures, issues, and trends; Environmental Ethics, Values, and Policy, ed. by Holmes Rolston, III: a series that explores ethical issues related to use and preservation of the natural environment.

THEOSOPHICAL PUBLISHING HOUSE

306 W. Geneva Rd.
Wheaton, IL 60189

Tel. 708-665-0130
Fax 708-665-8791

Date of founding: 1925

Jour Publ: *The American Theosophist; The Quest*

Ser Publ: Commentaries on Living, Series I, II, III, by J. Krishnamurti: a series whose purpose is to disseminate this *avant garde* study of the purpose of life; Collected Writings of H. P. Blavatsky, I-XV, ed. by Boris de Zirkoff: a series whose purpose is to keep in print the writings of Blavatsky, principal founder of the Theosophical Society.

Other info: TPH also publishes under the "Quest" imprint. This series of high-quality paperbacks contains numerous books on spiritual philosophy, concentrating on discussions of "awareness" and on "consciousness."

THOMAS JEFFERSON UNIVERSITY PRESS

Truman State University
MC111L, 100 E. Normal Street
Kirksville, MO 63501

Tel. 816-785-4665
Fax 816-785-4181
E-mail SS18%nemomus@academic. nemostate.edu
http://www.truman.edu/tjup/home. html

Date of founding: 1988

Jour Publ: Annual: *Mediterrranean Studies*

CHARLES C. THOMAS, PUBLISHER

2600 South First St.
Springfield, IL 62794-9265

Tel. 217-789-8980
Fax 217-789-9130

Date of founding: 1927

Other info: Toll-free telephone number: 800-258-8980

TRANSACTION PUBLISHERS

Rutgers University
New Brunswick, NJ 08903

Tel. 908-445-2280
Fax 908-445-3138

Date of founding: 1965

Ser Publ: Social Philosophy and Policy Series, ed. by Ellen Frankel Paul; Social and Ethical Thought, ed. by Abraham Edel; Library of Conservative Thought, ed. by Milton Hindus.

TRINITY FOUNDATION, THE

P.O. Box 1666
Hobbs, NM 88241-1666

Tel. 505-392-7274

Date of founding: 1977

Jour Publ: *The Trinity Review*

Other info: Forty-five titles in print.

TWAYNE PUBLISHERS

866 Third Avenue
New York, NY 10022

Tel. 212-702-2000
Fax 212-605-9350

Date of founding: 1948

Ser Publ: Studies in Intellectual and Cultural History, ed. by Michael Roth: to provide concise interpretations of major developments or themes in intellectual history for undergraduates. In-house editor: Margaret Dornfeld, Ext. 7997.

UMI, A BELL & HOWELL COMPANY

300 N. Zeeb Road, P.O. Box 1346
Ann Arbor, MI 48106-1346

Tel. 313-761-4700 Ext. 3895
Fax 800-308-1586
http://www.umi.com/

Ser Publ: As publisher of record for doctoral dissertations in North America, UMI offers full-text copies of virtually every philosophy dissertation published since 1861. Other philosophy offerings include xerographic reproductions of out-of-print books and filmed collections of primary research materials that are otherwise unavailable.

Other info: Call for free catalogs and more information.

UNIVERSITY OF ALABAMA PRESS*

Box 870380
Tuscaloosa, AL 35487-0380

Tel. 205-348-5180
Fax 205-348-9201

Date of founding: 1945

UNIVERSITY OF CALIFORNIA PRESS

2120 Berkeley Way
Berkeley, CA 94720

Tel. 510-642-4247
Fax 510-643-7127

Date of founding: 1896

Jour Publ: *Representations*, ed. by Stephen Greenblatt and Carla Hesse, University of California, Berkeley; *Rhetorica*, ed. by Craig Kallendorf, Texas A & M University

UNIVERSITY OF CHICAGO PRESS

5801 South Ellis Avenue
Chicago, IL 60637

Tel. 312-702-7700
Fax 312-702-9756
http://www.press.uchicago.edu/

Date of founding: 1892

Jour Publ: *Ethics; Perspectives on Science–Historical, Philosophical, Social*

Ser Publ: Science and its Conceptual Foundations, ed. by David L. Hull: a series to encourage and develop interdisciplinary analyses of the foundations of science, using philosophical, historical and sociological, psychological or anthropological techniques. The series invites submissions in studies of the biological, physical, and social sciences and mathematics.

Other info: The Press publishes translations from the French, German, and Italian in addition to work in philosophy and philosophy of science written originally in English.

UNIVERSITY OF GEORGIA PRESS

330 Research Drive, Suite B-100
University of Georgia
Athens, GA 30602-4901

Tel. 706-369-6130
Fax 706-369-6131,
E-mail ugapress@uga.cc.uga.edu
(inquries only)

Date of founding: 1938

Other info: E-mail address for inquiries only. Toll-free order number: 800-266-5842

UNIVERSITY OF HAWAII PRESS

Journals Department
2840 Kolowalu St.
Honolulu, HI 96822

Tel. 808-956-8833
Fax 808-988-6052

Date of founding: 1947

Jour Publ: *Philosophy East and West*, ed. by Roger T. Ames

Ser Publ: Monographs of the Society for Asian and Comparative Philosophy, ed. by Henry Rosemont, Jr.: a monograph series on specialized topics in Asian and comparative philosophy.

Other info: Quarterly. 1996 rates: Individuals $31/year; Institutions $40/year.

UNIVERSITY OF ILLINOIS PRESS

54 E. Gregory Drive
Champaign, IL 61820

Tel. 217-333-8935
Fax 217-244-8082

Date of founding: 1918

Jour Publ: *The Journal of Aesthetic Education*

UNIVERSITY OF MASSACHUSETTS PRESS

P.O. Box 429
Amherst, MA 01004

Tel. 413-545-2217
Fax 413-545-1226

Date of founding: 1964

Ser Publ: Critical Perspectives on Modern Culture

UNIVERSITY OF MICHIGAN PRESS

839 Greene St., P.O. Box 1104
Ann Arbor, MI 48106

Tel. 313-764-4388
Fax 313-936-0456

Date of founding: 1930

UNIVERSITY OF MINNESOTA PRESS

111 Third Avenue South
Minneapolis, MN 55401

Tel. 612-627-1970
Fax 612-627-1980

Ser Publ: Minnesota Studies in the Philosophy of Science: a series comprised of volumes that derive from ongoing research sponsored by the Minnesota Center for the Philosophy of Science, Ronald Giere, General Editor.

UNIVERSITY OF MISSOURI PRESS

2910 LeMone Blvd.
Columbia, MO 65201-8227

Tel. 314-882-7641
Fax 314-884-4498,
E-mail orders@ext.missouri.edu

Date of founding: 1959

Other info: Most of our publications would fit into the general category of political philosophy.

UNIVERSITY OF NEBRASKA PRESS

312 North 14th Street
Lincoln, NE 68588-0484

Tel. 402-472-3581
Fax 402-472-6214
E-mail press@unlinfo.unl.edu

Date of founding: 1941

UNIVERSITY OF NORTH CAROLINA PRESS

P.O. Box 2288
Chapel Hill, NC 27515-2288

Tel. 919-966-3561
Fax 919-966-3829
E-mail uncpress@unc.edu

Date of founding: 1922

Jour Publ: *High School Journal; Studies in Philology; Journal for the Education of the Gifted; Southern Literary Journal; Social Forces*

UNIVERSITY OF NOTRE DAME PRESS

P.O. Box L
Notre Dame, IN 46556-0774

Tel. 219-631-6346
Fax 219-631-8148

Date of founding: 1949

Ser Publ: Boston University Studies in Philosophy and Religion, ed. by Leroy Rouner; University of Notre Dame Studies in the Philosophy of Religion, ed. by Frederick Crosson; Revisions: A Series of Books on Ethics, ed. by Stanley Hauerwas and Alasdair MacIntyre; Soundings: A Series of Books on Ethics, Economics, and Business, ed. by Thomas Donaldson; Library of Religious Philosophy, ed. by Thomas V. Morris; Midwest Studies in Philosophy, ed. by Peter A. French, Theodore E. Uehling, Jr., and Howard K. Wettstein; Studies in Science and the Humanities, from the Reilly Center for Science, Technology, and Values; Medieval Philosophy and Theology, ed. by Mark D. Jordan.

Other info: Before submitting a manuscript for publication, please send a letter of inquiry with a table of contents and an introduction or foreword.

UNIVERSITY OF OKLAHOMA PRESS*

1005 Asp Avenue
Norman, OK 73019-0445

Tel. 405-325-5111
Fax 405-325-4000

Date of founding: 1929

UNIVERSITY OF PUERTO RICO PRESS

Box 23322, UPR Station
San Juan, PR 00931-3322

Tel. 809-250-0550
Fax 809-753-9116

Date of founding: 1932

Jour Publ: *Dialogos*: Journal of the Philosophy Department of the University of Puerto Rico, Río Piedras Campus

UNIVERSITY OF ROCHESTER PRESS*

P.O. Box 41026
Rochester, NY 14604

Tel. 716-275-0419
Fax 716-271-8778

Date of founding: 1989

Ser Publ: Library of the History of Ideas, ed. by John W. Yolton: a series of volumes on major themes of intellectual history drawing on influential articles published in the *Journal of the History of Ideas* since its inception in 1940.

Other info: Editorial contact: Robert Easton, 716-275-6208; Marketing Contact: Janet Armstrong, 716-275-0419; Orders: Barbara Graver, 716-275-8272

UNIVERSITY OF SCRANTON PRESS

Linden and Monroe
Scranton, PA 18510-4660

Tel. 717-941-7449
Fax 717-941-4309
E-mail rousseaur1@uofs.edu

Date of founding: 1988

Jour Publ: *Diakonia*

Other info: Member of Association of Jesuit University Presses; editorial policy: theology/religious studies; philosophy/philosophy of religion; the culture and history of northeastern Pennsylvania

UNIVERSITY OF UTAH PRESS

101 University Services Bldg.
Salt Lake City, UT 84112

Tel. 801-581-6771
Fax 801-581-3365

Date of founding: 1949

Ser Publ: The Tanner Lectures on Human Values, ed. by Grethe B. Peterson: a series whose purpose is to advance and reflect upon the scholarly and scientific learning relating to human values and valuation; Ethics in a Changing World, ed. by Margaret Battin and Leslie Francis: a series that responds to issues dealing with the ethical implications of developments in science and technology.

UNIVERSITY OF WASHINGTON PRESS

P.O. Box 50096
Seattle, WA 98145

Tel. 206-543-4050
Fax 206-543-3932

Date of founding: 1920

UNIVERSITY OF WISCONSIN PRESS

114 North Murray St.
Madison, WI 53715-1199

Tel. 608-262-8782

Fax 608-262-7560

Date of founding: 1937

UNIVERSITY PRESS OF AMERICA

4720 Boston Way
Lanham, MD 20706

Tel. 301-459-3366
Fax 301-459-2118

Other info: Publishes scholarly monographs, festschriften, conference proceedings, bibliographics, and reference works.

UNIVERSITY PRESS OF COLORADO

P.O. Box 849
Niwot, CO 80544

Tel. 303-530-5337
Fax 303-530-5306

Date of founding: 1969

UNIVERSITY PRESS OF FLORIDA*

15 N.W. 15th Street
Gainesville, FL 32611

Tel. 904-392-1351
Fax 904-392-7302

Other info: Book-length works in contemporary (20th-century) philosophy.

UNIVERSITY PRESS OF KANSAS

2501 W. 15th St.
Lawrence, KS 66049-3904

Tel. 913-864-4154
Fax 913-864-4586

Date of founding: 1946

Other info: UPK publishes titles in ethics, political and social philosophy, and moral theory. Authors of manuscripts in these areas are encouraged to send a letter of inquiry describing their work and a curriculum vitae.

UNIVERSITY PRESS OF NEW ENGLAND

23 South Main St.
Hanover, NH 03755

Tel. 603-643-7100
Fax 603-643-1540
E-mail
university.press@dartmouth.edu

Date of founding: 1970

Ser Publ: Collected Writings of Rousseau

UNIVERSITY PRESS OF VIRGINIA*

Box 3608 University Station
Charlottesville, VA 22903

Tel. 804-924-3469
Fax 804-982-2655

Date of founding: 1962

Other info: Nancy C. Essig, Director; Cathie Brettschneider, Acquisitions/Humanities

VANDERBILT UNIVERSITY PRESS

Box 1813, Station B
Nashville, TN 37235

Tel. 615-322-3585
Fax 615-343-8823,
E-mail vupress@vanderbilt.edu

Date of founding: 1940

Ser Publ: The Vanderbilt Library of American Philosophy

VERSO

180 Varick St.
New York, NY 10014

Tel. 212-807-9680
Fax 212-807-9152

Date of founding: 1970

WADSWORTH PUBLISHING COMPANY

10 Davis Drive
Belmont, CA 94002

Tel. 415-595-2350
Fax 415-592-3342
E-mail eide_chavez@wadsworth.com
http:www.thomson.com/wadsworth/default.html

Date of founding: 1956

Other info: A general college publisher specializing in undergraduate textbooks. Publishes a substantial number of works for the philosophy curriculum.

WASHINGTON INSTITUTE PRESS*

1015 18th St., NW, Suite 300
Washington, DC 20036-5203

Tel. 202-293-7440
Fax 202-293-9393

Date of founding: 1982

Jour Publ: *In Depth*, 3 times per year

WAVELAND PRESS, INC.

P.O. Box 400
Prospect Heights, IL 60070-0400

Tel. 708-634-0081
Fax 708-634-9501

Date of founding: 1975

Other info: Publishes college-level textbooks and supplements.

WEATHERHILL, INC.*

568 Broadway, Rm. 705
New York, NY 10012-3225

Tel. 212-223-3008
Fax 212-223-2584

Date of founding: 1968

WEISER, SAMUEL, INC.

P.O. Box 612
York Beach, ME 03910-0612

Tel. 207-363-4393
Fax 207-363-5799

Date of founding: 1956

Other info: Toll-free order number: 800-423-7087

WESLEYAN UNIVERSITY PRESS

110 Mount Vernon St.
Middletown, CT 06459-0433

Tel. 860-685-2420
Fax 860-685-2421

Date of founding: 1957

WESTMINSTER/JOHN KNOX PRESS*

Presbyterian Church USA
100 Witherspoon St.
Louisville, KY 40202-1396

Tel. 502-569-5000

Date of founding: 1838

WESTVIEW PRESS

5500 Central Ave.
Boulder, CO 80301-2847

Tel. 303-444-3541
Fax 303-449-3356

Date of founding: 1975

Ser Publ: Dimensions of Philosophy, ed. by Norman Daniels and Keith Lehrer: main texts covering the fundamental concepts and issues of a particular subject. An emphasis on modern, forward-looking treatments for the next generation of teachers and students; The Focus Series, ed. by Norman Daniels and Keith Lehrer: supplementary texts that focus on specific topics common to the undergraduate curriculum; Feminist Theory and Politics, ed. by Virginia Held and Alison Jaggar: insights from contemporary feminism confront mainstream scholarship in those disciplines most engaged in contemporary social analysis.

WORLD BOOKS

1915 Las Lomas Rd. NE
Albuquerque, NM 87106-3805

Tel. 505-242-9983
Fax 505-839-9450,
E-mail ajbahm@carina.unm.edu

Date of founding: 1974

WORTHINGTON PUBLISHING COMPANY*

Box 1661
6907-202 Halifax River Dr.
Temple Terrace, FL 33687-6691

Tel. 813-988-5751

Date of founding: 1989

YALE UNIVERSITY PRESS

P.O. Box 209040
New Haven, CT 06520-9040

Tel. 203-432-0960
Fax 203-432-0948

Ser Publ: Terry Lectures: a lecture series at Yale University on the subject of religion in the light of science and philosophy. The lectures are edited by The Terry Committee, Yale University.

Other info: A brochure of philosophy titles is available on request.

ZONDERVAN PUBLISHING HOUSE*

5300 Patterson Ave. SE
Grand Rapids, MI 49530

Tel. 616-698-6900
Fax 616-698-3454

Date of founding: 1931

ZONE BOOKS

611 Broadway, Suite 608
New York, NY 10012

Tel. 212-529-5674
Fax 212-260-4572
E-mail urzone@aol.com

Date of founding: 1985

Ser Publ: Zone, ed. by Sanford Kwinter, Jonathan Crary, Hal Foster, and Michel Feher: an interdisciplinary investigation of ideas in contemporary culture.

ACADEMIC PRINTING AND PUBLISHING

P.O. Box 4218
Edmonton, AB T6E 4T2

Tel. 403-435-5898
Fax 403-435-5852

Date of founding: 1975

Jour Publ: *Apeiron: A Journal for Ancient Philosophy and Science; Canadian Philosophical Reviews; Man and Nature*

BROADVIEW PRESS

P.O. Box 1243
Peterborough, ON K9J 7H5

Tel. 705-743-8990
Fax 705-743-8353

Date of founding: 1985

Other info: Broadview Press publishes a broad range of textbooks and other academic books in the arts and social sciences. US: 3576 California Rd., Orchard Pk., NY 14127. UK: BRAD Book Rep. & Distr., Ltd., 244A London Rd., Hadleigh, Essex SS7 2DE.

EDITIONS BELLARMIN*

165 rue Deslauriers
Saint-Laurent, PQ H4N 2S4

Tel. 514-745-4290
Fax 514-745-4299

Date of founding: 1891

Jour Publ: *Science et Esprit, Philosophiques*

Ser Publ: Cahiers d'Etudes Médiévales, ed. by Guy H. Allard, veulent atteindre un public diversifié composé aussi bien de spécialistes, professeurs, chercheurs et étudiants que de personnes intéressées à un aspect ou l'autre de la civilisation médiévale; Noesis, ed. by Yvon Lafrance: cette collection se consacre à la publication des travaux de recherches en langue français sur la pensée grecque et latine.

EDITIONS FIDES*

165 rue Deslauriers
Saint-Laurent, PQ H4N 2S4

Tel. 514-745-4290
Fax 514-745-4299

Date of founding: 1937

Ser Publ: Héritage et Projet, ed. by André Charron, Richard Bergeron, and Guy Couturier: Cette collection regroupe des ouvrages se situant à deux niveaux d'écriture: un niveau de rigueur scientifique en des champs de recherche qui correspondent aux requàtes de la société et l'Eglise contemporaine; un niveau de vulgarisation rendant accessible à un assez large public des matériaux et un contenu de réflexion théologique substantiels et pertinents; Cahiers de Recherche Ethique, ed. by Rodrigue Bélanger: Une collection pour permettre une meilleure approche des problémes d'ordre moral ou éthique qui se font jour autour de nous.

MCGILL-QUEEN'S UNIVERSITY PRESS

3430 McTavish St.
Montréal, PQ H3A 1X9

Tel. 514-398-3750

Fax 514-398-4333
E-mail mqup@printing.lan.mcgill.ca

Date of founding: 1960

Ser Publ: McGill-Queen's Studies in the History of Ideas: a series that aims to present a wide range of important scholarly monographs in Western intellectual history and philosophy and will also include scholarly bibliographies and critical editions. McGill-Queen's also publishes works of contemporary philosophical interest. Preference is given to authors resident in Canada, but others will be considered.

Other info: Additional address: Queen's University, Kingston, ON K7L 3N6; 613-545-2155 Fax 613-545-6822; E-mail: mqup@qucdn.queensu.ca

MCMASTER UNIVERSITY LIBRARY PRESS

Mills Memorial Library
McMaster University
Hamilton, ON L8S 4L6

Tel. 905-525-9140 Ext. 24738
Fax 905-546-0625
E-mail blackwk@mcmaster.ca

Date of founding: 1971

Jour Publ: *Russell: The Journal of the Bertrand Russell Archives*

PRESSES DE L'UNIVERSITÉ DE MONTRÉAL

Case Postale 6128, Succ. Centre-ville
Montréal, PQ H3C 3J7

Tel. 514-343-6929
Fax 514-343-2232

Date of founding: 1962

UNIVERSITÉ LAVAL

c/o Lionel Ponton
Faculty of Philosophy
Cité Universitaire
Sainte-Foy, PQ G1K 7P4

Tel. 418-656-2131 Ext. 4775
Fax 418-656-7267

Date of founding: 1945

Jour Publ: *Laval Théologique et Philosophique*, ed. by Lionel Ponton: extensive research articles, book reviews, and chronicle of items of prime interest in all fields of philosophy and theology.

UNIVERSITY OF CALGARY PRESS

2500 University Drive NW
Calgary, AB T2N 1N4

Tel. 403-220-7578
Fax 403-282-0085
E-mail
75003@ucdasvm1.admin.ucal gary.ca

Date of founding: 1971

Jour Publ: *Canadian Journal of Philosophy*

UNIVERSITY OF MANITOBA PRESS

15 Gillson St., Suite 244
University of Manitoba
Winnipeg, MB R3T 5V6

Tel. 204-474-9495
Fax 204-275-2270

Date of founding: 1967

Ser Publ: Manitoba Studies in Native History; Publications of the Algonquian Text Society; University of Manitoba Studies in Icelandic

UNIVERSITY OF OTTAWA PRESS/LES PRESSES DE L'UNIVERSITÉ D'OTTAWA

542 King Edward
Ottawa, ON K1N 6N5

Tel. 613-564-2270
Fax 613-564-9284

Date of founding: 1936

Ser Publ: Philosophica, ed. by Daniéle Letocha and Graeme Hunter: since 1973, Philosophica has published some 40 monographs and collective volumes, in English and French, on a wide range of philosophical topics. The co-editors are committed to publishing works of high quality. They share a very broad conception of philosophy, one that encompasses both historical and systematic studies, and that recognizes all the major contemporary traditions.

Other info: The Press also publishes other monographs and textbooks in philosophy, in English or French.

UNIVERSITY OF TORONTO PRESS INCORPORATED

10 St. Mary St., Suite 700
Toronto, ON M4Y 2W8

Tel. 416-667-7791
Fax 416-667-7832
http://www.library.utoronto.ca/www/
utpress/depthome.htm

Date of founding: 1901

Ser Publ: The Collected Works of Erasmus, the purpose of which is to translate into English, with introductions and notes, the complete correspondence of Erasmus, and his principal writings, ed. by James K. McConica et al.: The Collected Works of John Stuart Mill, a series to present fully collated texts of those works that exist in a number of versions and to provide accurate texts of those works previously unpublished and that have become relatively inaccessible, ed. by John M. Robson. The Mill Series is now complete.

WILFRID LAURIER UNIVERSITY PRESS

Wilfrid Laurier University
Waterloo, ON N2L 3C5

Tel. 519-884-1970 Ext. 6124
Fax 519-725-1399
E-mail press@mach1.wlu.ca

Date of founding: 1974

Jour Publ: *Dialogue*: quarterly journal of the Canadian Philosophical Association

PUBLISHERS: UNITED KINGDOM

ABERDEEN UNIVERSITY PRESS*

Farmers Hall
Aberdeen, Scotland AB9 2XT

Date of founding: 1860

AIDAN ELLIS PUBLISHING

Cobb House, Nuffield
Henley-on-Thames
Oxfordshire, England RG9 5RT

Tel. 0491-641496
Fax 0491-641678
E-mail aidan@aepub.demon.co.uk

Date of founding: 1971

APPLEFORD PUBLISHING GROUP*

Appleford
Abingdon
Oxford, England OX14 4PB

Tel. 0235-848319

Date of founding: 1963

Ser Publ: Courtenay Library of Reformation Classics; Evangelicals & Society from 1750, both ed. by G. E. Duffield. Both series are historically oriented, Ph.D. level or above, usually based on doctoral studies and often including rare texts.

ARIS & PHILLIPS, LTD.

Teddington House
Church Street, Warminster
Wiltshire, England BA12 8PQ

Tel. 0985-213609,
Fax 0985-212910

Date of founding: 1972

Ser Publ: Series of classical texts includes works by Plato, Cicero, Seneca, Lucretius, and Aristotle. The original text in Latin or Greek is accompanied by a parallel English translation, introduction to author and work, and commentary.

ASHGATE PUBLISHING LIMITED

Gower House
Croft Road, Aldershot, Hants
England GU11 3HR

Tel. 01252-331551
Fax 01252-344405
E-mail ashgate@cityscape.co.uk

Date of founding: 1967

Ser Publ: Avebury Series in Philosophy/Philosophy of Science, ed. by David Lamb

ASHGROVE PRESS, LTD.*

7 Locksbrook Rd.
Trading Estate
Bath, England BA1 3D2

Tel. 0225-425539
Fax 0225-319137

Date of founding: 1980

ATHLONE PRESS

1 Park Drive
London, England NW11 7SG

Tel. 0181 458 0888
Fax 0181 201 8115

Date of founding: 1950

BIBLIAGORA

P.O. Box 77
Feltham
Middlesex, England TW14 8JF

Tel. 081-898-1234,
Fax 081-844-1777,
E-mail
100525.1225@compuserve.com

Date of founding: 1973

Other info: Specializes in the tracing of out-of-print philosophy titles. Also supplies new titles published in the UK or US.

BLACKWELL PUBLISHERS

108 Cowley Road
Oxford, England OX4 1JF

Tel. 0865-791100
Fax 0865-791347

http://www.blackwellpublishers.co.uk/

Date of founding: 1921

Jour Publ: *Analysis; Metaphilosophy; Philosophical Investigations; The Philosophical Quarterly; Modern Theology; Social Philosophy & Policy; Philosophical Books; Praxis International; Ratio; Mind and Language; Nous; European Journal of Philosophy; Journal for the Theory of Social Behaviour; Journal of Applied Philosophy; The Heythrop Journal; Business Ethics; Journal of Philosophy of Education; Journal of Political Philosophy; Bioethics; Pacific Philosophical Quarterly; Proceedings of the Aristotelian Society; Constellations; Zygon*

Other info: Blackwell publishes about 30 books per year in analytic and continental philosophy, most in paperback.

BRITISH ACADEMY

20-21 Cornwall Terrace
London, England NW1 4QP

Tel. 0171-487-5966
Fax 0171-224-3807
E-mail basec@britac.ac.uk

Date of founding: 1901

Jour Publ: *Proceedings of the British Academy*

Ser Publ: Auctores Britannici Medii Aevi, ed. by D. E. Luscombe

BURNS & OATES, LTD.

Wellwood
North Farm Rd., Tunbridge Wells
Kent, England TN2 3DR

Tel. 01892-510850,
Fax 01892-515903

Date of founding: 1847

CAMBRIDGE UNIVERSITY PRESS

The Edinburgh Building
Shaftesbury Road
Cambridge, England CB2 2RU

Tel. 01223-312393
Fax 01223-315052
http://www.cup.cam.ac.uk/

Date of founding: 1534

Jour Publ: *Philosophy; Religious Studies; Science in Context; Economics and Philosophy; Social Philosophy and Policy*

Ser Publ: Cambridge Studies in Philosophy; Stanford from Cambridge: The Complete Works of Friedrich Nietzsche; Cambridge Studies in Philosophy and Biology; Cambridge Studies in Philosophy and the Arts; Cambridge Texts in the History of Philosophy; Cambridge Studies in Philosophy and Law; Cambridge Studies in Philosophy and Public Policy

CARFAX PUBLISHING COMPANY

P.O. Box 25, Abingdon
Oxfordshire, England OX14 3UE

Tel. 01235-521154
Fax 01235-401550
E-mail sales@carfax.co.uk

Jour Publ: *Cogito; Philosophical Psychology; International Studies in the Philosophy of Science; Asian Philosophy*

CENTAUR PRESS

Fontwell, Arundel
Sussex, England BN18 0TA

Tel. 01243 543302

Date of founding: 1954

Ser Publ: The Kinship Library: to further humane education by stressing the need for a return to a more compassionate philosophy, in particular to the subject of "animals' rights" and the connection between human treatment of other creatures and our interpersonal relationships

COLIN SMYTHE, LTD.

P.O. Box 6, Gerrards Cross
Buckinghamshire, England SL9 8XA

Tel. 01753 886000
Fax 01753 886469

Date of founding: 1966

CONSTABLE & CO., LTD.

3 The Lanchesters
162 Fulham Palace Road
London, England W6 9ER

Tel. 081-741-3663
Fax 081-748-7562

Date of founding: 1890

DARTON, LONGMAN & TODD, LTD.

1 Spencer Court
140-142 Wandsworth High Street
London, England SW18 4JJ

Tel. 0181-875-0155
Fax 0181-875-0133

Date of founding: 1959

DUCKWORTH

48 Hoxton Square
London, England N1 6PB

Tel. 0171-729-5986
Fax 0171-729-0015

Date of founding: 1898

EDINBURGH UNIVERSITY PRESS

22 George Square
Edinburgh, Scotland EH8 9LF

Tel. 0131-650-4218
Fax 0131-662-0053
E-mail kathryn.maclean@ed.ac.uk

Date of founding: 1946

Jour Publ: *Edinburgh Review* (litera-
ture/aesthetics/arts); *Paragraph* (critical
theory); *Utilitas* (moral and political
philosophy); *Studies in World
Christianity* (religious philosophy)

Ser Publ: World Ethics; Philosophy
of Religion; Aristotle Studies;
Hellenistic Philosophy; Constructive
Theology; Asian Philosophy;
Speculative Metaphysics

ELEMENT BOOKS, LTD.

The Old School House
The Courtyard, Bell Street
Shaftesbury
Dorset, England SP7 8BP

Tel. 01747 851448
Fax 01747 855721

Date of founding: 1978

ELSEVIER/PERGAMON*

The Boulevard
Langford Lane, Kidlington
Oxford, England OX5 1GB

Tel. 865-843000,
Fax 865-843010

Date of founding: 1948

Jour Publ: *Studies in History and
Philosophy of Science; History of
European Ideas; New Ideas in Psychology*

FABER AND FABER, LTD.

3 Queen Square
London, England WC1N 3AU

Tel. 071465-0045
Fax 071465-0034/0043

Date of founding: 1929

FONTANA*

HarperCollins Publishers
77 Fulham Palace Road
Hammersmith
London, England W6 8JB

Tel. 081-741-7070
Fax 081-307-4440

Date of founding: 1967

Ser Publ: Philosophy Classics, ed. by
Anthony Quinton

FRANK CASS PUBLISHERS*

Newbury House
890-900 Eastern Ave.
Newbury Park, Ilford
Essex, England IG2 7HH

Tel. 081-599-8866
Fax 081-599-0984

G. W. FOOTE & COMPANY*

702 Holloway Road
London, England N19 3NL

Tel. 071-272-1266

Date of founding: 1881

Jour Publ: *Freethinker*

GEORGE RONALD PUBLISHER, LTD.

46 High Street, Kidlington
Oxford, England OX5 2DN

Tel. 44-1865-841515
Fax 44-1865-841230
E-mail sales@grpubl.demon.co.uk

Date of founding: 1948

GOLDEN COCKEREL PRESS

16 Barter Street
London, England WC1A 2AH

Tel. 0171-405-7979
Fax 0171-404-3598
E-mail lindesa@ibm.net

HAIGH AND HOCHLAND, LTD.*

The Precinct Centre, Oxford Rd.
Manchester, England M13 9QA

Tel. 061-273-4156
Fax 061-273-4340

Date of founding: 1950

Jour Publ: *Journal of the British Society for Phenomenology*

HARCOURT BRACE & CO., LTD.

24-28 Oval Rd.
London, England NW1 7DX

Tel. 0171-267-4466
Fax 0171-485-4752
E-mail college@hbuk.co.uk

HARVESTER WHEATSHEAF*

Campus 400, Maylands Avenue
Hemel Hempstead
Herts, England HP2 7EZ

Tel. 0442-881900 Ext. 3237
Fax 0442-252544

Date of founding: 1970

Ser Publ: Philosophers in Context, ed. by Stephen Korner; The Developing Body and Mind Series, ed. by George Butterworth; Theoretical Imagination in Psychology, ed. by Gun Semin

J. RICHARDSON*

9 Begbroke Crescent, Begbroke
Oxford, England OX5 1RW

Tel. 08675-4847

Date of founding: 1985

Ser Publ: Study Aids, bibliography books on philosophy

JAMES CLARKE & CO., LTD.

P.O. Box 60
Cambridge, England CB1 2NT

Tel. 01223-350865
Fax 01223-366951
E-mail lutterworth.pr@dial.pipex.com

Date of founding: 1859

JOHN CALDER PUBLISHERS, LTD.*

18 Brewer Street
London, England W1R 4AS

Date of founding: 1950

Jour Publ: *Journal of Beckett Studies*

JOHN MURRAY PUBLISHERS, LTD.*

50 Albemarle Street
London, England W1X 4BD

Tel. 071-493-4361
Fax 071-499-1792

Date of founding: 1768

KONGORYUJI TEMPLE

29 London Road, East Dereham
Norfolk, England NR19 1AS

Fax 01362 693962

Date of founding: 1958

Jour Publ: *Flowing Star* (studies in
esoteric Chinese Buddhism and
Philosophy), ed. by W. Hertzog,
Quarterly

Other info: Regular monographs
upon ancient Chinese medical theory
and therapies, doctrinal evolution, rit-
ual art and translations of Sutra texts.
Current details upon request.

LAWRENCE & WISHART

144A Old South Lambeth Rd.
London, England E9 SLN

Tel. 0181-533-2506
Fax 0181-533-7369
E-mail 1-w-bks.demon.co.uk

Date of founding: 1936

LUCIS PRESS, LIMITED*

Suite 54, 3 Whitehall Court
London, England SW1A 2EF

Tel. 071-839-4512
Fax 071-839-5575

Jour Publ: *Beacon*

Ser Publ: Esoteric Philosophy,
by Alice Bailey

THE MACMILLAN PRESS, LTD.

Houndmills, Basingstoke
Hampshire, England RG21 6XS

Tel. 01256-29242
Fax 01256-810526

Date of founding: 1843

Ser Publ: Library of Philosophy and
Religion, ed. by John Hick; Swansea
Studies in Philosophy, ed. by D. Z.
Phillips; Macmillan Studies in
Contemporary Philosophy, ed. by
Alan Millar and Peter Lamarque;
Claremont Studies in the Philosophy
of Religion, ed. by D. Z. Phillips

MANCHESTER UNIVERSITY PRESS

Oxford Road
Manchester, England M13 9NR

Tel. 0161-273-5539
Fax 0161-274-3346,
E-mail mup@man.ac.uk
http://secure.bookshop.co.uk/
MUP/DEFAULT.HTM

Date of founding: 1912

Other info: Publishes in areas of
cultural, feminist, and post-colonial
theory.

MERLIN PRESS

2 Rendlesham Mews
Rendlesham, Nr. Woodbridge
Suffolk, England IP12 2EA

Tel. 01394-461313
Fax 01394-461314
E-mail jgm@merlpres.demon.co.uk

Date of founding: 1956

Jour Publ: *Socialist Register*, ed. by
R. Miliband and L. Panitch

METHODIST PUBLISHING HOUSE*

20 Ivatt Way
Peterborough, England PE3 7PG

Tel. 0733-332202
Fax 0733-331201

MICROFORM ACADEMIC PUBLISHERS

Main Street
East Ardsley, Wakefield
West Yorkshire, England WF3 2AT

Tel. 01924-825700
Fax 01924-871005
E-mail
micro_image@cix.compulink.co.uk

Date of founding: 1956

Jour Publ: *Philosophy*

Ser Publ: Transactions of the
Cambridge Philosophical Society,
1821-1928

Other info: Publications are in
microfilm. *The Journal of the Royal
Institute of Philosophy*, 1926-1980, is
available on 10 reels plus 92 fiches.

NEW ATLANTIS FOUNDATION

7 East End Lane
Ditchling, Hassocks
West Sussex, England BN6 8SX

Tel. 0273-844778

Date of founding: 1954

Ser Publ: Foundation Lectures:
appreciation of important writers

OCTAGON PRESS, LTD.

P.O. Box 227
London, England N6 4EW

Tel. 0044-81-348-9392
Fax 0044-81-341-5971
E-mail octagon@schredds.demon.co.uk
http://www.bookshop.co.uk/octagon/

Date of founding: 1972

Other info: Titles published are
generally, but not exclusively, translations of works of near-Eastern
philosophy that are of interest to
students of Sufism.

OPEN UNIVERSITY PRESS

Celtic Court, 22 Ballmoor
Buckingham, England MK18 1XW

Tel. 0280-82338
Fax 0280-823233
E-mail enquiries@openup.co.uk
http://secure.bookshop.co.uk/
OPENUP/DEFAULT.HTM

Date of founding: 1977

Other info: Publishes books in the
fields of philosophy of science,
philosophy/women's studies, and
philosophy/education.

OXFORD UNIVERSITY PRESS

Great Clarendon Street
Oxford, England OX2 6DP

Tel. 01865-556767
Fax 01865-556646
http://www.oup.co.uk/

Date of founding: 1478

Jour Publ: *British Journal of Aesthetics;
Mind; British Journal for the Philosophy
of Science; Journal of Semantics*

Ser Publ: Oxford Readings in Philosophy; Clarendon Library of Logic and Philosophy, ed. by L. Jonathan Cohen; Oxford Studies in Ancient Philosophy, ed. by Christopher Taylor; Marxist Introductions, ed. by Steven Lukes; Oxford Logic Guides, ed. by Dov Gabbay, Angus Macintyre, Dana Scott and John Shepherdson; Clarendon Aristotle Series, ed. by J. L. Ackrill and L. Judson; Clarendon Plato Series, ed. by Lesley Brown; Clarendon Later Ancient Pilosophers, ed. by J. Barnes and A. Long; Odeon (Interdisciplinary Series on Continental and American Thought), ed. by J. V. Harari & V. Descombes; Clarendon Edition of the Works of John Locke, ed. by M. A. Stewart; Clarendon Edition of the Works of Thomas Hobbes; Oxford Ethics Series, ed. by Derek Parfit; Studies in Bioethics, ed. by Peter Singer; Oxford Theological Monographs; Oxford Philosophical Monographs; Oxford Readings in Politics and Government; History of Western Philosophy; Classical and Medieval Logic Texts; Mind Association Occasional Series; Oxford Studies in the History of Philosophy, ed. by M. A. Stewart; plus others

PATERNOSTER PRESS

P.O. Box 300, Carlisle
Cumbria, England CA3 0QS

Tel. 0228-512512
Fax 0228-514949
E-mail
100526,3434@compuserve.com

Date of founding: 1935

PENGUIN BOOKS, LTD.

Bath Road, Harmondsworth
Middlesex, England UB7 0DA

Tel. 081 899 4000
Fax 081 899 4099

Date of founding: 1935

PICKERING & CHATTO PUBLISHERS, LTD.*

17 Pall Mall
London, England SW1Y 5NB

Tel. 071-930 3088
Fax 071-839 4509

PRENTICE HALL

Simon & Schuster Internat'l. Group.
Campus 400, Maylands Avenue
Hemel Hempstead
Hertfordshire, England HP2 7E2

Tel. 0442-881900
Fax 0442-257115
E-mail ibd_order@prenhall.co.uk
http://www.prenhall.com/

QUARTET BOOKS, LTD.

27 Goodge St.
London, England W1P 2LD

Tel. 0171-636-3992
Fax 0171-637-1866
E-mail quartetbooks@easynet.co.uk

Date of founding: 1972

RATIONALIST PRESS ASSOCIATION*

88 Islington High Street
London, England N1 8EW

Jour Publ: *New Humanist*

ROUTLEDGE

11 New Fetter Lane
London, England EC4P 4EE

Tel. 0171 842 2168,
Fax 0171 842 2300,
E-mail philosophy@routledge.com
http://www.routledge.com

Jour Publ: *The International Journal of Philosophical Studies*

Ser Publ: Arabic Thought and Culture; Arguments of the Philosophers; Collected Papers of Bertrand Russell; Continental Philosophy; Critics of the Twentieth Century; Environmental Philosophies; Ideas; International Library of Philosophy; Issues in Ancient Philosophy; Opening Out: Feminism for Today; Philosophers in Focus; Philosophical Issues in Science; Points of Conflict; Problems of Modern European Thought; Problems of Philosophy; Professional Ethics; Routledge History of Philosophy; Routledge History of World Philosophies; Routledge Nietzsche Studies; Routledge Philosophy GuideBooks; Social Ethics and Policy; Thinking the Political; Topics in Medieval Philosophy; Warwick Studies in European Philosophy; Warwick Studies in Philosophy and Literature

Other info: See also Routledge, Inc., in the *Directory of American Philosophers.*

RUDOLF STEINER PRESS*

P.O. Box 955
Bristol, England BS99 5QN

Tel. 0272-466663
Fax 0272-466668

Other info: Publishes anthroposophi-
cal books. Represented in North America by Anthroposophical Press, R.R. 4, Box 94A1, Hudson, NY 12534, USA.

SAGE PUBLICATIONS, LTD.*

6 Bonhill St.
London, England EC2A 4PU

Jour Publ: *Philosophy of the Social Sciences; Political Theory*

SHEPHEARD-WALWYN PUBLISHERS, LTD.

Suite 34, 26 Charing Cross Road
London, England WC2H 0DH

Tel. 0171-240-5992
Fax 0171-379-5770

Date of founding: 1972

253

Ser Publ: The Letters of Marsilio Ficino, originally published in Latin during the Florentine Renaissance, the first English translation of this major Renaissance philosopher. Five volumes published so far and still in print; sixth volume due for publication in October 1997.

SIDGWICK & JACKSON, LTD.*

Macmillan General Books
18-21 Cavaye Place
London, England SW10 9PG

Tel. 071-373-6070
Fax 071-370-0746

Date of founding: 1908

SOUVENIR PRESS, LTD.*

43 Great Russell St.
London, England WC1B 3PA

Tel. 071-637-5711

Fax 071-580-5064

Date of founding: 1952

T. & T. CLARK, LTD.

59 George Street
Edinburgh, Scotland EH2 2LQ

Tel. 0131-225-4703
Fax 0131-220-4260

Date of founding: 1821

Jour Publ: *The Expository Times; The Scottish Journal of Theology; Studies in Christian Ethics; Journal of Feminist Studies in Religion; Communio*

THOEMMES PRESS

11 Great George St.
Bristol, England BS1 5RR

Tel. 117-929-1377
Fax 117-922-1918
E-mail
100633.1133@compuserve.com

Date of founding: 1989

Jour Publ: *The British Journal for the History of Philosophy*

Ser Publ: Key Issues, ed. by Andrew Pyle: to republish the contemporary responses that met major works and key areas of debate; Bristol Introductions, ed. by Ray Monk: short original texts that aim to present challenging perspectives on philosophical themes, intended to be of interest to the new student and advanced scholar; Key Texts: facsimile paperback editions of books that have not been available for many years, with particular emphasis on less popularized works of thinkers in the history of ideas; Wittgenstein Studies: an invaluable resource for the Wittgenstein scholar, collecting many major texts of recent years that have proved to be of enduring relevance to the study of Wittgenstein; Idealism Series, ed. by Peter Johnson: old and new works that find new features of interest in Idealism and a perspective that is germane to current philosophical concerns; Cambridge Platonists, ed. by G. A. J. Rogers: works of the seventeenth century English philosophical school, including the classic texts of Cudworth and More, indispensable for a proper understanding of the relationship among the natural sciences, religion, and philosophy in the period from Galileo to Newton

Other info: Alongside a list of newly commissioned titles, Theommes Press also has an extensive reprint programme of over 400 titles encompassing philosophy, religion, education, economics, Scottish thought and culture, and social and political thought.

UNIVERSITY OF EXETER PRESS

Reed Hall, Streatham Drive
Exeter, England EX4 4QR

Tel. 01392 263066
Fax 01392 263064
E-mail uep@ex.ac.uk

Date of founding: 1990

Other info: UEP titles are available in North America through Northwestern University Press.

UNIVERSITY OF WALES PRESS

6 Gwennyth Street, Cathays
Cardiff, Wales CF2 4YD

Tel. +44-0-1222 231919
Fax +44-0-1222 230908

E-mail press@wales.ac.uk
http://www.swan.ac.uk/uwp/info.htm

Date of founding: 1922

Ser Publ: Political Philosophy Now,
ed. by Howard Lloyd Williams,
Wolfgang Kersting, Stephen B. Smith,
and Peter Nicholson

VALLENTINE MITCHELL PUBLISHERS*

Newbury House
890-900 Eastern Ave., Newbury Park
Ilford, Essex, England IG2 7HH

Tel. 081-599 8866
Fax 081-599 0984

VERSO

6 Meard St.
London, England W1V 3HR

Tel. 0171-437-3546
Fax 0171-734-0059
E-mail
100434.1414@compuserve.com

Date of founding: 1970

VOLTAIRE FOUNDATION

99 Banbury Road
Oxford, England OX2 6JX

Tel. +44-0-1865 264600
Fax +44-0-1865 284610
E-mail email@voltaire.ox.ac.uk

Jour Publ: *Studies on Voltaire and the Eighteenth Century*

Ser Publ: Oeuvres complétes de
Voltaire; Libre pensée et litérature
clandestine; Bibliographica

VRINDAVANUM BOOKS*

7-11 Kensington High Street
London, England W8

Tel. 071-584-8136

Date of founding: 1985

W. S. MANEY & SON, LTD.

Hudson Road
Leeds, England LS9 7DL

Tel. 0113-2497481
Fax 0113-2486983

WILFION BOOKS PUBLISHERS*

4 Townhead Terrace, Paisley
Renfrewshire, Scotland PA1 2AX

Tel. 041-889-0950

Date of founding: 1975

WOBURN PRESS*

Newbury House
890-900 Eastern Ave.
Newbury Park, Ilford
Essex, England IG2 7HH

Tel. 081-599-8866
Fax 081-599-0984